OUT OF MY
DEPTH

Anne Darwin with David Leigh

Published by Mirror Books,
an imprint of Trinity Mirror plc,
1 Canada Square,
London E14 5AP, England

www.mirrorbooks.com
twitter.com/themirrorbooks

Executive Editor: Jo Sollis
Editor: Charlotte Cole
Art Director: Julie Adams
Image Production: Paul Mason

ISBN 9781910335468

First paperback edition

Printed and bound in Great Britain
by CPI Group (UK) Ltd, Croydon, CR0 4YY

Every effort has been made to fulfil requirements with regard to
reproducing copyright material. The author and publisher will be
glad to rectify any omissions at the earliest opportunity.

Front cover images: The Mega Agency, Getty

Contents

DEDICATION

For Mark and Anthony, with love and gratitude

FOREWORD

In 30 years working as a journalist, I've covered some amazing stories across the world. But in terms of sheer breath-taking audacity, none come remotely close to the incredible, globe-trotting antics of the seemingly most ordinary of couples from the seaside town of Seaton Carew on England's north east coast.

Mother-of-two Anne Darwin is a softly spoken and unassuming former doctor's receptionist, who helped her now infamous 'canoe man' husband John pull off one of the most brazen frauds you're ever likely to read about.

Little did I know that when I knocked on the door of a fourth-storey apartment in Panama, Central America, shortly before Christmas in December 2007, I would play a central role in uncovering a gobsmacking, trans-Atlantic adventure that, quite literally, beggars belief.

Anne's often heart-wrenching story is one of extreme regret, remorse, shame and, finally, redemption. She deserves great credit for being brave enough to tell her side of a story that engrossed millions of people across the world, but that left her in the very depths of despair.

David Leigh

Prologue

Seaton Carew, March 22, 2002

Feeling the chill of the evening drawing in as their lifeboats churned through the waves, the men who had been scouring the North Sea for almost 18 hours were growing increasingly tired and frustrated. A lot of things weren't making much sense that day, yet still they refused to give up hope. Come on, they muttered to themselves under their breath, where the hell is this guy?

Approaching dusk on a still March evening, they were all too aware that, as the light faded, so too did their hopes of success. Including land-based support crew, some 65 Royal National Lifeboat Institution volunteers were involved in a massive sea search, one of the biggest off the north-east coast of England in years: six rescue boats using tried and tested search patterns, methodically criss-crossing 200 square miles of ocean for any trace of a local man last seen paddling out to sea in a red canoe. Worryingly, he was apparently heading towards the mouth of the River Tees – one of the busiest shipping channels in the United Kingdom. The possibility of a gruesome death, sucked into a ship's propellers, could not be ruled out. No one wanted to admit it but they all knew that the outcome of the rescue mission was looking bleaker by the minute.

Spotters screwed up their eyes in the vain hope it might help them see something. But there was nothing to be seen: nothing at all. According to the local news, everyone was puzzled. It had been a text-book operation in what the men considered ideal rescue conditions: only partly cloudy, with a 'sea state' of two to three, meaning only a gentle swell, with no hint of the mountainous waves or icy conditions they so often had to contend with. It was, they all agreed, the perfect day for a rescue. So where was he?

The operation, being coordinated by the Humber coastguard, had grown steadily in scale throughout the day. Three aircraft had been called in to assist: a bright yellow Royal Air Force Sea King search-and-rescue helicopter, a small fixed-wing Cleveland Police spotter plane and an RAF Nimrod reconnaissance aircraft. Even a Royal Navy warship, HMS *Explorer*, which happened to be in the area on exercise, had joined the search, all surely adding, rescuers felt, to the chances of success. Dozens of RNLI and coastguard shore teams were combing the coastline for debris or worse. Nothing was being left to chance.

Shortly after lunch, at 1.15pm, there was finally a breakthrough when a double-ended paddle, typically used by canoeists, was retrieved from the sea near North Gare, just a mile or two along the coast from Seaton Carew, the little seaside town from where the missing man was seen paddling off the previous day. But, if, as feared, it was his, it could mean he had been left at the mercy of the sea and the notoriously strong tidal currents that could quickly have dragged him out towards the shipping lanes. It didn't look good.

As the hour approached 6pm, the men, who had worked in shifts throughout the day and the previous night, were weary through lack of sleep. But it was the worry that somehow, someone had missed something, maybe the tiniest of clues, that bothered them most. Back at Redcar HQ, wives and girlfriends had been to the local ASDA supermarket to stock up on pies and sandwiches, for it wasn't just the boats that needed refuelling. They brewed piping hot tea and coffee for the men who had put their day jobs on hold to join the search. Some of the more experienced hands had niggling doubts about their mission, wondering if, perhaps, there was a little more to this 'disappearance' than met the eye. There hadn't been a single sighting of either the missing man or wreckage from his canoe and they were baffled. The nagging doubts continued but each and every man was well aware of the RNLI ethic that call-outs are never criticised, no matter how suspicious they may appear, for fear of dissuading future callers. Their job was to save lives and, acutely aware the missing man was a local, said to be about 50 years old, with a wife and probably a family at home, worrying themselves sick and hoping against hope for the miracle they too were praying for, they tried to push such thoughts to the back of their minds.

The boatmen had all been involved in rescue operations before and some recalled previous occasions when, just as they had all but given up hope, their luck had suddenly changed and they had plucked a fortunate soul to safety from the unforgiving sea. But as the night began to draw in along the Cleveland coastline, most were beginning to fear in their hearts, that it was not destined to be one of those days.

Folk taking a late afternoon stroll along the promenade in Seaton Carew stopped to lean against the blue-painted iron balustrades and gaze out to the cold and grey North Sea. In the distance, and through the haze thrown skywards by the surf's spray, rising up and merging into the smoke billowing out of the giant oil refineries and nuclear power station at the mouth of the River Tees, they could just about make out the outlines of some of the rescue boats involved in a search that was making headlines in newspapers, and on local television and radio stations. The talk of the town, in the pubs and hotels, fish-and-chip shops and seafront stores selling candyfloss and brightly coloured sticks of rock, was of nothing else. 'Any news on that bloke who went out in his canoe?' countless customers asked the shopkeepers. 'No, nothing, it's not looking good,' they were each told, as the sound of the rescue aircraft lingered in the distance.

Looking out from the drawing room window of her Victorian sea-front home, watching the flashing lights from the massive search operation underway, Anne Darwin was a nervous wreck. She knew very well the brave men and women risking their lives looking for her 'missing' husband were not going to find him that night, the next… or anytime soon.

She thought to herself, What the hell have I done?

Here, for the first time, Anne tells her extraordinary and heart-wrenching story.

Chapter 1

Courtship and Marriage

Horse and carts were still a common sight on the streets when I was growing up in the seaside mining villages of Horden and Blackhall Colliery, on the north-east shoulder of England. Horden Colliery was one of the biggest mines in the country, employing thousands of workers and, at its height, producing more than 1.5 million tonnes of coal a year: it was known as the 'Jewel in the Crown' of the British coal mining industry. Today, of course, the mines are long since closed and the villages of my childhood, on the shores of the North Sea, have changed beyond all recognition. For a start, they're an awful lot cleaner. It wasn't until I was 15 that I even realised starlings weren't always jet black. The only ones I'd ever seen in my early years were always coated in soot from sitting on the chimneys of the villages' terraced homes and I didn't know they could actually be speckled. But then, few things in our villages escaped the dust and soot that constantly billowed from the chimneys, such was the life of communities that had been home to generations of mining families.

I was born on 3 July 1952, in Hartlepool and christened Anne Catherine. My Dad, Henry Stephenson, known as Harry, worked at the mine from leaving school as a young boy. He trained originally as a blacksmith and later as a welder, and worked mainly on the surface but occasionally had to go underground to repair machinery. My Mam, Catherine, known as Kathleen, was a full-time mother to me and Michael, who was three years older than me. My sister Christine was born nine years later. When Mam left school she looked after her ailing mother; she didn't have the chance to work.

Until I was three we lived in Blackhall Colliery, and then we moved to the neighbouring village of Horden, where my parents were given the opportunity of living in a colliery house that was more suitable for a growing family. It was from here that my early memories come.

Monday was always washing day, with the ironing sometimes spilling over into Tuesday. There was a washing-line in the yard for drying the clothes so they always smelled fresh, although having coal fires was a problem as often soot fell from the chimneys onto the washing. We had an indoor line in the kitchen where the ironing would hang, to be aired, before being folded and put away the next day. Friday was the day for doing the housework. Mam started upstairs and worked her way down; dusting, hoovering, polishing and cleaning windows. As I grew older I was encouraged to help, and it was rewarding to see the shiny surfaces reappear from beneath the dust. Mam had crocheted doilies on her dressing table. I very carefully lifted them off to reveal the pattern they left behind, before dusting it away.

Grandma, Dad's mother, usually came to visit on a Friday. She stayed for tea and sometimes gave us a sixpence or a shilling when she left to go home. When we first moved to Horden, Grandma and Granda lived just a short walk away. They moved to a modern house in the new town of Peterlee when we were still quite young, that's when her Friday visits became part of our routine. She was a plump lady and I loved to sit on her knee for cuddles. Granda was a blacksmith at Horden Colliery. When he retired he spent time in his garden, growing roses. My favourite was the variety called Blue Moon. To me it looked so exotic.

The weekend usually began with doing the shopping on Saturday, and sometimes we'd go for a walk with Kim, our Manchester Terrier. I loved to go through the bluebell woods in spring. Originally belonging to Grandma and Granda, we had Kim for fourteen years.

Sunday was the one day when we ate in the front room. It was a roast dinner, of course, followed by homemade rice pudding with a skin on top – delicious. Mam cooked it on the gas stove in the kitchen, moving the whistling kettle out of the way, and my brother, Michael, and I helped by shelling peas and peeling vegetables, sitting at the kitchen table or in the one armchair. There was a set pot in the corner – built from brick, it was a big pot over a coal fire, and heated the room and water for baths and washing clothes. Kim was often lying on the hearth-rug in front.

In the morning we'd have been to church, where we always wore our Sunday best. For me this included a hat and gloves – even in the summer, when I'd wear lace gloves – and my Easter present was always a new hat. The afternoon was spent playing or listening to the radiogram, or later watching the television, while Mam baked pies and cakes for tea. When she called 'Who wants to clean the bowl?' we raced to scrape out the remains of the cake mixture from the bowl and I sometimes cut out the scones. They were happy times with simple pleasures. Like another world now.

We used a little tin bath in front of the kitchen fire each night, always hoping no one needed to pass through the kitchen to use the outside toilet. Once a week the long bath was dragged in from the yard for us all to use. It felt like luxury to be able to sit in and stretch out. The downside was the time it took to fill it from the set pot, and to empty it. (Bath time often felt quite awkward when I was a girl in her early teens. It wasn't until we moved again, when I was fifteen, that we had the convenience of a modern bathroom.)

The houses had a yard at the back with an outside toilet and coal house. There was little traffic about and we played outside in the long terraced streets – we occasionally had to stop what we were doing when a horse and cart needed to pass along the road to make doorstep deliveries. It was only a short walk to the local park, where we played on the swings and slides and roundabouts.

The Catholic infant and junior school was next to the church we attended. My first classroom had a high ceiling and a coal fire in one corner, which always roared away in winter. We sat either side of long tables rather than at desks. These were the days when 'Nitty Nora' visited the schools on a regular basis to inspect the children's heads.

What sticks in my memory was the toilet block in the yard. It fascinated me that the toilets graduated in size, one for each year group. There was a separate playground for boys and girls, boys preferring to kick footballs and the girls using skipping ropes or trying to juggle with three balls, singing rhymes and chasing each other. One year we had an open-air concert of singing and dancing in the school playground. The parish priest came and all our families were there to watch. It was a glorious summer day.

During the summer months we often went to Crimdon beach. We met Aunty Mary and Uncle Jim and our two cousins and played beach ball, rounders, piggy-back races and jumped over the waves. We sometimes went to the pavilion where we bought chips or ice cream. But more often than not we walked to Aunty Mary's house, in Blackhall Colliery, for tea before going home to Horden, exhausted after a long day in the sun. We hadn't heard of skin cancer and always suffered from sunburn.

Occasionally my other uncle and grandad came too. My Mam's father lived with Aunty Mary, as did her brother. Grandad was from Ireland, and worked as a miner at Blackhall. His wife, who I was named after, had died before I was born.

Every summer holiday we went away for a week to Scarborough with Aunty Mary, Uncle Jim and our cousins. We travelled either by train or coach and we always stayed in the same guest house. It felt like going home, everything was so familiar and just a short walk from the beach. Holidays were always good fun; we got to spend more time with Dad.

I was too young to be aware of it, but the mines were producing too much coal and there were not enough people who wanted to buy it. For many mining families, wages all but dried up as Horden Collieries management drastically cut back on overheads and shut the pits for three weeks in every month. Many miners either moved away or tried to find work in the heavy industries of Hartlepool, Middlesbrough or Sunderland. My father stuck it out. All I knew about it was that there was never very much money. Mam was always waiting for the next payday. But there was home-cooked food on the table and we never went without life's necessities. My Aunty Mary used to sew, she often made me dresses, and Mam would knit.

When I was 11 years old I sat an entrance exam to attend St Joseph's Convent Grammar School in Hartlepool. I remember feeling greatly relieved to pass and was excited to be able to go. We were taught by nuns and had to wear a stuffy old-fashioned uniform of dark brown tunic, cream blouse and a blue, brown and gold tie and hat. I joined the school choir and discovered I loved singing, and once a year there was an annual theatre production where I was involved, usually as part of the choir or the chorus. I was an average student – it was the practical subjects I enjoyed. I learnt to sew and started to make my own clothes, and when I reached the sixth form I found I had an aptitude for shorthand and typing. As a child I wanted to be an air hostess or a nurse, but as a teenager I decided on office work and wanted to be a secretary.

My one special friend was Kathleen, who I met when I started grammar school. We would talk of being married and living next door to each other and raising our children together. She followed the Sunderland football team, and I occasionally went to home matches with her. We both enjoyed Irish ceilidh dancing and this is how we spent most Sunday evenings – travelling to the local parishes who took it in turns to host the dances. It could be exhausting but it was always enjoyable. Neither me nor Kathleen were particular fans of wearing make-up – we were quite reserved and didn't do the girly things. I had long dark hair, and it was miniskirts with flat shoes for the ceilidhs, occasionally a maxi dress if it was a Christmas do.

Mam and Dad's pleasure was dancing, too. Old Time ballroom dancing on a Saturday evening. Occasionally I went with them if there was a special dance on. One particular week was the choosing of Miss Blackhall. I went along to be a spectator and have a couple of dances with my Dad. When it came to the judging, the girls were invited to walk around the room in a circle. I was just sitting watching, with no intention of participating whatsoever. Someone came round asking me and others sitting down if we'd join in. I refused, but they said, 'Please get up, we need to make up the numbers.' So, with encouragement from my Mam and Dad, I did.

To my surprise I was chosen to be Miss Blackhall. I won £10, was presented with a silver cup and had my picture in the local paper. The only duty was to appear in another parade in the holiday camp at Crimdon Dene the following summer – with all the winners from the surrounding villages – but I didn't win anything there.

I was 16 when I had my first boyfriend and was heartbroken that he ended the relationship when he went to college. It was an innocent relationship, which I think lasted almost a year but it will always be special because it was the first. A couple of years passed before I had another boyfriend, then a few followed in fairly quick succession. I didn't enjoy going to pubs and I couldn't see anything meaningful developing with any of them.

John Darwin and I first crossed paths on the bus going to our respective grammar schools – John was two years older than me and went to St Francis' Roman Catholic Grammar School. We always acknowledged one another, but often with nothing more than a nod of the head as John boarded the bus in the next village. That was as far as it went. John later told me that I often caught his eye, but I never really gave him much thought. He wasn't really good looking and was a little too cocksure of himself for my liking. One day he knocked off my school hat on the bus and I quickly turned round and glared at him. John just laughed.

He left school when I was 14 to attend a college in Teesside, where he studied for A levels before going to teacher training college in Manchester. He was later taken on as a maths, science and religious studies teacher in Leadgate, near Consett in County Durham. I didn't see him during this time, apart from the odd Sunday morning at church when he'd come over and talk to me after mass. My parents were friendly with John's, having known them throughout their lives. His dad had been a bricklayer for the council but was now retired. His mam was a cook at Hartlepool General Hospital, preparing the meals for special diets.

I took a Sunday job in the sweetshop next to John's house when I was 16. It was a five-minute walk from where we now lived in the coastal village of Blackhall Rocks. John would often come in and pass the time of day.

He was cheeky and self-assured and frequently asked me out, but I always said no. Because he was two years older than me, I didn't feel comfortable about going out with him and I didn't feel good enough. I suppose I was a bit in awe of him. My only encounters with teachers had been as a pupil. I wasn't really attracted to him either – he was taller than me but slightly built, which is probably why he had the nickname 'Dinky'. I actually never knew his first name until after our first date. He had a mop of curly hair a bit like Jimmy Hendrix's. John could be very persuasive and charming and he didn't seem to be put off, no matter how many times I said no. He always asked for sweets from the top shelf, knowing I would have to climb a ladder to get them.

Leaving school at 17 with qualifications in shorthand and typing, I landed a job as a typist at a printing firm in Hartlepool, William Barlow and Son. I continued studying at night school and gained English O level and higher speeds in shorthand and typing. I was lucky to get a job so quickly and it felt good to be earning my own money, even if it was less than £5 a week. I gave some money to Mam, paid my own bus fares and still managed to save a little each week.

After countless times asking me to go out with him, I eventually agreed. I was 20. On our first date, we went to a bowling alley in Billingham with a young married couple, who had a baby. I hadn't met them before – Martin had been to college with John – so it was an anxious evening for me. But it was a good night. I felt I shouldn't have worried about not being an equal just because he'd been to college and I hadn't; we could still have fun together. I wasn't expecting a long-term relationship, but after that first time we began seeing each other quite regularly. We used to walk for miles at Blackhall or Crimdon over the cliffs or along the beach.

We were officially 'an item', and family and friends suspected it wouldn't be long before they heard the sound of wedding bells. John had a good sense of humour and was attentive. He told me stories of his childhood adventures with his brother or his friends. Always one for loving the outdoors, he grew up as a bit of a daredevil. They went off to the beach to spend the day, lighting fires, cooking potatoes in the embers, climbing rocks and playing in the caves. For me, he made romantic gestures like collecting heart-shaped stones from the beach when we were out walking.

One summer's evening, John drove us to a pub in Dalton Piercy where, after a few drinks, he asked me to marry him. There was nothing overly romantic about his proposal, but I had half-expected it and said yes. I had always wanted to be married and to have a family. I'm sure I loved the thought of being married far more than I actually loved John, but I was very happy.

We married later that same year at St Joseph's Catholic

Church in Blackhall Colliery, on 22 December 1973. It was a small wedding, just family and friends – about 60 of us in total. Christine, now twelve years old, was a bridesmaid and Kathleen, my friend from school, was chief bridesmaid. I wore a white dress with lace trim, a veil and headdress, and carried a bouquet of red roses.

Straight after the wedding we were driven to Newcastle airport and flew to Magaluf in Majorca for our honeymoon. It was the first time I had ever flown. We spent the evenings in the company of a young couple from Newcastle. John and I went on a few trips organised by the hotel to take in the local culture or walked along the beach. The sea was bright and blue, not like the cold, grey North Sea of home.

On returning, we stayed with my Mam and Dad for a couple of days before moving into the house John already owned, 187 Durham Road, Leadgate. It was a Victorian terraced house with high ceilings. It had originally been a three-bedroom house, but one bedroom had been converted into a bathroom and there were two reception rooms and a kitchen downstairs. It had a coal fire in the room at the rear of the house and a gas fire in the front sitting room. There was a yard at the back with an outside toilet and coal store and a pretty little garden at the front. John's parents had provided the deposit, as they did again later with his first car, a dark green Hillman Imp. John had lived there for a few months, going home to Blackhall for the weekends, but he didn't have much in the way of home comforts, so we gathered bits and pieces of furniture together and moved in on 6 January 1974.

Chapter 2

Confronting John's Mistress

To be married and living in my own home was everything I had ever dreamed of and John and I talked excitedly about having children to make our family complete. But while I was perfectly content, I quickly discovered that John was never quite satisfied with his lot.

I had to leave my job in Hartlepool as it was too far to travel from Leadgate. I had risen through the ranks to become secretary to the deputy managing director, and now found a job as a secretary at Shotley Bridge General Hospital. Although we were both earning a fair wage, money was still tight, and I repeatedly told John not to be so foolish when he said he wanted me to have the best of everything. To me, it really didn't matter if we went without the latest washer or television, but it clearly mattered to John.

When we were first married we had mostly second-hand furniture donated by friends and relatives, which we gradually replaced when we could afford to buy new. Not like today, when young couples have fully furnished homes before getting married. But since his late teens, John had been desperate to break away from his working-class roots and the stigma, as he saw it, of council homes and being poor. I remember going to buy a washing machine and choosing one that was middle of the range, but John suggested a much more expensive model. It appeared to me to have an excessive amount of programs that I would never use, but he said, 'If you have this one at least you'll always have the option to use them. Buy a cheaper one and you won't have that choice.' Which was a fair comment but to me it was still an unnecessary expense, yet after some debate we bought the more expensive one. I was quickly learning, what John wanted he usually got.

I remembered, just before we were married when I was promoted at work, John's dad, Ronnie, saying, 'Oh that's much better isn't it, to be able to tell people you're a secretary.' Social standing meant a lot to him, he always wanted to stand out from the crowd. Thinking about it now, perhaps John's need for the best came from his dad.

Ronnie, originally a builder's labourer, had been determined to make something of himself and had no intention of leading what he considered to be the grimy life of a miner. He had married well, to a girl who lived in one of Blackhall's posh private houses. According to his family, John was later brought up in an atmosphere of money, money, money – that's what mattered above anything else.

At the time, I discovered that if we talked about something we liked at his parents' house, John's Mam sometimes gave him the money. Unknown to his dad, she said, 'Go and get what you want.' I soon learnt not to mention things we'd quite like if she was in earshot. It made me feel uncomfortable to be always taking money.

It was still early days in our marriage when, out of nowhere, he dropped a bombshell, the prospect of which terrified me: 'Why don't we up sticks and emigrate to Australia?' There were plenty of opportunities for qualified young teachers, he said, and I would easily find secretarial work and we could start a new life in the sun.

I was horrified. It wasn't something I had ever given any thought to. I told John I'd miss my parents and friends and was very happy and content with the way things were. As a concession, I did say, 'Perhaps later, in a few years.'

Thankfully – for once – he didn't press the matter. I didn't have the slightest desire to go anywhere, let alone thousands of miles away to the other side of the world.

In 1974 I got the news I had been praying for when I fell pregnant, but was devastated when I miscarried. John, very coldly, was relieved. He said, 'It's too early to start a family.' But for me the pain didn't really ease until the following year, when I fell pregnant again.

I think we were both a bit surprised but John was more accepting this time around. Being a biology teacher, he was keen to follow the progress of the pregnancy quite closely. We painted the spare bedroom, bought a cot and all the other necessities. We had an old chest of drawers that had belonged to my grandfather. We painted it white to give it a fresh look and began choosing names.

As it got closer to the expected date of delivery we packed a bag in readiness for the short ride to the hospital. However, two weeks' later I had to be admitted for inducement. John stayed with me all day and we played cards on 'the bump' to pass the time.

About mid-afternoon, I was told the baby was becoming distressed and was at risk. The doctor advised a c-section, which needed to be performed immediately. John said, 'If that's the case, I'm going home.' I was distraught and asked, 'Why leave now, you've waited all day?' At that time, fathers were permitted to be in the delivery room, but they were not allowed in the operating theatre. He said, 'There's no point staying if I can't witness the birth.' I replied 'The baby will be born in the next few minutes and you'll be able to see it soon after.' (We had chosen not to know the sex, in advance of the birth).

I was whisked off to theatre, but John went home. I believe he phoned the hospital later to find out what happened, but he didn't visit until the following day and had no regret about leaving me. I was heartbroken.

Our first son, Mark, was born on 23 November 1975. Ten days later, I went home with my baby and gradually the sadness at being left alone for the birth disappeared as I cradled Mark in my arms and looked forward to the rosy future ahead. Now we really are a family, I thought. As was the usual thing to do at the time, I gave up my job to stay at home and be a full-time mother. I was happy to be at home washing nappies and loved my son unconditionally.

One day a week, Mam would make the two-hour journey by bus to visit for the day and help me with the baby. If the weather was good we'd go for a walk pushing the pram, often going into Consett, a former mining town on the edge of the Pennines, to do some shopping. If it was too cold or wet, she'd help me with some housework or cooking. After a long day at work, Dad would come by car to take her home. We would speak on the phone every day but I always looked forward to the days she came to see us.

Two years later, John decided we needed a bigger, more modern home and so we moved to a newly built, three-bedroom house, with central heating and a good-sized back garden, in the smart village of Witton Gilbert, on the outskirts of Durham. Around the turn of the year I was expecting again, and our second son, Anthony, was born on 3 September 1978. The boys were my life and I now wanted for nothing. My family was complete.

John, however, was becoming progressively more restless. He was increasingly disillusioned with the teaching profession, forever muttering about a lack of standards and lack of discipline in the classroom. But, equally important to John, was the need to earn more money. He had even taken a weekend job as a doorman at a local cinema in Hartlepool to earn some extra cash.

The years after Anthony's birth were not particularly happy ones. John seemed to have little time for the boys and hated the fact that I was always nagging him about smoking around them in the house. We began to argue more, but John always seemed to overlook my views. 'It's my house and if I want to smoke, I will,' was how he put it. He wouldn't shout, it was always more of a lecture. Through his teacher training he had learned how to control disruptive pupils and that's pretty much how he made me feel at times – a second-year pupil in one of his classes. I would just be talked down to. Whatever John wanted to do he did and I reached the stage where it felt pointless even arguing with him. I had lost touch with my friend Kathleen by now, and felt very isolated.

John still had a passion for adventure and arranged a camping trip in the Lake District with his brother. I'd been looking after the boys on my own all week, and it was the middle of winter and there was snow on the ground.

'You can't go camping in this weather,' I said, when he told me about it the week before.

'Of course we can,' was his reply, 'we'll be fine.'

'You could both freeze to death!' I insisted.

'We'll be all right, we've got a camping stove, and it'll be good fun. You have no sense of adventure.'

He was right, I didn't, I worried about the future for

the boys. 'You might be buried alive and what am I supposed to do with the boys when I'm on my own?'

'You can always go to visit your mother, you'll have the car.'

There was no way I could talk him out of it, he was going and that was it whether I liked the idea or not. They went away but, as it turned out, the trip resulted in a row between the two brothers and it ended earlier than expected. However, it didn't stop them from having more adventures, which involved sailing or cycling together, though they seldom went to plan. I would either spend the time at home on my own with the boys or sometimes, if he left the car, went to stay with my parents for a few days.

In May 1982, I had my first 'solo' adventure with the boys. John's parents took a villa in Spain for a month and invited the four of us to join them during the spring bank holiday week. They were always generous with the boys and enjoyed being part of their lives. They'd invite them to stay for a night or two, and when they visited they'd often bring a present for them, even if it wasn't a special occasion.

I was thrilled that they'd asked us to join them in Spain, but John said it was too far to go for just a week. He arranged one of his excursions with his brother instead, but fortunately for me, his parents arranged for me and the children to join them anyway. It meant flying with the boys on their very first flight and a train journey in Spain to meet Ronnie and Jenny. I was extremely nervous about making the journey, but I didn't want to disappoint my in-laws or the boys. Ronnie was proud to have been able to afford this villa in his retirement.

We had a great time. Ronnie didn't enjoy driving very much and didn't want to drive in Spain. I, on the other hand, loved to drive and was very happy when he decided to hire a car listing me as the named driver. We spent the week exploring the local sites and on the beach with the boys. They enjoyed spending time with their grandparents and the adventure of being on a plane and a train.

This was the second time we'd spent a holiday with John's mam and dad, the first one being two years earlier in France when the six of us travelled together by car. John and his dad shared the driving. We had been joined by John's sister, Sheila, Laurence, her husband, and John's brother, David. Anthony celebrated his third birthday during this holiday. It was a happy time.

When we returned home from Spain we found four rabbits in the garden, which John had bought as a surprise for the boys. I didn't know what to make of them at first, but they provided a lot of entertainment and pleasure for us all. Even the rabbits couldn't just have a hutch, they were eventually given a purpose-made rockery to live in, with carefully constructed tunnels and had the freedom of the garden to roam. John made car tracks over the rockery for the boys to drive their remote-control cars over the top.

I was pleased he was taking more of an interest in the

boys as they were growing older. In winter he would take them sledging down the steepest hills he could find and built an igloo in the garden that the boys and the rabbits could explore.

We enjoyed family camping holidays in Northumberland and Scotland. One year we went to Wales but the car broke down and we had to be relayed back home. As the boys grew older we had several holidays in Brittany, France. They would play on the beach, but while I watched them, John would usually be sat in a deckchair, his nose buried in a book. That was pretty much the state of our marriage for many years.

When Anthony was seven I decided I wanted to go back to work, at least on a part-time basis, and John was only too happy at the prospect of me once again earning some extra money. After ten years being a full-time mother, I found a job, first as a sales assistant at Marks & Spencer and then at Boots. They were both temporary positions – about six months later I started work as a part-time receptionist at Gilesgate Medical Centre in Durham. Soon after that we moved to another – yet again bigger – house in the village, a four-bedroom home on Glebeside. Being out of the house was a breath of fresh air for me.

John, on the other hand, was miserable at work and eventually said he couldn't go on being a teacher for very much longer. He started applying for new jobs, and when a letter arrived one morning in 1990, offering him a position as a financial advisor at Barclays Bank in Newcastle upon Tyne, he took the plunge and resigned after 18 years of teaching. I was happy for him because he had been so miserable. 'If it's what you want, a change will do you good,' I reassured him.

But it didn't take him long to discover that the grass isn't always greener on the other side. I think he thought a change in career would make everything better, but it didn't. He just didn't take to the bank. He felt he was being asked to sell products to people who didn't really need them or couldn't afford them, and he wasn't prepared to do that. In hindsight, he must have learned a lot about how banks operate though. He stuck it out for a year but was pretty unhappy the whole time. He started looking for other jobs and totally surprised me one day when he said he had decided to join the prison service. It was his decision and I was happy for him.

So in 1992, at the age of 42, John embarked on another complete change of career and, after finishing his training, he started work at Holme House Prison in Stockton-on-Tees. Like any job, it could be stressful at times, but John seemed to enjoy his work, at least at first.

John had dabbled in stocks and shares for years but only risked small amounts of cash, because that was all that was available to him. Retirement was constantly on his mind – he'd long bragged he'd be a millionaire by the time he was 50. But he knew his two index-linked pensions wouldn't give us the comfortable life he craved. He needed something else.

As Mark and Anthony grew older, they were roped in to help with their father's latest money-making schemes. There were two in particular that raised eyebrows, the first being garden gnomes. John bought rubber moulds and enlisted the boys to paint the resulting figures in bright colours. He'd then sell them on his stall in Durham market or at car-boot sales. Later, realising gnomes were never going to make him rich, he tried his hand at breeding snails, having read an article about how you could make a tidy side income in doing so. Needless to say, he made little or no money and soon decided snails were not for him.

When Anthony was aged 15, he began looking for a way of earning some pocket money and applied for a job with a door-to-door catalogue company. He was too young to do it on his own so the local agent suggested John and I could help with some of the ordering. As time went by, John appeared to be spending a lot of time with the local agent, making up excuses as to why he needed to see her.

I began to be suspicious, which came to a head when John said he needed to go away to a weekend conference with the woman. I asked outright if he was having an affair: 'Is there something going on between you two?'

He denied it. 'Don't be ridiculous, we're going to a conference and she's taking her daughter with her,' he said, and went away regardless.

But I knew in my heart something was going on. I could see it in their eyes when they looked at each other – there was a glint in John's eyes that I hadn't seen in a long time. He didn't look at me in that way anymore. I could see my marriage dissolving in front of my eyes and I decided I had to do something if I wanted to save it. I didn't want it to end and I realised I had to fight to keep us together.

So one day, I decided to go to the woman's house and confront her. I drove to the nearby village where she lived, and knocked on the door. When she answered, I was shocked. I had met her several times before and noticed immediately that her once blonde curly hair had been straightened and dyed almost the same colour as mine.

At first, she denied there was anything going on with John. She said they had decided to set up another business together selling items for personal protection: personal alarms, pepper spray and some noxious spray that gave off a horrid odour that was impossible to wash off. According to her, she had the ideas and John had the ability to make the business work.

I guess he thought he'd found a kindred spirit and became infatuated with her. I said to her it was plain by the way they looked at each other and the amount of time they spent together that they were more than business partners. Eventually, she confessed to having an affair. We didn't shout, I didn't even raise my voice, but I felt I had made a stand.

I went home to make tea for the boys and was ironing when John arrived home that evening. I told him what I had done, leaving him with little option but to admit that it was true.

Even then, despite his assurances to the contrary, the affair carried on for some weeks. It was only when the woman's husband found out and came to our house and confronted John, warning him in no uncertain terms to keep away, that John realised he had to end the relationship. I didn't get involved, but I was in the next room and could hear the argument. John knew I could hear it, too.

Of course, I was angry and heartbroken and thought about leaving him, particularly when I realised the affair had been going on despite John's promises. But married life was all I'd known for nearly 20 years. I doubted my ability to cope on my own and I worried about what effect it would have on the boys if we separated.

One evening, at John's instigation, we sat down and started to examine where things had gone wrong in our marriage. I was shocked when John confessed to having had another affair, soon after we married. I realised I didn't even want to be with him anymore, but was still worried about the impact on the boys and how I would cope on my own. Where would I live? Who would the boys live with? I didn't want to see the boys hurt, and the last thing I wanted was to tear the family apart. I felt I had failed as a wife. In turmoil, I felt totally trapped: it was without doubt the lowest point of my life so far.

After much soul searching, I eventually forgave him. My marriage vows were for better for worse, till death us do part, and I wanted to honour them. We agreed to make a fresh start, where we'd both make more of an effort and try to make things work. However, I wasn't sure if I'd ever be able to trust him again.

Chapter 3

Get Rich Quick

John always knew that while his part-time sidelines helped pay the bills, they would never make him a wealthy man. He remembered his father telling him you couldn't go wrong with bricks and mortar and decided to turn his attention to building a mini-property empire. It was the mid-1990s when he started investing in this latest get-rich-quick venture.

The first house he bought was in the historic market town of Chester-le-Street, which he suggested would provide me with an alternative to a pension. It had four bedrooms and we converted a downstairs room to make five in total. The rooms were let to mostly young, unemployed people. John thought it would provide us with a steady income as they were claiming housing benefit, which could be paid directly to us as landlords.

Within the space of a year he had bought 11 more houses, this time in poor former mining villages. Five of them were among the cheapest homes in the village of Easington, where pit owners had been notorious for providing the most basic housing they could get away with. John liked to boast that he bought one on a credit card for £6,000. They were simple 'two up two down', brick-terrace properties. There was a sitting room at the front of the house with a small kitchen and bathroom extension at the back and two bedrooms upstairs.

Easington had been devastated by the demise of the mining industry, which in 1951 employed 81,000 people in the county. Those jobs had simply vanished, leaving appalling levels of economic, social and environmental deprivation and rising crime rates. This was where John foolishly believed his rental homes would make him a millionaire. It was easy money, he bragged. I was far from sure.

I thought it was too much to take on. I already wasn't happy dealing with the tenants in the house we rented out in Chester-le-Street. The income John was expecting was slow to arrive as the tenants wouldn't complete the necessary application forms for housing benefit. There was a constant change of tenants as they never seemed to agree with one another, and they had no idea about how to care for themselves or the property. We'd spent a long time preparing the house and it was upsetting to see the way it was being treated. All I could foresee was a huge multiplication of our problems happening in Easington.

John reasoned that they would be different because he would look for couples or young families, as the houses only had two bedrooms. As with all his ventures, John relied on working out everything on a spreadsheet and then producing it as evidence. 'It's plain to see, it's there in black and white. I've looked at every possibility,' he'd say. He did manage to get a few houses let to long-term tenants that gave us no hassle. If only it could have been the same for all of them.

We were spending less and less time together. We were either at work or John was doing repairs on the houses. He tried to do as much as possible by himself to save unnecessary expense. Then he got frustrated with me because I couldn't help out.

By this time I had two jobs. I worked 25 hours as senior receptionist at the surgery and I did two evenings a week, finishing at midnight, in addition to one full day on a weekend at the out-of-hours centre for GPs. I enjoyed the work, the responsibility of making sure everything was prepared for the next day's surgery and helping patients at their most vulnerable. We had angry people to deal with as well, disappointed that they couldn't get an appointment immediately, but there was always a way to spot those genuinely in need so we could sort things out for them there and then. It was very rewarding. Obviously it gave us some extra income, too, but I certainly didn't have time for maintenance on the rental properties. With John working shifts, we were often like ships passing in the night. We had never had much of a social life – John once joked to someone that he only took me out when it was voting night. I kept my sanity by singing in a local choir and the occasional meal out with the girls from the surgery.

It was late summer or early autumn 2000 when John announced he had found the perfect seafront home for us in nearby Seaton Carew. I was very happy where we were and didn't want to move – we had just got our own house the way we wanted it and I felt we had put down roots in Witton Gilbert. Although the move would mean a much shorter journey to work for John, it wouldn't be practical for me to do my second job. Our home was big enough for our needs. Anthony had already left, to find work near to his girlfriend, Louise, and I knew it was likely that Mark would also soon move away.

I was shocked to discover he also wanted us to buy the property next door. Nos 3 and 4 The Cliffe were in a row of five majestic Victorian terraced houses, he told me, with magnificent views over the sea. They had been built in the 1890s, so local legend had it, for the five daughters of a wealthy industrialist. Next door, but just far enough away to block out the noise from departing guests, was the town's best known hotel, the Staincliffe, built in the same gothic style by the same wealthy pillar of the community.

Still, John persuaded me to visit the houses to see for myself. I took one look and thought, *He must be crazy*. I found the prospect of living there totally daunting. The two houses were huge and very run down. Branching off the once-grand staircase of No 4 were 13 low-rent rooms, spread over four levels and across the top floor of No 3. I didn't want to be surrounded by live-in tenants and all the problems that I knew would come with that. I asked the owners lots of questions about the rental income, occupancy rates and valuations, trying to establish whether they were, at least, a good investment. Meanwhile, John ignored the shabby front door and peeling paint, and waxed lyrical about them being self-funding properties that could be money-spinners.

John was very focused, you might even say single-minded, when he was working on a project. Nothing else mattered. Every waking minute would be spent working out the pros and cons as far as finance was concerned, but he failed to realise his practical capabilities and, as a result, work usually took much longer than imagined.

Seaton Carew might have been sad looking, dirty and run down, but John had been drawn to the town since the days when it was a place anyone would be proud to visit. Before the nuclear power station was built, before the fun fair was ripped out and the vast chemical complex mushroomed on the south side of the bay, the town's bright lights and penny arcades offered everything a child could wish for. The town's three-mile arc of sand, sheltered to the north by Hartlepool's headland and to the south by Coatham Sands, was a world away from the pit village, eight miles up the coast, he had called home.

John saw buying the properties as an ideal opportunity to start making the kind of real money he had long craved.

I think he saw it as a chance to live a life of leisure handed to him on a plate. In his head, he was already making plans to retire on the profits he would make from the £2,000-a-month rental income, imagining the look on the faces of the other prison officers when he drove out of the car park of Holme House Prison for the last time. In his mind, I could tell, living at The Cliffe would prove to everyone that John Darwin had made a success of his life. The big front doors, the stone-mullioned windows and the imposing balconies added up to the perfect image for John to show the world.

Armed with the current owners' accounts, John approached the Yorkshire Bank to make his claim for a new mortgage. House prices were rising steadily, his 12 existing rental properties were now worth much more, on paper at least, and John discovered he could get a 'global mortgage', bundling all the properties we owned into one loan. Instead of a messy range of borrowing that would be complicated to control, he would have just one lump sum every month to pay. I really didn't think it was a good idea and told John we shouldn't rush into it. It was a huge mortgage and the thought of not being able to pay it filled me with fear and dread. But to him it all sounded nice and simple – and that was that.

There was an initial interest-only period, which John said would tide us over to the following summer, by which time we expected to have sold our house in Witton Gilbert. However, John was not paying off the money he owed on a growing number of credit cards, which he hadn't mentioned to the Yorkshire Bank. He knew that if he had confessed to any financial difficulties, there would have been little chance of getting the loan. So he had said nothing, reassuring himself that everything would sort itself out eventually.

The debt was quickly rising and I couldn't believe his cavalier attitude. He was burying his head in the sand. I told him if it didn't work out, we'd lose everything. He just told me to stop worrying and that everything would be fine.

We moved to Seaton Carew on 20 December 2000. For John, the first Christmas of the new millennium, celebrated in his grand new house on the seafront, was undoubtedly the proudest of his life so far. Living there was proof that he was a success. He'd moved his family from a humble house in a former mining village to the Victorian splendour of a seaside resort.

Parked outside and looking suitably expensive was his pride and joy, a gleaming dark blue Range Rover with the number plate B9 JRD, for John Ronald Darwin. He had a steady job at the local prison, an impressive portfolio of rental properties and two handsome grown-up sons. Our marriage had been through rocky times, but we were still together. At the age of 50, he was well on the way to having everything he wanted. At least that's how it may have appeared to an onlooker.

For me, Christmas that year was a non-event. The house was bare of festive decorations and we were surrounded by packing cases. We hadn't even managed to get the cooker connected before Christmas Day. Thankfully, we had a microwave oven so we didn't go hungry. I think Anthony spent the day with his girlfriend Louise's family and came to visit us at New Year, and both John and Mark were working.

The Cliffe was cold and drafty. With its high ceilings and large rooms with badly-fitting windows, the house was never warm unless the heating was on for about twelve hours a day. Often the radiators felt hot to touch but the rooms still felt cold. We developed the habit of just heating the room that we were in, using gas fires, unless we had visitors. I missed our Witton Gilbert home with good insulation and double glazing. Preparing for the move had been quite stressful and it wasn't a happy time. Now, I wandered from room to room slowly realising the enormity of what we were facing. How would we ever decorate and furnish the house?

Each floor of No 3 had a connecting door to No 4, and to me it felt there was no privacy. We could hear the comings and goings of the tenants so they must be able to hear us. Some of them would come in late at night rather the worse for alcohol. They were all single men, mostly unemployed, though a couple of them had jobs. I was glad we had two Rottweilers. I knew most people would be deterred by them, even though they were very gentle dogs and by no means lived up to the reputation of the breed.

We wanted to improve the image of No 4, but didn't have the capital to refurbish the bedsits to a high enough standard. We were turning some prospective tenants away, but we weren't able to attract the sort of people we would have preferred. Working shifts in the prison service often gave John several consecutive days off, which he would spend working on the houses, or if he was on night shift he would survive on just a couple of hours sleep each day for a whole week. But John soon discovered he just didn't have enough time to look after all the houses on his own. We appointed a property management agent to look after some of the houses in the northern-most villages, but they proved to be just as unsuccessful at re-letting them when they became vacant. And they were slow to pass on the rental income, which didn't help our situation.

Financially, before we moved to Seaton Carew we at least had some room for manoeuvre. Now, having the huge global mortgage, and with even more responsibilities, we were quickly getting into more debt than ever. It wasn't long before John fell out with the people who were supposed to be paying our mortgage, and with bedsits left empty at No 4, and extra bills to pay for repair and maintenance, we were completely out of our depth. A tidal wave of financial ruin was fast approaching.

Chapter 4

'I'll Have to Do a Reggie Perrin'

Finding the strength to face each day was getting harder and harder. To the outside world we were an ordinary, hard-working couple, with ordinary, everyday problems. But the truth was so very different.

My stomach would turn over at the sound of the post being delivered, or the phone ringing. We were being chased and hassled by many different companies, and I struggled to put on a brave face and carry on as if everything was OK – all the while my husband, John, along with our situation, was becoming more and more desperate.

Every penny that was coming in was going out twice as fast. John had accumulated various property investments – in a bid to make his longed-for fortune and secure our future. But, by March 2002, it was obvious John's investments were a disaster. He was so reckless. It had never ceased to amaze him how easy it was to add another credit card to his collection; it had never ceased to terrify me. He owed £64,000 on 13 different cards and various high-interest loans, but now the credit had run out. No one would lend him another penny.

But John was never the sort to take no for an answer. He wouldn't be seen as a failure. And my inability to talk sense into him was about to sink my living nightmare to a whole new depth.

We kept this problem hidden from everyone, including our sons, but it was at the forefront of my mind all the time. If we could have sold one or two of the rental properties, we could have paid enough of our debt to keep people happy. But we couldn't sell even one, because they were all tied up in a global mortgage with the house we were living in. The bank wasn't budging an inch. I had no idea how we could ever get ourselves out of this mess and knew bankruptcy was beating at our door. It seemed the only option left.

I hated coming home from work, dreading what new bills or threatening letters were waiting on the doormat. I never knew what kind of a mood John would be in. He often used to ignore me and sulk, preferring to spend time playing internet games. I never wanted the houses in the first place, and I didn't know how or why John's plans had got so out of control. There was no pleasure in my life and nothing to live for.

Sometimes I walked across the road and sat staring at the sea, contemplating what it would be like to walk straight into it and not come back – I never learned to swim, so there would be no second chance. I didn't love John and certainly didn't love myself. It was only the thought of Mark and Anthony that stopped me, and that I was a coward. All I wanted was to go back to a time before rental properties and live a simple life.

We looked at every possible way to alleviate our debt. John rang Range Rover to see if he could refinance his cherished vehicle. They said no. He contacted the teachers' union about claiming a lump sum of his pension, but was told it was out of the question.

John's ideas started to get more extreme. One evening he said, 'I think I should crash the Range Rover on the way home from work. If it's written off, we could claim the insurance money.' Then he added, 'But I might actually kill myself doing it. I don't want to do that.'

I said, exasperated, 'John, don't be stupid. There has to be a better way to work things out. Bankruptcy might be painful and humiliating, but at least we'd still have each other and could start again with our slate wiped clean.'

But John wouldn't even consider it. He said he'd never be able to live with the shame.

In December the previous year, John had taken out a £50,000 fatal accident policy in joint names. I had always thought the policy was linked to the mortgage, but with hindsight I can't be completely sure. Maybe that was when John first started thinking of his plan to 'do a Reggie Perrin' and disappear. Either way, he definitely knew he was worth more dead than alive.

From time to time he'd mention faking his own death, but I didn't think for a minute he was serious. I assumed that sooner or later we'd simply have to file for bankruptcy. But John was serious.

Sitting in front of the roaring fire one evening, he told me that his mind was made up: he really was going to fake his own death. He knew it couldn't look as if he had committed suicide, as that would invalidate his insurance policy. He said if he could just vanish for a while, and then come back again, I could claim the life insurance money, pay off the debts and everything would once again be hunky-dory. He knew he would have some explaining to do and maybe some money to repay, but he'd think of something, he always did.

I was speechless. He had it all worked out in his mind. He was convinced he could get away with it and all he needed was my help because he couldn't do it alone. 'If we opt for bankruptcy, we'll lose everything, including our home,' he said. 'So, too, would our tenants. I'd hate to see those people out on the streets.'

I was sure he couldn't have cared less about them. I couldn't believe what I was hearing.

'What about the boys?' I asked, horrified. Furious! 'You're not seriously saying you'd let them believe you are dead? And what about the police? You'll be found out and locked up – we both will. For God's sake, John, you'll have to think of something else. You can't just disappear!' I really thought John had lost his mind.

'Well it's either that or I do it for real,' he replied.

I was so angry. 'I'm the one who will have to do the

lying. You can't honestly expect me to tell the boys you are dead? What sort of mother do you think I am?'

I stormed out of the room in frustration, in floods of tears, and locked myself in the bathroom. What the hell was he thinking?

John knocked on the door but I was having none of it. 'Go away and leave me alone!'

'OK, well, I'll do it for real then,' John said, 'and then you'll be free of me and the debts.'

At that point I was thinking, *Go ahead and do it!* But I couldn't actually speak the words. And then I felt guilty for having such thoughts. I was confused. I no longer knew what I really wanted, I just didn't want to be in this mess.

When I calmed down a little, I unlocked the door and found John back in the drawing room.

'Tell me you won't do it, you won't just disappear,' I said. He was my husband after all.

'OK, OK, I promise,' he replied, but I wasn't sure I believed him.

We had the same argument numerous times during the following weeks. I really couldn't believe he was going to go through with it. It was just too unreal to be true. Of course, I kept trying to talk John out of it, but whenever I protested, he simply insisted there was no alternative. It was often the only topic of conversation; I would become so upset and emotional, that some days, if we didn't talk about it, we barely spoke at all. He refused to take the only sensible option of bankruptcy and as usual, thought he knew best. We both knew that time was running out as far as our dire financial situation was concerned, but nothing I could say would make him change his mind.

The truth was, he simply could not contemplate the thought of losing everything and being seen as a failure. His mind was already made up.

Chapter 5

The Vanishing Act

Neither of us were sleeping. We were both at our wits' end. Piles of bills arrived daily, along with a smattering of bailiffs' demands threatening eviction and court proceedings. We had run out of options.

Nothing I could say would persuade John to take the sensible route of bankruptcy. I thought he had lost his mind when he told me he'd decided to fake his own death. We argued furiously for weeks. I asked how he could possibly think we could do this to his boys, and to his own father, but he wouldn't listen. 'I'll only need to vanish for a couple of weeks,' he'd say, 'and then we'll have the money.' He couldn't see what was wrong with this.

I knew I would eventually give in and help. I always did.

I lay awake at night wishing he'd really have the fatal accident he talked about. Terrible, horrible, thoughts, I know, but that's how I felt. I had long since fallen out of love with John, but I couldn't work out how I'd survive without him. I felt helpless and trapped. He was so different to the man I'd married. At times he had been good humoured and witty, and even quite romantic. But all that had changed and those attributes were long gone. I'm sure the stress we were under didn't help. But I really didn't want to go through with this madness, and right up to the last minute I did all that I could to dissuade him, although I knew, deep down, I was fighting a lost cause.

On the morning of 21 March 2002, after one last vain attempt to talk him out of it, I left for work still not really believing I had agreed to go through with his plan. John had been keeping a close eye on the weather and the tides, and felt conditions today were as good as they would get for his vanishing act. The next day the sea would be much calmer and wouldn't lend itself to his plan. Quite how I made the journey to work that morning I don't know. I arrived at the surgery car park at about 8.40am with absolutely no recollection of how I'd got there.

Once the early morning flurry of phone calls requesting appointments and prescriptions had subsided, I found it increasingly difficult to concentrate on my work. I was hoping against hope that John would call to say he couldn't go through with it. Up until now, work had been a distraction from the problems at home, but today thoughts of what was happening at home were all that occupied my mind.

I could feel my heart beating in my chest and I had a pounding headache, but I tried my hardest to remain calm and carry on with the daily routine. No one appeared to notice that I was actually trembling as I drank a cup of coffee. I had no appetite for my lunch.

I was in the middle of a phone call when I was told John was on another line. He was asked to hold until I was free to speak to him. I wasn't expecting him to call, and my immediate thought was that – thank goodness – he'd changed his mind and couldn't do it. But I was mistaken. He was calling to remind me to be at the pick-up point on time, or earlier if at all possible. He wanted me to be there by 6.30pm. I knew that was impossible, and the soonest I could get there would be 7pm. I told him I'd been ill all morning, literally worried sick at the thought of what he was about to do and the lies I was going to have to tell. I asked him again, 'Is there no other way?'

'No, there is no alternative. It will all be over in a couple of weeks. It will be fine. Please, just be there,' came the reply.

I was constantly watching the clock, time weighed heavily, yet all of a sudden it was time to lock up and leave.

I left the surgery in Gilesgate at about 6.20pm, and arrived at the North Gare car park, just a five-minute car ride from our home, around 7pm, as promised. I flashed the car's headlights as I saw John's outline trudging towards me. He looked a little like a bedraggled Milk Tray man, wearing his thick, quilted black cotton jacket, jeans and a black woolly hat, and carrying a rucksack, a tent attached to the bottom and a sleeping bag on top.

He got in the car, and sounded exhilarated as he described what had happened. He told me that several walkers had seen him struggling down to the sea with his canoe, and he hoped they'd be vital witnesses. He laughed as he told me how he'd packed so much gear for his getaway that the canoe simply wouldn't budge. The tide was coming in and, no matter what he did, he couldn't get the canoe to move. He pushed his hands into the sand on either side, but it was so weighed down it wouldn't shift. He bounced up and down, rocked back and forth, and dug his hands into the sands harder, trying desperately to get some movement. There was nothing for it but to get out and try again.

Eventually, after what seemed a lifetime, he had finally caught a wave, and then another, and the canoe slowly lurched forwards. He was off. He paddled out to sea, northwards towards the pier at North Gare, about a mile along the coast. The sea was actually quite choppy and both he and most of his belongings, including the small tent and sleeping bag he'd taken, were soaked by the waves by the time he paddled into shore. A few items of clothing and a spare pair of trainers had somehow stayed dry, so he'd changed out of his sodden apparel and sat hidden in the dunes for the rest of the day, waiting for the light to fade. When it did, he had thrown the paddle out to sea, only for it to wash straight back to shore on the next wave.

He tried again, but the same thing happened, so he told me he'd had to cut his losses and leave it where it was. With the canoe itself, he forced it downwards, so it quickly filled with water and threw in a few rocks for good measure. There was too much buoyancy for it to sink completely, he thought, but he hoped it would drift out to sea a little with the outgoing tide. He had packed what he had left into his rucksack. After many hours hidden away in the dunes, he headed off to find me.

I could see he was still running on adrenalin. 'For God's sake, John, you can't do this,' I begged. It still wasn't too late.

But there would be no going back for John. He had decided to head across country by train, so he told me to drive towards Durham Railway Station. I asked why not Hartlepool, which was much closer, but he said that would be the first place police would look to see if anyone had seen him. He would go to Newcastle, across the country to Carlisle, then on from there the next day.

'Unfortunately, it will all be up to you then,' he said. 'I'm sorry.'

Still not really believing what I was actually doing, I headed to Durham, stopping en route to dump some of his wet clothing in a skip I spotted at the side of the road.

His mood became subdued as we drew closer to the railway station, no doubt pondering what lay ahead. Wary that there were CCTV cameras in the station car park, I parked in an unlit side street. We had an emotional hug goodbye, not knowing quite how long it would be before we would see each other again, and I set off for home. I think I cried all the way. I don't know if I was crying for John and his uncertain future or for me and what I was about to do and everything that was about to unfold. Or, for everyone that would be impacted by my actions. My mind was in turmoil. I was frightened. I was being asked to do something I didn't want to do and I didn't know how to get out of it. I knew it was wrong, of course I did, and I knew I'd hurt everyone with the terrible lies I was about to tell.

Why did I do it? is the question I still ask myself today. Why did I make that phone call? I was never motivated by money, that wasn't the reason. John's voice was ringing in my ears, 'Just make the call, make it sound convincing, it'll be all right.' Incredible as it may sound, the only reason I had was my loyalty to John. While I'd questioned his actions in the past, things had usually worked out OK. That's illogical, I know, but I wasn't in my right mind. I felt I had a duty as his wife to do what he had asked. I now realise how totally stupid I was and that I should have had the courage to stand up for what I believed in – the truth. Never before had I done anything so utterly wrong and I certainly never will again. My Mam had always said I was easily led by others. How right she had been. But I did go along with everything John asked of me, and I fully accept I was therefore complicit in the crime.

In the week running up to that fateful night, John had concocted the story I would tell the police when I arrived home. I was to say I had gone window shopping, which would account for my late arrival home; had seen his car in the drive, when he should have been at work; and then noticed his canoe was missing and started worrying that something had happened.

Now, I put the story into motion, calling the police to report his disappearance. I told the emergency operator my fears over John's safety had grown when I picked up the home phone and dialled 1471 to see if anyone had called. I said I had recognised the last number received as that of Holme House Prison.

'I have to admit, I am getting a bit worried,' I told the 999 operator. 'I called the prison where he works, and they said they had tried to contact him as he hadn't turned up. This isn't like John at all.'

When two officers arrived at my house a short while later, I told them it was all a bit of a mystery and, although I was trying to reassure myself everything would be fine, I was growing increasingly worried he might have had an accident. I said at first, when I saw his car, I assumed that a work colleague must have passed by to give him a lift, as had happened once or twice in the past. I was greeted at the door by our two dogs, so I knew John couldn't be at home. But then I spotted the canoe was missing from the hallway and now I thought that perhaps he had taken it out and got into some difficulty. He had only brought the hand-built red canoe into the house from the garage a week or so earlier, after using it for the first time in years, I said. 'He's a very experienced canoeist but I'm starting to worry something dreadful might have happened,' I added. I was shocked at how easily I perfectly repeated the concocted lie.

Police quizzed neighbours and quickly established John had indeed been seen leaving our home, carrying his canoe and paddling off from the shore in the direction of Teesmouth earlier that morning.

The police agreed there was a real risk that something must have happened, and a full-scale search-and-rescue operation was quickly launched. Neither John nor I had the slightest idea how big this would become.

I told the police I had decided against telling the boys anything that night as I didn't want to unduly alarm them and put them through the torment I myself was going through. To be honest, I couldn't face the thought of speaking to them yet. I was sure everything would be fine, I said to the police, and any moment John would come bounding through the door with a simple explanation about what had happened.

Early the next morning, after a fraught and sleepless night, I was told by the police that the search was continuing but there there was still no word of John or sightings of the canoe. They urged me to call someone, so still not wanting to speak to the boys I decided to call Mam and Dad. That was a difficult call to make, telling the lie to the two people who had nurtured me and brought me up to be honest. They were totally shocked and in disbelief. I'd forgotten Dad was due to attend a hospital appointment that morning and said for them to keep the appointment and come as soon as they could. In the meantime, one of John's colleagues arrived to offer moral support. I didn't know him very well, as I'd only met him and his wife a few weeks earlier when John invited them for a few drinks.

In the end, I couldn't bring myself to call the boys at all. Mam took the decision to ring my brother Michael, and asked him to call Mark, who I knew would be at work in London.

Letting Anthony know was a different matter altogether. He was on holiday in Canada, visiting Niagara Falls, where he planned to ask his girlfriend, Louise, to marry him. I couldn't contemplate how on earth I could break the news to him, ruining what was meant to be one of the happiest times of his life. Michael agreed with me to leave Anthony in peace for now.

I was in a wretched state and my lies, to Michael, the police, to everyone, were very quickly spiralling out of control. I don't really know what I expected but it was far, far worse than I dreamt possible. Police officers were searching my house for clues, looking under every bed and in all the cupboards, and a detective was still gently pushing me for any information I might have neglected to tell them, which was scaring the life out of me. 'I've told you everything I know,' I sobbed. 'He's not coming back, is he?'

The matter most concerning me was that Mark would soon be here, and the thought made me nauseous. It wasn't as if telling Mark his father was missing, presumed dead, was a little white lie. It was going to leave him and Anthony absolutely devastated. How could I do this to my own sons? It was a question I would ask myself many, many times, in the days, weeks and months ahead. It was just about the worse thing a mother could do to her children.

Michael drove Mark up from London, and when they arrived later that afternoon I didn't have to pretend to be upset. I was already crying my eyes out because of what I had to do. I couldn't speak, we just held each other close, while I sobbed, Mark tried hard to hold back his tears. I felt wretched and loathed myself for what I was doing. What kind of a mother does this deliberately and totally unnecessarily? I felt helpless. Eventually Mark spoke, 'Where is he, Mam? You know what he's like, he'll turn up and wonder what all the fuss is about.'

'I don't think he will,' I replied, 'he's been gone too long,' all the while knowing he wouldn't be returning and, if his escape plan had worked, he wouldn't be found any time soon.

When there was still no sign of John the next day, Saturday 23 March, we knew we had to inform Anthony.

We were all in the living room, on the ground floor at the front of the house. Mark thought he should be the one to do it. I imagine he was trying to spare me from further pain. But as soon as he heard his brother's voice, words failed him and, his hand shaking, he handed the phone to my sister, Christine. I sat with my head in my hands, trying to shut out the scene, but couldn't avoid hearing the conversation. I felt trapped in a nightmare. As soon as they realised the seriousness of the situation, Anthony and Louise immediately cancelled the rest of their holiday and booked flights back to the UK. They arrived late the following day, having flown back to Heathrow, then driven for five hours to be with the family as soon as they could. All because of my terrible, unforgivable lies.

I think it was the police who broke the news to John's dad – possibly the family liaison officer, I'm not sure. Mark and Anthony went to visit him, but I didn't go until some time later. John's mother had died a few years earlier, and his relationship with his parents had deteriorated a few years before her death. I hadn't seen any of his family for several years, but his brother and sister, and her husband, came to see me. Obviously, they were upset, even though there had been little contact between John and them over recent years.

My home was a buzz of activity as police, family, neighbours and work colleagues came to show their support. I certainly looked like a convincing desperate wife – I wasn't eating or sleeping, so I was pale and drawn, my eyes red-raw from crying. I didn't know what else to do, so I spent hours sitting in a chair in the front room, staring out to the sea, which everyone – except me – was now convinced had claimed John's life. I was in a terrible state, that's true, but not for the reason everyone thought.

Some 65 RNLI volunteers had spent 85 hours looking for John, six rescue boats and three aircraft had assisted, nothing was left to chance. But four days after John's disappearance, on Monday morning, 25 March, the coastguards finally terminated the search-and-rescue operation, admitting that the chances of him being found alive had passed and he was presumed drowned at sea.

Chapter 6

Learning to Play the Grieving Widow

It was about a week after his disappearance that John called the mobile phone. When I answered it I was shocked to hear his voice at the other end of the line. He tried to disguise it, saying, 'Can I speak to Anne please?' I went into the bedroom to take the call.

I couldn't think straight, 'Why are you ringing? Are you coming back? What's wrong?'

He replied, 'It's too soon to come back. I just want to know what's happening? Has everyone gone home yet?'

'Are you mad? Of course they haven't gone home yet. I've got a house full of people and the police are in and out all day long. I can't talk to you like this.'

'Write this number down and ring me tomorrow at 9pm. It's a phone box, I'll be waiting.'

'I can't promise to be able to ring at that time.'

'Just try. Say you have to go to the shop and ring me from a phone box, not from home or the mobile.'

His money ran out and I was left exasperated. I returned to the drawing room, where the rest of the family were wondering who the call was from. I told them it was just a friend enquiring how I was.

The next evening, just before nine o'clock, I announced I needed to pop out to the shops to pick something up. Someone, though I don't recall who, offered to go with me, but I said I just needed to get out of the house and wanted to go alone. It was late and there wouldn't be many people around. I needed to do something normal. Of course, the real reason was that I had to make that call to John. I knew if I didn't, he would ring the mobile again and I didn't want that to happen.

'Where are you?' I asked. I had no idea where he'd gone after leaving Newcastle.

'In the phone box, near the pub, in Silloth.' I'd never heard of Silloth, and John had to explain where it was. At first, he had checked into bed and breakfast accommodation, using a false name, John Allen, and now he was camped out on the beach in the small Cumbrian town. 'Tell me what's going on?' he asked.

'What do you think is going on? The house is full of people, police, everyone's asking questions. It's all over the television and radio, I can't carry on. Please come back and just give yourself up,' I pleaded, in tears.

'I can't,' he said. 'I haven't come this far to give in now and lose everything.'

'It's easy for you, all you have to do is hide away. I'm the one being interrogated and having to face people and lie to them all the time. Let me tell Mark and Anthony. It's terrible watching them not knowing whether to think you are dead, while hoping you're still alive. Thinking you're lying somewhere, injured.'

'No, you can't do that. They'll get over it. The police will stop looking soon and everyone will go home and get back to normal. Trust me,' he said, 'We'll work it out. You just need to stay calm. I love you, don't abandon me now, I need you to do this.'

I couldn't say 'I love you' back to John, I felt totally exhausted and void of all feeling towards him, except anger. But still I carried on, agreeing to call again in a couple of days.

For three weeks after his disappearance, the boys had stayed with me to offer what comfort they could. They were dreadful days because I knew I was the cause of their pain and everything I was doing was an act. I hated myself for doing it. The days seemed to pass in a blur. I wasn't eating, drinking and barely sleeping, not out of grief, of course, but because of the terrible lies I was telling. Everyone just seemed to be wandering around the house in a daze. I felt so helpless and just wish I'd been strong enough to put an end to it all.

Anthony appeared a little stronger than Mark, with a part of him refusing to believe his father was really dead. He kept himself busy by checking websites for news from the coastguard or missing persons organisations. In the weeks that followed, he searched the internet for any information about people missing at sea and contacted the UK Missing Persons' Bureau. He said he hoped his dad would turn up somewhere in a hospital with amnesia. However unrealistic he thought it was, as long as there wasn't a body he refused to give up.

Before disappearing, John had given a great deal of thought to the secretive life he would be forced to lead on his return. Along with his list of options on how best to disappear, and where to hide until the dust had settled, he also had to figure out the rather more difficult and longer term concern of where he was actually going to live once he was 'dead'. He quickly decided the simplest – and cheapest – option would be to move back home. Well, almost. No 4 had a number of vacant bedsits, which could be used to hide in, especially with the properties' connecting doors. When John told me of his plan, I was horrified. 'Don't be ridiculous,' I told him. 'Someone will spot you straightaway and then we'll have the police at our door.' But John wasn't going to let my silly doubts stand in his way.

John phoned several times asking if he could come home, but I told him he couldn't because the boys were still there. He was finding camping out, with the few provisions he had, very hard, and was getting desperate.

The boys had stayed with me to offer what comfort they could for three weeks after his disappearance. Eventually, Mark had to leave to return to work and, a couple of days later, Anthony also headed south to his home. For the first time since John's vanishing act, the house was empty.

When John called that day, he tearfully begged me to come and get him, and I relented. Truth was, John couldn't wait for his grieving sons to return to their homes, so he could return to his.'

I drove cross country to Cumbria and discovered John had changed so much in just three weeks that I hadn't even recognised him. I sat waiting at our pre-arranged pick-up spot in a car park and watched an elderly gentleman limp towards the car and walk past. Then he came past a second time and, as he passed and glanced towards me, I recognised John. He had grown a beard and he was wearing baggy clothes that I didn't recognise, which he later told me he had bought in a charity shop, and sunglasses.

He had lost a lot of weight. It seemed he hadn't had a proper meal since disappearing and said he was starving. I had been driving for over two hours and needed a break before the return journey, so we decided to stop at a pub to get some food. I felt very uneasy, constantly looking around to see if people were watching us and, to be honest, I was embarrassed to be with him. He had been living rough and obviously hadn't washed in weeks. He looked like a tramp and smelled to high heaven. It really was overbearing and I couldn't wait to get out into the fresh air.

I was pleased to see he was alive and in one piece, but I was also very angry and told him it was time to put an end to the lies. But John said he couldn't and the worst was now over. I knew that wasn't the case and there would be much worse to come if we carried on.

'We need to at least tell the boys, John,' I begged him. 'They are grieving and suffering so much.'

But he said that was impossible. If we told them, they were likely to persuade me to tell the truth. He also said that if they agreed not to say anything, it would implicate them in the crimes and that was the last thing either of us wanted. This wasn't something we'd considered before because we hadn't expected things to go on for so long, but it was now clear that the lying had to continue. I felt totally trapped, powerless to do anything.

Back home, John needed a bath and I certainly wasn't going to disagree. I think I put his filthy clothes straight in the wash. As soon as he was out, he started quizzing me about how I was getting on with claiming the insurance. I couldn't believe what I was hearing. The stress of lying in such a terrible way to the boys and everyone else had taken its toll. I was a bag of nerves and furious with him for even bringing it up so soon after coming home.

'I haven't done anything!' I yelled at him, through

tears. 'Nothing. Nothing at all. How the hell could I?'

John knew it would be unwise to push things further. For now, anyway.

We settled into an awkward routine. John spent most of his time in No 3 with me but he had also made regular forays to the bedsit in the basement of our house next door, which he planned to make his bolt-hole. He knew there would soon come a time when he might have to rush through one of the connecting doors in a hurry, and he made trial runs to help eliminate the risk of errors when he had to make that quick getaway for real. The ground-floor living-room window had vertical blinds fitted, and to make it easier for John to move around, I fixed net curtains to the bay window in the drawing room on the second floor.

Just three days after he returned home, I received a call from the police that sent me into a blind panic. The next day, a team of officers would be coming round for a renewed top-to-toe search of the house, looking for any clues they might have initially missed. It seemed incredible that the police were telegraphing their visit, but John was very glad they did. We quickly set about methodically walking through every room, making sure there were no tell-tale signs of John being there.

John knew it was far too dangerous, and too early, to risk hiding next door. He wasn't happy at all, but knew the only option was to disappear again. After the last disastrous camping expedition, he said taking to a tent again wasn't an option, so he decided to head south an hour to Morpeth and lay low in a B&B for a week.

Incredibly, knowing the police would soon be knocking on the door, John didn't even leave that night. But I knew I couldn't take any chances, so I changed the bedding, putting the dirty linen in the washing machine, and told John he couldn't sleep with me in the bed as I didn't want any give-away indentations in the fresh sheets. Instead, after packing a rucksack with a few things, John curled up on a sofa in the drawing room and tried to get some sleep. When he woke, realising he might need some identification, he quickly printed out two copies of a tenancy agreement for the bedsit, one for him and one for me, using another fake name, Karl Fenwick. He even printed out the name to stick on the bedsit's front door to try to create some authenticity.

It was still dark and time to go. I unbolted the ground-floor connecting door to No 4, checked the coast was clear, and John tiptoed to his hideaway in the basement to collect his disguise garments and a walking stick. He then crept up the stairs, and adopted his staged limp as he quietly shuffled out of the door and off down the street towards the bus station. As soon as he had gone, I went to the bathroom to check he'd put the toilet seat down. After all, he was a man.

The search had been far more extensive than I had

imagined it would be. Four police vans had arrived just over an hour after he left, and teams of officers, wearing blue forensic overalls, went through every room of the four-storey house, including the loft and storage space in the back garden (which had once been a chapel, then a garage).

One of the first things they did was search the bedroom, carefully pulling back the duvet – obviously there were some who still felt there was more to John's disappearance than met the eye. Officers went through every drawer, bagging up dozens of letters and bills, tenancy agreements, receipts and taking away John's prized computer. I panicked when they briefly went into No 4 through the connecting door on the ground level, and was mightily relieved they hadn't searched all the bedsits, probably because they would have each needed individual search warrants. The whole experience left me badly shaken. It also left me in no doubt that some officers still weren't totally convinced about John's disappearance.

Unbeknown to the police, we actually had two telephone lines into the house, having discovered by chance that there was a socket in one of the back bedrooms that had an old number, which for some reason had never been disconnected. I only ever plugged a handset into that line when I needed to secretly receive or make a call. John had set times to call, and he knew if there was no answer, it was because I had someone with me in the house and I hadn't plugged the phone in. John called that night and, once again, found me frantic. The search had taken all day to complete and was extremely thorough. I was concerned about the letters and documents they had taken away, and the computer they had removed for forensic examination. John told me not to worry, that they probably wouldn't find anything, the computer would be returned and their investigations would soon be ended. I wished I had his level of calm.

I didn't know this at the time, but while he was in Morpeth, John was finalising plans for his new identity. He had decided on stealing the plot from Frederick Forsyth's *The Day of the Jackal*, a novel he had read and reread. He loved how the book's protagonist, the Jackal, played in the film by Edward Fox, trawled graveyards looking for the headstone of a baby boy who, had he not died, would have been about the same age as the assassin. Using the details of the late Alexander James Quentin Duggan, the Jackal bought a copy of the deceased's birth certificate – all the proof he needed to successfully apply for a passport. If it was good enough for the Jackal, thought John, it would certainly be good enough for him. He had given much thought to where he was going to live and felt it might actually be cheaper, and certainly safer, to travel abroad if he needed to disappear for long periods of time. To do this he needed a new name and new passport.

He decided to stick with John, so would just need a new

surname. A John who, like him, was born in 1950, but
who had died at a very young age. He called Morpeth
council and made an appointment to search through
microfiche files in the genealogy and archives department.
Once there, he spent several hours trawling through
records for a likely candidate. He finally hit on a baby
called John Jones, born just five months before him, on 27
March 1950, at his grandmother's home in Sunderland,
where John was also born. The baby had tragically died
just five weeks later, on 30 April, from enteritis, or
inflammation of the small intestine, at the city's Hospital
for Infectious Diseases. The Christian name was spot on
and the surname, Jones, one of the commonest names
going. It couldn't have been better for his purposes. He
jotted down the date of birth and the reference numbers
necessary to pull a birth certificate and left feeling rather
pleased with himself. And, unlike the Jackal, John didn't
even have to get his shoes dirty by trudging through
graveyards in the dead of night. The following day, he
travelled to Sunderland and made straight for the office of
births, deaths and marriages, where he duly applied for
and was given the birth certificate. He had folded and
re-folded the certificate many times, and rubbed both
sides into a grubby bit of carpet, so it looked old and worn.
John Jones, mark two, was born.

Several days later, when he returned home, John
decided he needed to join the library at Hartlepool. With
so much spare time on his hands, he'd have access to as

much reading material as he needed but, more importantly, John was well aware librarians were public figures and able to vouch for people on passport applications. On 22 April, John filled in an application form, showed librarian Susan Garrington his birth certificate and a copy of a tenancy agreement for The Cliffe, and was told his membership card would be ready next time he visited. He was also overjoyed to realise that, the police having taken his home computer, he would once again have access to the internet using one of the library's computers.

It was six weeks after John disappeared that an early-morning walker spotted a broken-up red canoe being tossed around in the waves tumbling ashore at Blue Lagoon Sands at the mouth of the River Tees. After dragging it out of the water and up on to the beach, the man called 999.

Hartlepool's inshore lifeboat was immediately launched and Coastguard and RNLI volunteers searched the coastline for several miles in each direction, while a police spotter plane flew overhead. A yellow waterproof jacket was also discovered a little further along the shore (which did not actually belong to John)… but, of course, there was no sign of a body. It was a remote spot, but quite why the canoe had taken so long to wash ashore was something of a mystery.

I was at home when I received a phone call from my police family liaison officer, saying he had some bad news. He asked if I would mind coming to the police station to see if I could identify a dark red canoe, with toggles at either end, that had just been washed ashore. A shiver ran down my spine. I hated any contact with the police and knew I would again have to put on another grief-stricken performance. I had a terrible feeling of trepidation, thinking that there may be some evidence that I hadn't been told about that would expose John's disappearance and all my lies. My stomach was in knots.

The family liaison officer collected me from home and took me to Hartlepool Police Station to identify the canoe, which was in a basement car park. I nodded that yes, it was his. I could see the name *Orca*, which John had christened the canoe and painted on the side, next to his drawings of a mother and two baby killer whales. It was broken apart and really did look flimsy, battered and holed. I think I even said as much, keeping up the pretence of the grieving widow.

The family liaison officer offered words of comfort, but I was sure he felt that any lingering hopes that John might have miraculously survived were now gone. This was the first time I'd been to the station and while there I was asked if I would give a statement about the night John disappeared. That really set my heart racing but I knew I couldn't refuse. I started to think I'd been tricked into attending and I was going to be arrested. But I was guided through the process of making the statement, and then, much to my relief, the officer drove me home. Once I was sure the coast was clear, John emerged and I told him what had happened. He didn't have anything to say in the way of words of comfort for my ordeal. He saw it as another milestone passed. They would surely give up hope of finding him alive now.

He was happy, feeling that the discovery of the broken canoe would add credit to the belief that he was lost at sea, but I felt sick, knowing I had to tell the boys of the latest development, which meant telling more hurtful lies. Mark sobbed as he told me it was as if he had not only lost his father but also his best friend. Anthony, too, was distraught. I felt terrible lying to them again and wondered how it would ever end. I reminded myself that I couldn't tell them the truth, as they'd then be accessories to the crime. Not to tell them was protecting them now. I was getting in deeper and deeper, and now I felt I had reached a point of no return.

John quickly settled in to life back at The Cliffe. It wasn't long before he started bugging me that we needed to start claiming for the insurance and pension monies, which of course was why he had staged his death in the first place. He pushed me to make phone calls, helped fill in the application forms and even drafted letters for me to rewrite and send off.

John always enjoyed doing research, so he had done a lot of investigating into what was necessary to make the claims. He would stand over my shoulder as I was making the necessary telephone calls and, if I appeared to be getting into any difficulties, he would put the phone on speaker phone and write notes for me about what to say. Sometimes he would dial the numbers for me. I hated making the calls, but he couldn't do it himself, obviously. It was down to me.

Then there were the letters to the insurance companies. He would either tell me what the contents of the letters had to be or draft a copy on the computer. John's typing skills left a lot to be desired, so because of my secretarial training I'd correct and adjust them before signing. I didn't want to sign letters that didn't look right.

I was playing my own vital role in the growing number of crimes we were committing at every step of the way. But I found it increasingly difficult to live with the shame of what we were doing. One day, soon after he had returned, everything came to a head and I ran out of the house and crossed the road, sitting on that beach and looking out to sea, wishing John really had drowned. Once again, I considered walking into the sea myself. I felt so desperate, so very ashamed. But then I thought about the effect it would have on the rest of the family, particularly Mark and Anthony, and I didn't have the courage to carry it out.

Mark and Anthony were still visiting every week.

These later became monthly trips, backed up by regular phone calls, taking turns to make sure I was coping.

Then in August, I received a phone call from the police informing me a male body had been found off the coast of Hartlepool and they were trying to identify it. When the family liaison officer later told me it wasn't John's body, which of course I knew it couldn't be, I tried to appear distraught and said I wished it had been, so I could at least lay him to rest and move on with my life. I was ashamed of myself for making such comments but it felt necessary to do so.

The following month Cleveland Police decided to make a fresh appeal for witnesses. From the moment John vanished, I had declined all requests for interviews from journalists. But now the police encouraged me, I felt I had no choice but to agree. I put out a statement, written with the help of police press officer Charlie Westberg, a former journalist.

I said the nightmare of John's disappearance was ongoing and, despite his body not being found, I felt sure he must have met with an unfortunate accident in the sea and died. I also said I had no reason to think John would have stage-managed his disappearance. This was a question some officers continued to ask, which obviously panicked me a great deal. I wondered whether those same officers thought I was involved in some way – this worry was never far from my mind.

My employers had been incredibly compassionate and kind, allowing me as much time off work as I needed. As the months passed, however, I decided I wanted to go back, on a part-time basis to start with. I needed something to distract my mind. I went back to work but there were days when I simply couldn't cope and had to leave. I hated lying to everyone and playing the role of a grieving widow. I had hoped to slip quietly back into the normal routine but I was frequently overcome when everyone, including patients who I had known for many years, offered condolences. I hated what my life had become and didn't deserve their kindness.

Chapter 7

The Inquest

It was somewhat ironic that for 'John Jones' to get on with his life, he now needed just one thing – John Darwin to be dead. Because a body had never been found, for very obvious reasons, the police case officially remained open. It seemed that every inquiry I made, whether seeking a payout on the £50,000 life insurance policy he had taken out just eight months earlier, or a claim on one of his pensions, was met with the same response: there was no way it would even be considered without an inquest first being held, as there was no proof John was dead. I hated making the calls because I knew what I was doing was wrong. It was fraud and I was digging a deeper and deeper hole for myself. Each one left me feeling sick to my stomach, but John just seemed to grow increasingly angry because the bills were still piling up and the debt – now my debt – was continuing to rise.

Nevertheless, he still found it hard to believe how easy it had all been for him. He'd faked his death, moved back home and the police, whom he considered pretty stupid, had seemingly very quickly lost interest in the case. As far as he was concerned, the glare of attention that briefly awakened our sleepy little seaside town had quickly fizzled out. He knew I was living on my nerves, lying to all and sundry, but he didn't seem to give any thought to the fact that I was the one under all the pressure, constantly playing the role of the grieving widow.

The man with our fate in his hands was Hartlepool coroner Malcolm Donnelly. We were now under no illusions that he would have to officially declare John dead before we could claim the life insurance and pension payouts that would free us of our crippling debt and make a new life possible. But it wasn't at all straightforward. The coroner explained to me that, in the case of a missing person, any request for an inquest had to be personally sanctioned by the Home Secretary. Such cases were relatively rare, just a handful a year, he said, and everyone would first have to be totally satisfied the police really believed that the case was closed. I doubted that would ever happen but John kept telling me not to worry, insisting it was just a matter of time, a few months at most, before things would improve. He was confident he'd done such a good job in making it look like he'd met his maker that the police would quickly close the case. They would then tell the coroner they were satisfied John Darwin drowned at sea, and Mr Donnelly would agree to petition the Home Secretary for an inquest, saying one was needed to bring closure for his 'poor widow' and to allow her to pick up the pieces of her life.

But John's optimism was ill-founded and he was livid when the coroner told me it was highly unlikely anything would happen in the very near future. John told me I would have to work on the police family liaison officer, who was sympathetic to my plight. And so I tearfully phoned the officer to tell him that until an inquest was held, life would forever remain in limbo.

As the weeks passed, I became increasingly convinced John's plan had been an unmitigated disaster. There was even less money coming in now. Naturally, John's salary had ceased to be paid and my part-time wage wasn't enough to live on. I was advised that I could take three months' compassionate leave on full pay and then there would be a gradual reduction in line with the amount of time taken. After numerous phone calls, I had managed to persuade most of the credit companies with whom John had cards to suspend payments until an inquest had been held, and the bank had agreed to keep the mortgage on interest only repayments. But I was still struggling to pay the bills and was warned if I didn't keep up with the insurance premiums, I wouldn't be able to make a claim in the future – and that was something we could ill afford to happen.

Waiting for the inquest was awful. I dreaded every knock on the door, fearing it would be bailiffs who would force their way in and seize property, or worse still, the police, there to arrest me having uncovered the truth about John's sham disappearance. When the doorbell rang I jumped out of my skin, forever fearing the worst, then always peeping through the curtains to see who was there. If I didn't recognise the face, I would inch back, hardly daring to move. When the telephone rang, I would always let the answer-machine kick in, to see who it was rather than accept the call. The deception seemed to snowball by the day, and I wondered whether it would ever end.

John remained furious that the police still had his computer, which was where he kept all the records for our rental properties and our tenants. I had never really had much to do with the running of John's mini-property empire and didn't even know where some of the houses were. 'How do the police expect you to carry on the business when they have confiscated the wretched computer?' he said, adding, without a hint of intended irony, 'if I hadn't been alive, how on earth would you have coped?'

We had also become aware that a couple of cars were often parked across the road from The Cliffe. I grew convinced they were being used either by undercover detectives or perhaps private investigators from the insurance company, watching for suspicious comings and goings. It had prompted me to buy net curtains for all the front-facing windows.

As the year progressed, with me a bag of nerves and John constantly moaning about being a prisoner in his own home and furious that there was still no word on an inquest, it's hardly surprising our relationship deteriorated. We constantly argued about money and John infuriated me with his dramatic mood swings. Sometimes he was as happy as Larry, confident it was all just a matter of time before his plan fell into place, while on other occasions, he was depressed and miserable.

I didn't stop worrying, not for one day. I lost all interest in our love life, leaving John – who never seemed to stop thinking about sex – angry and frustrated. He hated being banished from No 3, which he often was. If I bolted the door, which I did when I was angry with him, there was nothing he could do about it. His bedsit next door – by this time he'd moved to a room on the second floor – was cramped and smelly and he hated being trapped in there. Although he had painted the walls and ceiling soon after returning to The Cliffe, it still had a distinctly unpleasant odour, a remnant of the previous occupant, a chain-smoking alcoholic.

Extremely bored, John began painting other vacant rooms, shuffling around and pretending to be my odd-job man. He was taking a stupid risk, and that none of the residents ever once appeared to recognise him as their former landlord is quite staggering.

Occasionally, if I had family or guests staying, meaning it was unsafe for John to be in No 3, he was forced to head off into town to buy food or other provisions. Again, leaving a house next door to the one we believed was possibly being watched was an incredible risk. But he continued to get away with it and, the longer he did, the more his confidence grew. 'I really am the invisible man,' he told me.

When family came to stay at Christmas, John had to spend a miserable festive season alone in his cramped little bedsit. But even when the coast was clear for him to return, our relationship had deteriorated to such an extent that I didn't exactly welcome him back with open arms. Waving the family off and seeing the sadness in their eyes was more than I could bear, and it didn't endear John to me. There were many rows and I sometimes suggested John should simply move away, so both of us could start new lives separately. I feel guilty that I even thought it, but there were many times when I wished he really had simply disappeared.

John was basically a prisoner in our home. After the eventual return of his computer by the police, he spent hours on the internet because he had so much time on his hands. The arguments got worse and seemingly more frequent.

One day, after John had told me flippantly to 'pull yourself together', I stormed out of the house in a rage and 30 minutes later found myself at the steering wheel of my car sobbing uncontrollably.

'I can't go on, I can't go on,' I kept repeating to myself. I thumped the wheel, in a blind rage at the hopelessness of my situation, then held my head in my hands, in a mixture of anger, self-pity and desperation. 'Why does it have to be like this, why can't everything be just like it used to be?'

I'd had ups and downs in my life like anyone but, on the whole, before 'all this', I had been happy, working as a doctor's receptionist and raising two fine sons, who had both done well and gone on to get good jobs. Now my life had become one long succession of lies. I was terrified of speaking to anyone, especially my family and friends, lest I inadvertently let something slip. Every time I went out, I nervously looked over my shoulder. I couldn't bear John's remarks any longer. Why was he always so inconsiderate and overbearing?

'Relax, the worst is over,' he would tell me.

'Who for?' I'd reply. 'Maybe for you but not for me. I'm having to lie to everybody, every minute of my life. Can't you understand how hard that is?'

John never had time for what he called 'my mild hysterics' and would simply roll his eyes, then walk off. Yes, he was trapped, a prisoner in his own home, but he didn't have to lie to anyone – because no one knew he was still alive. John Darwin didn't talk to anyone because John Darwin was dead. Other than me, there wasn't a soul in the world who knew he had secretly come back to life and returned to his family home. He was living there, right under the noses of the loved ones who missed him the most – and the police who were supposedly still looking for him. When someone came to visit, he could simply scuttle off to his bedsit. One minute he was there, the next he was gone. For John, it was as simple as that. If a visitor turned up when he was out, he always knew because he'd devised a warning code using our living room curtains. If they were tied back, it was safe to come home, but if they were dangling freely, it was a warning that I had unexpected company and he should lie low until the danger had passed. It saved his bacon on more than one occasion.

For me, everything I did or said involved deception. Every time someone visited, I would have to remember to change those damned curtains while having to play the grieving widow, putting on an act to gratefully accept people's kindness and consoling words. I hated every last minute of it, but as time passed I admittedly got better and better at it.

It was towards the end of February 2003 that everything suddenly changed. Mr Donnelly announced he would be holding an inquest. He informed me that he had sought permission from the then Home Secretary, David Blunkett, after being assured by the police that the case was pretty much closed and the chances of finding John had, sadly, long passed.

The date was set for 10 April 2003, a little over a year since John had disappeared. Initially pleased with the news, I then became panic-stricken at the thought of having to give evidence and be cross-examined in court.

John, however, was cock-a-hoop. In the days running up to the inquest, he kept an incredibly low profile. The last thing he could afford to happen was to have his cover blown at this late stage. I was a bag of nerves, convinced that something would go badly wrong. The boys and their partners were coming to stay at No 3 for a few days, so it was imperative John shut himself away in his 'foxhole', as he often referred to his bedsit. From there, on the eve of the inquest, he would undoubtedly have heard the voices of his sons through the walls as they chatted with me late into the night. I used to lock the doors but they were only bolted and the boys could have easily pulled them open and walked through to next door at any time.

The morning of the inquest was a sombre affair at No 3. Neither I, nor the boys, were looking forward to it – though for very different reasons. For Mark and Anthony, it would officially mark the end to any glimmer of hope that their father had miraculously survived. For me, giving evidence would be a case of adding to my rapidly increasing portfolio of monumental lies, only this time in a courtroom. I had been dreading the day – and having to lie publicly in front of the boys – for weeks.

Initially, I had told John I couldn't go through with it: I could not go and sit through an inquest and ask for probate because there was no will. But, of course, I did go through with it. Fortunately, I didn't have to give evidence under oath, instead being called to simply make a brief statement.

In presenting their evidence to the coroner, the police said there were four possibilities. 1) John had staged the whole affair. 2) He had committed suicide. 3) He'd had an accident and died. 4) He had died at the hands of persons unknown.

Options one, two and four were then discounted. There was no evidence to prove he had planned anything, not one person the police had spoken to said he appeared suicidal. And there was nothing to link anyone else with involvement in his death. The police therefore concluded a tragic accident was the most likely occurrence, whether through a heart attack (he was known to have angina), or having got into trouble in the canoe and drowned. Mr Donnelly said he agreed an accident was most probable and recorded a verdict of accidental death, declaring John Darwin to be 'missing presumed dead', meaning very soon I – now officially a widow – would have the all-important death certificate in my hands.

As the boys and I made our way out of the coroner's

court, we bumped into John's sister, Sheila, his brother, David, and his aunt, Margaret Burns. The time of the inquest had been changed a few days earlier but it transpired the coroner's office had neglected to inform the other relatives, who were angered at having missed the hearing. I had no idea they hadn't been informed but there was a heated exchange of views, ending with Sheila, David and Margaret, who suspected I had deliberately not wanted them there, rejecting my offer to return to the house for a low-key wake. When I got home, I did feel a tremendous sense of relief. I knew full well the financial importance of John being declared dead.

What the inquest verdict meant, as far as John was concerned, was that everything was falling very nicely into place. Now officially 'dead', and with a death certificate in my hands, the money started to come in.

Between 19 May and 29 August 2003, I received a total of £90,867.35 in payouts from pension and life insurance policies, and the mortgage protection policy paid out a further £137,400.42, paying off all but £130,000 of the global mortgage. It included a cheque for £25,000 from John's life insurance policy. The policy was for £50,000 but the company would only pay 50 per cent as his body had never been found. John, of course, was delighted. For him, all the deception had been worthwhile. He had always been confident of getting away with his disappearing act and he'd been proven right. Everyone had fallen for it, hook, line and sinker. 'I'm a genius!' he'd congratulate himself, seemingly with little regard for the sons, whose hearts he had broken, or anyone else. It did dawn on him, however, that with me now officially a 'widow', there was nothing to stop me from leaving him and marrying someone else. After all, I was the one now in complete control of the purse strings.

So, that August, John also opened a Lloyds TSB bank account in the name of John Jones. At his bank interview, he'd described himself as a labourer, employed by a Mrs A. C. Darwin. His cheek knew no bounds. Now we could move some of the money from my account into his, and he started buying Premium Bonds. Reducing the global mortgage so considerably also meant I could start selling off some of the rental properties, further easing our debt. The first one sold for £21,510. Everything was coming together very nicely indeed as far as John was concerned.

He now turned his attention back to getting a passport and obtaining it proved as ridiculously easy as everything else had been. Having got to know the librarian, Susan Garrington, quite well, John got her to vouch for his identity as John Jones by signing the back of the two required passport photos. He filled in a passport agency application form and sent it off with a copy of the birth certificate and the two photographs.

Just a few weeks later, on 13 October, a shiny new passport for Mr John Jones arrived in the post at our home address. It was as simple as that.

The one joyful occasion during this time was Anthony and Louise's wedding day. To say we'd spoilt Anthony's engagement plans is certainly an understatement, and I'll regret that for evermore. I was determined nothing would spoil their wedding day. I was delighted when Anthony asked for my help in making the 'Order of Service' booklets, but unknown to him John also had input in the process. It was the only way he could be part of things, behind the scenes. It was sad to think Anthony couldn't know anything about the part he'd played.

In September 2003, the wedding day finally arrived. It was a glorious sunny day and they were married in Louise's home town of Basingstoke, Hampshire. That meant leaving John on his own in Seaton Carew for a few days. To be honest, it was a relief for me to be away from him. The two boys had grown closer over the last few years and Mark was his brother's best man. It was a wonderful day but tinged with sadness, albeit for different reasons for me than everyone else. I had two handsome sons and was proud to be photographed with them.

Almost a year after the inquest, in March 2004, the boys and I held a small memorial service for John, walking to the end of the pier in Seaton Carew and each throwing wreaths into the choppy waters below. We had talked about what was best to do to mark John's 'death' for a while, and I think the boys felt it would give them some closure. God know what the boys would have thought of me had they known their dad was inside the house behind us, possibly even watching from the window for all I knew.

Chapter 8

A Conman Is Conned

John knew he would have to move abroad if he was to have an existence he could enjoy. He didn't want to be a shuffling, shaggy bearded character for much longer. Now he had a passport he could get out of the country, so next he needed to work out exactly which was the best location we could move to without attracting too much suspicion.

He avidly watched any travel programmes he could find, and one on Cyprus particularly caught his eye. The climate was good, and although property in the Greek-governed south was expensive, the north, governed by Turkey, looked a much better bet, with both housing and the cost of living far cheaper. In November 2003, he decided we should check it out.

Having resigned from the surgery the previous month I told family and friends I needed a holiday, which I knew they'd find understandable, and that I'd decided to travel alone to Cyprus to get some sun and escape for a while. I told everyone I was flying from Manchester Airport but in fact drove to Manchester with John, then caught a train to

London, as we were flying from Stansted.

We were taking a huge risk by travelling together and I felt John's beard would in fact draw attention to him rather than offer a disguise. It was the first time he had used his John Jones passport and I was convinced he would be stopped and arrested for travelling with fake documents, or we'd bump into someone who'd recognise us. Sometimes, I wished that would happen and it would bring everything to a head. However, the journey was uneventful.

We stayed in a small hotel in the harbour city of Kyrenia, in Northern Cyprus. Our days were split between lazing by the pool and visiting potential properties and plots of land to buy. John was always drawn more toward the blank canvas that a plot of land offered, hoping to fulfil a dream of one day building his own home. I enjoyed looking at the finished properties and comparing them with homes back in the UK, but I couldn't get excited about a plot of land. John decided we should put down £500 on one plot that took his eye. He was the one with the vision, or so he thought. I doubted we would be able to build a house in a foreign country where we didn't speak the language, and where work would be difficult to supervise, living so far away. The deal eventually fell through and, because of the complexities of buying in the north, John pretty soon gave up on Cyprus completely. I can't say I was disappointed; in fact, I was relieved. Memories of John wanting to emigrate to Australia, soon after we married, came flooding back and once more I was filled with doubt.

His thoughts turned to the USA, which had always been a bit of a dream for him. This had been helped along by a relationship he had struck up in the winter of 2003 with a woman from Kansas, called Kelly Steel. I'd often overheard them speaking online, while playing the internet game EverQuest. I didn't know the first thing about computer games but, evidently, John's character came to the rescue of Kelly's, and they began chatting over the web. Given his past history of affairs, I wasn't happy about it. John seemed fascinated with Kelly's life in rural Kansas and I later discovered he'd told her he was a widower and had always harboured an American dream to buy land, marry a pretty girl and settle on that side of the Atlantic.

It was quite incredible that John wasn't rumbled and our lies exposed in June 2004, when I had a phone call from the police informing me that they'd had a report of John being sighted outside our home. They asked if I'd heard anything from him. I said no, but the call sent me into a panic. My immediate thought was that the police would want to search the house. If they had come knocking on the door instead of phoning I don't know what I would have done.

It turned out a former colleague of John's, from the

prison, had spotted him as he drove along the Seaton seafront. The prison officer reported to the police that the man he saw had a long grey beard and resembled Saddam Hussein 'at the time of his capture', but he was '100 per cent certain' it was John Darwin.

I was amazed that something like this hadn't happened before. After all, John's appearance hadn't changed that much. But rather than coming to my home to check out the sighting, the police fortunately – or perhaps foolishly – simply rang me. Astonishingly, they didn't even follow up with a visit.

Fearing John's cover was about to be blown, we quickly agreed he needed to disappear, at least until the threat of being discovered had passed. John said he would fly to the States to check out some possible property investments he had been looking at online, through Kelly.

I was furious that he was taking off to see a woman who I'd heard him flirting with on the internet and asked what he was playing at, but he repeatedly assured me it was nothing but business and he was simply being friendly. I wasn't convinced. Would any wife?

But, at the same time, a part of me was actually glad to be rid of him for a few weeks. It meant he wouldn't constantly be under my feet and I could even relax a little with him out of the house. We needed an escape route, and maybe he would find it in America.

And once he was gone, I'm not sure I really wanted him to come back. For much of the time I was just angry with him and I wasn't loving towards him at all. There was a constant tension between us and I was tired of living on a knife's edge. Part of me wished he would just disappear for good.

After a couple of weeks John returned, with his tail between his legs. It wasn't until some time later that he sheepishly told me the money, which he'd had in his John Jones account, was gone.

He told me that before he had left for America, even before his colleague had spotted him, he and Kelly had discussed business opportunities, with Kelly suggesting renovating a farm and raising cattle. John had been impressed when Kelly told him she knew everything there was to know about horses and cattle and also about book-keeping and accounts. She said if he was prepared to invest some money, she could run the ranch and they could split the profits. John had leapt at the idea and wired her £28,000 ($50,000).

I don't really know whether it was the woman or the property he was really interested in, but I later discovered that she had sent John topless pictures of herself, so it certainly seems he had more than just property on his mind when he flew to America. To have entrusted such a large sum of money to a woman he hardly knew and had never even met was astonishingly reckless. For a man like John, after everything he had been through to get that money – and everything he had put me and the boys through – it defies belief.

When he reached America, and met Kelly – a 41-year-old mother of three – she took him to what he'd anticipated to be an idyllic Kansas ranch. It was instead, in his words, 'Crapsville'; apparently nothing more than a rickety shack of a house, with eight acres of land, bought for $14,000.

He claimed Kelly used one delaying tactic after another to stop him going to the lawyer's office, where the property was supposed to be signed over in his name. He was furious and demanded to know where was the rest of the money he had wired. He even employed a firm of local solicitors to try and get his 'investment' back, but to no avail.

Kelly had transferred the title of the property into the name of her supposedly estranged husband, and had used the rest for renovations and to pay off some of her debt. Because of various legal complexities, the lawyers warned John he had little chance of ever recovering any of the cash. John was furious but there was nothing he could do.

I couldn't believe his stupidity. I was even more horrified when he showed me some threatening emails he'd sent to Kelly in an attempt to recover his money. He'd claimed he was friends with a debt collector from the Bronx area of New York, who'd do virtually anything he'd ask for the right amount of money, and that he'd already sent 'some people' to Kansas to check up on her. 'I've asked for assistance in this matter and things WILL happen and continue to happen unless you repay me all of my money,' John's email said.

I'd never thought John capable of doing something like that. Sometimes it felt as if I didn't really know him at all and I wondered what other secrets he was keeping from me.

Despite the fact she had apparently stolen John's money, Kelly had gone to her local police department about the threatening emails, and they handed her on to the FBI. An agent advised her that John was making crank threats, and that she should tell him the FBI were involved. As soon as she informed a very panicked John, he very wisely, at last, decided his American dream was over.

By now, all of the insurance money had been paid out. John asked me whenever he needed money and I gave it to him. Actually, he could do any banking transactions whenever he wanted and frequently did. He had all of my passwords, which I had never changed.

Sometimes things at home were OK, I could cope with it all, but then all of a sudden they'd just come crashing down again on top of me. Sometimes we shared a bed – but it was sporadic. On occasions he would go storming off to his bedsit and I would bolt the door behind him so he couldn't get back in. But then I would feel guilty. I used to think about John and wonder to myself, *Well, what else has he got?* He was a prisoner within four walls. I pitied him. He didn't have a life. It was just an existence.

It became our way of life. I was in too deep and felt that I couldn't confide in anybody. I couldn't implicate the boys by telling them, nor the rest of my family. If I'd just been able to tell one person other than John, perhaps they'd have helped me see sense. But I had no one at all.

That October John turned his attention to the sea. His latest plan was to look at buying a sea-going boat in which to sail around the world. Such a voyage would be a huge undertaking for even the most experienced of sailors, and John knew next to nothing about boats. The only sailing experience he had was sailing a dinghy with his brother. But, as ever, he wasn't the kind of man to let such small matters get in the way of his dreams, even if I couldn't swim… and hated being at sea! If he read about something, he felt he could do it, no matter what it was.

The following month, on 12 November, John flew to Gibraltar, where he had seen a catamaran advertised for sale. He had exchanged a few emails with the seller and decided he needed to see the 60-foot boat, named *Boonara*, for himself. Within days of seeing it, he made an offer of £45,000 for the 1970s diesel-powered catamaran, which was followed up with me making a £1,000 transfer from my bank account as a deposit. But the deal fell apart when

John flew into a rage over some of the contents of the boat not being included in the sale. He was also infuriated at the red tape he was encountering while looking into registering as a boat owner.

Hardly surprisingly, I lost the deposit. Everything John touched, or so it seemed, ended in disaster. It was ironic, after all he'd put us through to get his hands on some money, that he was so adept at giving it away to strangers.

Chapter 9

Schemers, Dreamers and Misfits

When I offered my resignation from the surgery in July 2003, and was part-way through working my notice of three months, I was asked to consider working fewer hours in a purely admin role. I hadn't really wanted to leave my job. I had always enjoyed it, but John had insisted it would be better for me, saying I'd be less tired and less stressed. I knew that work wasn't the real problem, nonetheless I had given in to his wishes again as I so often did. I was excited at the opportunity of staying on in a different role and it was intended to be for a limited time only, probably about a year. John wasn't keen at first but I was granted permission to work on an ad hoc basis, which meant I could choose the days I wanted to work and take time off whenever I needed, so he agreed. I felt it was a way of repaying the kindness shown by the doctors and staff over the recent years. Above all, it meant I would still have periods of respite away from John and enjoy some normality in my life.

So, from January 2004 to the summer of 2007 I continued to work two days a week. John spent his days working his way through the various rooms, starting on the top floor of No 3 and then working his way throughout No 4, stripping off wallpaper, doing repairs and decorating. He also spent time redesigning the two rear gardens. The outside of the house was in great need of renovation and decoration, so we had scaffold erected at the front of both houses. It was a mammoth task and took about two weeks to erect. This had the added bonus of offering John some seclusion for moving around inside the house without the risk of being seen through the windows.

Initially I was scared to even set foot on the ladder, using the easier option of getting onto the scaffold through the windows, but on certain levels that wasn't possible. After a few weeks I overcame my fears and became quite adept at moving between levels and even managed to work at roof height on the four-storey houses. The bird's eye view over the sea was quite spectacular, certainly one I'd never expected to witness. When I was at home, John was even bold enough to work on the scaffold in full view of everyone, with his overalls and beard for his disguise. The work was arduous and lasted for at least six months. I was the one who went to the builder's yard and carried the bags of sand and cement.

It was now nearly four years since John had faked his own death. In that time, he had found it was impossible to register as a boat owner in Gibraltar, too difficult to develop in Cyprus, and his attempts to invest in Kansas had bordered on farcical. He had looked at France and

Spain but quickly ruled them out as being too close to home. He ordered books about emigrating to Canada and Norway, neither of which he felt would be safe places for someone living on a false passport, and then he started looking in earnest at Central America and in particular Belize, Guatemala, Costa Rica and Panama. Panama was the one that caught his eye.

He loved everything he read about the exotic-sounding Central American location, which, according to one guidebook, attracted 'adventurers and entrepreneurs, schemers and dreamers, misfits and full-on nutcases'. Perhaps an ideal home for John, who I have to admit ticked many of the boxes quite nicely. It is as if man and country were somehow destined to be together. John had a checklist – language, climate, currency, people, cities, prices, amenities, things to do and shopping – and after more internet research, he concluded that Panama did indeed appear to be the perfect place for us to start afresh. It was the sole topic of his conversation.

In 2006, more and more people were using websites that allowed them to ask questions and post answers. John joined an online forum called Viviendo en Panama – Living in Panama – which provided information for English expatriates about living and working in Panama. At 9.45pm on 31 January, the site's newest member posted that he was looking for information on the climate and the wildlife in certain parts of the country, describing himself as a 'bored Brit' looking at emigrating. In fact, John was incredibly indiscreet on a forum that could have been read by anyone. Despite his years as a teacher, John typed in a very childish manner. He had a habit of holding down the full-stop key mid-sentence, typing a mixture of upper and lower case words, making basic spelling mistakes, using smiley faces, and his favourite abbreviation 'lol' – laugh out loud – featured in almost every message he ever sent. Over the course of six months, John signed up with more than a dozen online forums, using his fake identity, John Jones, confident no one would ever know who he really was.

John was so excited at the thought he had finally found the ideal getaway destination, he was already dreaming of a new home in the rainforest. He sent off a request to Panama Realtor estate agents for information about a service they offered, to erect log cabins anywhere in the country. John was already thinking of buying some land and building – yet again – the home of his dreams.

I knew next to nothing about Panama, other than that it had a famous canal and was an awfully long way away. But once it became apparent that John was seriously considering it as somewhere to live, I began reading some of the books and emigrating material he'd bought or been sent. It appeared very exotic, with its rainforests, indigenous Indian tribes and tropical climate – probably an interesting place to visit on holiday – but I was far from certain it was a place we could put down roots and ever call home. John, however, seemed convinced it would be the perfect place for us to begin a new life, so it didn't really matter what I thought. As usual, I just went along with things. My opinion counting for little was the normal way of life, it was all that I'd been used to. Occasionally I'd be listened to, but rarely agreed with. If I dared to argue a point, John would always have a much stronger counter-argument and so my feelings of insecurity persisted. How on earth could I function without him? It sounds quite pathetic now, but that's how it was at the time.

As we made plans for a new life overseas, we knew we needed to have building work done to prepare both Nos 3 and 4 The Cliffe for sale. The housing market was slow and there was also a planning application in progress that might discourage buyers. In early March, we had both received letters from Hartlepool Borough Council advising us that the new owner of No 2 was seeking permission to turn his house into bed and breakfast accommodation. Using his false name, John Jones, and his electoral register address, 4 The Cliffe, John wrote a long rambling letter to the council, protesting about the plans. He also wrote a similar, but shorter, letter from me, using the same printed paper, which he told me to sign, using my address, No 3. Enclosed with each letter were similar photographs, obviously taken with the same camera, on the same day, which John had taken to illustrate concerns over parking congestion. I felt he was becoming dangerously blasé and putting us both in the position where we could easily have been caught out. The

impending change of use for the neighbouring house
didn't exactly thrill me, but it wasn't so objectionable to
me, either. But there was no point in me refusing to sign
the letter – John would simply have signed it in my name,
as he had done in the past when he was buying the houses.

We knew we would have to completely separate Nos 3
and 4 The Cliffe to get the best possible price. Selling
them individually with the flying freehold from No 4
extending over the top floor of No 3, would have been
very difficult. Big old houses in Seaton Carew were
difficult enough to shift as it was. But separating the
houses was a major issue that caused more stress for John.
The connecting doors on all the floors would have to be
blocked off – meaning he would have no escape route to
his bedsit next door. There was, however, no alternative,
so we hired a team of builders and plumbers to separate
the utilities and re-establish the house as two individual
properties.

For months, John had been looking into how best to
avoid paying tax, or at least as little as possible, when we
sold the houses, and this is when he selfishly dragged
Mark into his scheme. Although land registry records
show the two houses were together worth nearly half a
million pounds, John decided that I would sell them to
Mark for the giveaway price of just £30,000.

There was a strong possibility I would have left the
country before exchanging contracts. The mortgage had
been paid off in full now, so by putting the house into

Mark's name he would be able to sign to complete the deal and then transfer the proceeds to me. I don't understand why – for tax reasons, perhaps? – John said the house would have to pass to Mark as a sale (albeit for a small amount) rather than be gifted to him. I was merely following instructions and never understood all the ramifications.

I truly wished we hadn't involved Mark in any way, as it would later cast huge suspicion on whether he was involved in our scheming, which he absolutely was not. He simply went along with it because he felt he was helping me. Mark paid for the houses by cashing in Premium Bonds, which he'd bought with money that I had given him. At John's instruction I also gave Anthony £30,000 to invest in Premium Bonds. This money was given to them on the understanding that the bonds would eventually be cashed in and the money returned to me. The maximum amount of Premium Bonds that one person could hold at the time was 30,000. That meant between us we could safeguard £90,000 for future use. We had effectively used both our sons as money launderers – it was an incredibly callous thing to do and I regret it bitterly.

Eventually, the time came to check out Panama for real. We had spent the previous day packing suitcases and carefully running through John's meticulous checklist of things needed for a two-week holiday in the sun. This wasn't any run-of-the-mill package deal to the Spanish

Costas or the Canary Isles. I'm sure John must have felt a little miffed that he was 'dead': it was the kind of trip he would have loved to brag about to everyone.

I had always been considered very much a home bird, so everyone, especially my family, had been shocked when I suddenly announced I was heading off to Panama for my summer hols. I was of course a widow, although not a particularly new one, and the fact that I planned to travel alone only added to the family's concern. I think the boys were both pretty astonished when I first told them. Mark said, 'Are you *sure* that's a good idea, Mam?' They were both concerned about me travelling alone in such a far-flung country, but I told them I'd looked into it very thoroughly and reassured them everything would be fine. The dogs had died by now, both of cancer of the shoulder joint, so I didn't have to worry about putting them in kennels. It was only natural my family should worry about me, but I told them I had to try and get on with my life and this trip might be just what I needed.

It was long before dawn on an English summer's morning, 12 July 2006, when John and I left Seaton Carew on the start of an adventure that would, once again, change our lives forever. When the alarm sounded at 4am, we were already awake and it wasn't long before we were up, showered and dressed. A quick slurp of hot tea and we were ready to go. I must have looked a somewhat comical figure as I tiptoed down the four steps of my seafront home that morning. I had a good look round, glanced up at the windows of the neighbouring houses, then, satisfied that the coast was clear, quietly went back inside, where John was waiting. We grabbed our luggage, loaded it into the boot of the Range Rover and slowly set off across the gravel drive, trying to make as little noise as possible.

My stomach was in knots by the time we reached Newcastle Airport after the 45-minute drive from Seaton Carew. I kept my head down and nervously glanced around, terrified someone would recognise one of us. Walking a few feet apart, we quickly made our way through the near-deserted terminal to the check-in desk, a good three hours early for our flight. Once again, I was extremely worried that John would be using his false passport. He told me to stay calm and everything would be fine. I responded, through gritted teeth, 'I'm trying my best.'

John had chosen a fairly obscure route, flying first to Paris with Continental Airlines, on to Caracas, the capital of Venezuela, with Air France, then finally boarding flight CM 0222 with the Panamanian state carrier, Copa Airlines, to Panama City. It was the cheapest one going.

We had both read guide books and relocation pamphlets and John had spent hours scouring the internet, but arriving at the frenetic and somewhat daunting Tocumen International Airport on the outskirts of the capital was still a massive shock to the system for both of us. With virtually no Spanish between us, even manoeuvring our way through the bustling airport and finding the Budget rental car desk was no easy feat. I was feeling very uncomfortable in such strange territory and quickly began wondering whether this trip had been such a good idea after all.

Over the years we were married, and long before any of this business started, John often talked about a hankering to move abroad but I'd never really been interested. There had been his idea to move to Australia not long after we were married. Then he wanted to go to the Falklands, next it was Canada. As the years went by, it was always a different country. There was always an issue – climate or language. He changed his mind so many times I lost count.

In advance of our visit, John had read that there were two factors key to making the narrow strip of land that made up Panama – often referred to as the 'Gateway to the World' – such an attractive destination. You could trek up Volcán Barú, a dormant volcano that is the country's highest peak, and get a unique experience: seeing, at the same time, the world's two largest oceans, the Atlantic and the Pacific, and the third and fourth largest continents, North and South America. There were miles of totally unspoiled white sandy beaches, 1,500 largely uninhabited islands, unexplored jungles and cloud-covered rain forests, where you could swim in chilly mountain streams.

Even the disastrous property dealing that had brought about John's 'death' hadn't dampened his enthusiasm for big ideas. He still planned to be a man of property, with acres of land he could call his own. Land that he could make money from was an even better prospect. 'It's going to be perfect for us,' he told me excitedly. 'A wonderful climate, beautiful countryside and a place we can spend the rest of our days together. It's perfect, absolutely perfect in every respect.' In his mind, John was already making plans to buy land and establish an eco-resort, with scattered log cabins and the offer of horse riding, boating and trekking for the guests who would come flocking. He rather wished he'd thought of it years ago.

By now I knew that John was an 'ideas' man, and although his ambition sounded wonderful in theory, I seriously doubted his ability to bring his plans to fruition. It was a massive project he was planning, in a foreign country where he didn't speak the language and wouldn't be able to communicate with builders.

Before setting off, he had been corresponding by email with Mario Vilar, head of a relocation and land agent company, movetopanama.com. John had asked Mario for help in finding accommodation for two, for the first five nights of our two-week trip (from 12 to 17 July).

Mario said he had the perfect accommodation and also offered to arrange a $25 taxi from the airport. John turned down the taxi, explaining he had already arranged a rental car, but confirmed his reservation for the room.

As romantic as ever, he was taking me to the country that might become our new home – and spending next to nothing on the cheapest bed and breakfast he could find. We actually got lost, had to park the car and find a taxi to take us to our destination, leaving the car in the banking district, next to recognisable buildings. Mario helped us to recover it the next day.

We discovered the accommodation was with Mario's parents, in their fourth-floor apartment, in the middle-class neighbourhood of Via Argentina. But it was clean and comfortable, and gave us an ideal base from which to explore the city and surrounding countryside. His parents were warm and friendly and offered us lots of advice on how to get around the city and suggested places that we might like to visit. We ended up staying with them for the full fortnight.

A few days later, we met Mario in his seventh-floor suite in a high-rise building in the heart of Panama City's banking district. When he asked if he could have a photo taken with his new British friends, we had no time to think or make an excuse as Mario's wife, Karina, appeared with a camera and took the picture. I was wearing a white vest top and had my brown leather handbag slung over my shoulder, and stood smiling between John, wearing a mauve, short-sleeved shirt, and Mario, who was wearing jeans and a blue-and-white striped shirt. The date, 14 July

2006, was automatically burned into the polaroid photograph in an orange font.

We were both conscious that keeping a low-profile was very important but we didn't have time to object to the photograph being taken. It was just a memento for Mario, we reassured ourselves, and after walking out of his office we didn't give it an awful lot more thought. Little could we have imagined how badly that seemingly innocent holiday snap would come back to haunt us seventeen months later.

Chapter 10

Panama -
A Mad New Plan

I have to admit, I was pleasantly surprised by Panama. I was enthralled by the countryside and thoroughly enjoyed visits to the Panama Canal and the capital's historic old town, with its charming bars and lively atmosphere. The country was breathtakingly beautiful and not at all what I had expected. It was no wonder more than 6,000 mainly retired Britons had already been lured there by good health care and land and property that was incredibly cheap.

We didn't find anywhere that was totally ideal to live: there was one issue or another with all the places we looked at. But during our break in the sun, we saw enough of the country to make us believe it really was somewhere we could make a fresh start. This time around I caught some of John's enthusiasm and enjoyed looking for a place to live in Panama City. The quest to find a plot of land was of less importance to me but John was determined to follow his dream. We were both filled with optimism as we flew home to England – and back to our double lives, me the widow and John the invisible man.

After unpacking, it wasn't long before I was on the phone to the boys, my family and closest friends, telling them all how much I'd enjoyed the trip. I think I had accepted now that the only way of having a life in which I could live without constantly looking over my shoulder, and to be with John and hopefully make our marriage work, was to move abroad. I was swept along by the idea that everything would, once again, be all right.

I felt like I had been reborn, I told the boys, and everything was so refreshing and new. I'd definitely be going back. It was a far cry from the nearby cities of Middlesbrough, Newcastle or Sunderland, and there were no menacing gangs of hooded youths lurking on street corners. But maybe, I had to admit to myself, that was something to do with the fact that every police officer in Panama was heavily armed. Not everything about the country was perfect.

John spent hours beavering away on the internet researching our future home and eventually discovered something that, to him, felt like he had struck gold. One lunchtime I received an email at work from John with the heading 'Corporation'. The email itself had no introduction and no sign off.

From: John
To: Anne
Time: 13:10:30 GMT. Date 11/10/2006
Holding Panama Real Estate in a Panamanian Corp

For a host of reasons– including confidentiality, estate planning, anonymity and, also, to protect your property against any legal proceedings or situations with creditors or recoveries aimed at a natural person's estate – it was becoming common practice locally to organise a Panamanian corporation to serve as the owner of a property.

John described it as a 'eureka' moment when I later got home from work. The ability to set up a corporation to protect property 'against any kind of legal proceedings' and make it safe from 'personal debts and obligations' was almost too good to be true. 'I've hit the jackpot!' he crowed.

It meant that if we set up a corporation to buy property, no matter what happened, and even if our fraud was ever rumbled, our property investments would be untouchable. Secretive, anonymous and beyond the reach of the British authorities, Panama was looking more and more like an ideal destination, John said.

With his mind made up, John was fired up with enthusiasm for the prospect of a new life in Central America, and we began the serious business of preparing to leave for good. We agreed that I should start talking about the country more and more so, when the time came for us to make our move, it wouldn't be quite such a shock for the boys or my family and friends. I was determined that if I was to move abroad, I should learn the language, so bought several teach-yourself-Spanish books. I spent at least an hour a day, usually early evening, learning basic sentences to help me with shopping, getting about and ordering meals in restaurants. I tried to get John involved but he wasn't really interested. All he could think about was getting back to Panama and so continued to spend hours on the internet looking for likely properties and land. 'Viviendo en Panama' was now in full swing.

Just before visiting Panama, John had used his John Jones alias to sign up for an online money-transfer service. Having tried his hand at stocks and shares from the spare bedroom of our house in Witton Gilbert, he knew the value of a good exchange rate and hated the thought of being at the mercy of overnight bank transfers. With a passport, a birth certificate, credit card statements, a few emails and a telephone interview, he was able to sign up with an international currency transfer company offering a live online feed of international interest rates.

He was now able to ship his cash abroad at the best rates at any time of the day or night. After barely touching the money we'd acquired for more than two years, there was now a flurry of activity. Less than a month after returning from Panama, John cashed in £30,000 of Premium Bonds he had held since the previous May in the name of John Jones and transferred the money to his John Jones Lloyds TSB account. The next day he started playing the money markets using his new online account. Lloyds TSB would only allow a maximum of £10,000 to be transferred on any single day – so on five separate days, between 10 and 18 August, John shipped £41,000 through the foreign exchange brokerage into his Commerce Bank account in Kansas. On top of $1,000 he'd moved as a test transaction in June, he now had almost $78,000 salted away in the United States.

Importantly for John, despite the rigorous anti-money-laundering regulations that were in force, the transfers failed to trigger any of the financial services sector alarms. No one had noticed that a man who was officially dead and was posing as a child who had died 56 years earlier was moving large amounts of money between two of the world's biggest economies. He must have thought Panama was going to be a breeze. Despite the unavoidable conclusion that we were getting deeper into the territory of organised crime – complete with conspiracy, fake identities, fraud, money laundering and offshore investments – John seemed to think it was no big deal.

John couldn't resist one parting shot at the banks he blamed for his downfall. The Yorkshire Bank had refused to extend his credit four years earlier – in his mind, forcing him to fake his own death – and now Lloyds TSB was offering loans. He had ignored two or three prior letters but now he decided to take what he could. In June he arranged for me to pay him £1,825 in three instalments to make it look as though I was his employer. He went along to his local branch and armed with documents that appeared to prove he was John Jones, he posed as my handyman in an interview for a loan. Without any further checks, the bank signed off on a £10,000 loan, which he agreed would be paid back in monthly instalments. Within two weeks, every penny had been converted into dollars and wired to Kansas. Eighteen months later, when police asked him why he'd taken out the loan and not paid it back, John simply claimed the bank got what it deserved.

It was six months later, in early 2007, that I decided to tell the boys that I was seriously thinking of emigrating. I said I was fed up with windswept Seaton Carew, the house held too many unhappy memories of their father and every day I couldn't help but look out over the very spot from where he had set off on his ill-fated canoe outing. 'It's as if my life is on perpetual hold,' I said. I was going to put both houses, 3 and 4 The Cliffe, on the market to see what the interest was – it was the only way I would ever be able to get on with my life, I told them. Though shocked, both Mark and Anthony supported my decision. Of course, it was just another of the many lies I had by now become accustomed to telling. I wasn't proud of myself but felt there was no other way.

By the spring of 2007, we had $130,000 – roughly £80,000 – in the John Jones bank account in Kansas, and

$50,000 in an offshore account I had opened in Jersey. But we knew it wasn't enough to provide for us in Panama. When in March that year we agreed a sale of £160,000 for No 4 The Cliffe – a bargain for the buyer, Gary Hepple – John was all set for his big move.

He flew to Panama, and a week later, on 15 March 2007, the day the sale of No 4 The Cliffe completed, I flew out to join him.

John had found a cheap hotel, the Costa Inn, on Avenida Peru, in a somewhat sleazy area of the city. He quickly discovered it was the red-light district at night. With prostitution legal and unemployment high, there was no shortage of women plying their trade. During the day armed police guarded the shops.

John had brazenly checked into the 90-room hotel under his real name, John Darwin – why on earth he used his real name I had no idea – paying £30-a-night for a small double room. I am sure the arrival of the balding Englishman, who spoke barely a word of Spanish and was obviously travelling alone, didn't go unnoticed by locals. In his dingy fifth-floor room, he had set up his big-screen Hewlett Packard computer (which he'd brought as hand luggage – it weighed a ton) and spent hours surfing the internet for remote properties to buy. Each morning, John exchanged pleasantries with the hotel's Spanish-born owner, Jose Carrera. John liked to visit the old town by taxi. In the mornings, he walked along the avenue to get a coffee for breakfast and have lunch in restaurants near the park. He spent the afternoons reading, writing and taking pictures of the city from the hotel's roof-top pool, always sitting alone in the sun around the same table.

When I arrived, we arranged to meet a string of estate agents and relocation experts. In between appointments, we spent as little time at the hotel as possible – although the staff were very friendly, it was budget accommodation by anyone's standards. With all the money earmarked for our new life together, we were making savings wherever we could. The money from No. 4 converted into well over $300,000. We planned to spend all of that, and more, on property – on an apartment in the city that would be our base, and on land to establish the eco-business itself. But until we could sell No 3, money – even stolen money – was tight. Instead of returning to the Costa Inn, we got into the habit of returning to the Dolce Coffee House, which we had discovered when we stayed with Mario's parents. It was modern, had air-conditioning and was light and bright. There was always a warm welcome from the lady who owned the business and the fruit smoothies were excellent.

John had narrowed his search for land to the coastal area of Colon, because we had always lived close to the sea. We met up with another estate agent, Diana Bishop, who I took to immediately. I felt Diana, a Panamanian who was born and raised in the canal-zone, was someone who really understood exactly what we were looking for. I told her that I was a widow, that I had two sons and that John was my partner.

We started looking round in lots of different places and then started reconsidering some of the ones we had already visited, plus there were a few on our list from our first visit that we hadn't managed to see. And that was when we found an apartment we liked in a city suburb called El Dorado. Diana found it for us and it suited our needs perfectly. I was particularly pleased because there was a small Catholic church within walking distance. That had always been one of my top requirements when looking for the right flat. It was a modern, top-floor apartment in a four-storey block with private parking underground. It was called PH Riazor, on Calle Arch Angel. There was a large open plan lounge/diner with a cloakroom off, a large fully-equipped kitchen with white units, two bedrooms, one with en-suite shower room. Leading off the lounge at the front of the building was a balcony covered with pot plants, which was a very pleasant space to pass the time and relax. It was high enough to offer a view over the rooftops of the surrounding streets on the edge of the city. Just beyond the kitchen was an open-air utility area with a Perspex roof to protect it from the rain. When it rains in Panama, you know about it – spectacular tropical storms were a regular occurrence. It was a short walk to the local shops and an easy commute into the city.

With the help of local lawyers, Gray & Co, of Panama City, I – because it was me controlling the purse strings – formed a corporation, Jaguar Properties, which we used to buy the fully furnished apartment for $97,000. But it was John's idea, and he chose the name, after his favourite car. He said it would be a nice touch to make Mark and Anthony directors of the corporation, as well as me, a move I deeply regret because it would later make Cleveland Police highly suspicious of the boys. I didn't think of that possible consequence at the time.

Shortly after we bought the flat, Diana showed us some land that she believed would be ideal for the eco-tourist destination we had talked about so much. By now, I have to admit, I was almost as enthused about the eco-business as John, though I still had doubts about the practicalities of building and running such a venture. The land, called 'Finca no. 1031', bordered the shores of Lake Gatun, in Escobal, a rural village two hours' drive from the capital. It was at the northern end of the Panama Canal, on the country's central, north coast. We really liked the area – it was pretty much virgin land with a bit of everything we were looking for. Well, at least that's how it seemed to our optimistic minds. It was partly jungle, there were steep ravines and swamps, but there were also wide-open spaces and some of the land bordered the shores of the lake, meaning it would be ideal for boating. There was also a tremendous variety of trees, birds, insects and other wildlife.

John also loved the fact that Colon was steeped in history. Sir Francis Drake had called the province 'the treasure trove of the world', and John rather liked the idea that he would be following in the footsteps of some of his more famous countrymen. But in reality, the idea of buying land and trying to establish an eco-resort in a remote and lawless part of a country we knew nothing about, was, I have to admit, insane. We had no experience in the tourism industry, John had already proved himself inept at running a business and he never listened to me. We were not exactly in the prime of our lives, and we didn't even speak the native language. Mowing the grass and pruning the roses was about as far as our gardening skills went, so quite how we planned to cope with looking after hundreds of acres of a tropical jungle, infested with dangerous snakes and poisonous spiders, is anyone's guess.

Christopher Columbus, decided to steer well clear of the Colon area after seeing what he described as a 'pestilential swamp filled with mosquitos, snakes and caimans' (a large reptile related to the crocodile). The English historian James Froude put it even more bluntly, writing in 1886: 'In all the world there is not, perhaps, now concentrated in a single spot so much swindling and villainy.' Perhaps we should have heeded Columbus and Froude's words.

In most guidebooks, tourists were advised to completely

avoid the region's capital, Colon, or risk being mugged at knifepoint. But, of course, we paid no attention to such warnings. Through our rose-tinted spectacles, it was easily the most attractive plot of land we had viewed. No matter that it covered a huge area, 481 acres, there was no running water and no electricity, and the road that led to it, through sleepy Escobal, was rutted with potholes. As per usual, John wasn't about to let reality get in the way of his dreams. And when he heard there were plans afoot to build an international airport at Colon and another bridge over the canal, making the area far more accessible, his mind was made up. It would mean that land prices would shoot up, he told me – so we'd better move fast. 'It will soon be worth millions,' he bragged. 'And we'll be laughing all the way to the bank.'

I later sent an email to my family, which had largely been written by John, saying the land could later be sold for monopoly money in excess of $2 million. The email must, I'm sure, have left everyone wondering about my new-found business acumen, as I wrote about 'carbon credits for trees' and the growth in eco-tourism.

I flew home via Caracas and Paris, arriving at Newcastle Airport on the morning of 2 April, in time for Mam and Dad's 60th wedding anniversary three days later. It was a beautiful sunny day, it felt more like summer than the beginning of April. It was good to be back home with all the family. My brother and sister had organised a private room in one of Durham's hotels for a celebration lunch. Michael made a DVD using family photographs with captions and music, mapping out the years since Mam and Dad had married. It was a total surprise to them. We all enjoyed watching it and requested a copy as a keepsake. Memories of happy times came flooding back to me – the beach holidays with cousins and the births of Mark and Anthony. Those pictures were full of happy, smiling faces, some of which included John. I did my best to keep at bay the thoughts of leaving them all behind in the not too distant future. I didn't want to spoil the atmosphere of the day.

John, had stayed on at the Costa Inn, and got the keys and moved into our new apartment ten days later. The lady selling the apartment wanted to move as quickly as possible and there was no chain so everything progressed without a problem. But setting up a new home for a man who was used to being waited on hand and foot wasn't easy, and in his emails – which became more and more frequent – it was clear he was struggling with the most basic domestic chores. Communication was also a major problem. He was trying to make do using the translation website babelfish.com. He wrote down questions he needed to ask in Spanish, but then found he couldn't understand the answers. Rather than use his time to learn the language, he dismissed the locals as stupid for not speaking English.

He emailed me a picture on 20 May of what looked like red lumps on his skin, saying, 'I'm sure I've got fleas. Haven't seen any but skin looks same as in picture… off to buy a hammer or something to kill the little buggers. Love you.'

His emails were often saucy and full of sexual innuendo: he even claimed to have typed some of them while sitting on the balcony in the nude. The very thought disgusted me. It seemed John was growing increasingly frustrated at being alone. He appeared to be becoming more insane by the day.

Chapter 11

Dreaming of
Jaguar Lodge

Back home in England, I knew I had to tell Mark and Anthony that I had made up my mind about emigrating, and broke the news to them on a weekend visit to Hampshire. They were pretty shocked that I had finally decided to leave the country, but they were, nonetheless, very supportive and promised they would come and visit.

I suppose I hadn't given a lot of thought to what John would do when they arrived at the airport: maybe he'd just have to disappear again. I told the boys I was heading back to Panama in the very near future to try and settle on some land to buy, but I'd be back before actually emigrating.

Throughout June, John kept me busy with lists of requests of what to bring with me on my forthcoming trip. He was growing increasingly excited about the land at Colon and after a solo visit to the area by bus – he only held a provisional driving licence in the name of John Jones, which wasn't valid in Panama – he sent me a copy of a report about planned investment and development in the region. 'There's never going to be a better time to buy here,' he wrote. 'We've really got to get in quick before land prices start to spiral.'

I returned to Panama for a month's trip, and moved into the apartment with John. Once again, after nearly six long years of hiding, we could openly live together as man and wife. It was lovely and I was very happy. For the first time in years, John seemed relaxed again. It was as if our marriage was reborn – as if a huge weight had been lifted off both of our shoulders. It was the first time I had felt normal in a very long time: life, now, was certainly a little bit different for us.

Because we had not yet sold our home in England, we had purposely bought a fully furnished apartment, deciding it was a far cheaper option than having to start from scratch. The living room was the most elegant, and had two white leather armchairs at either end of a matching sofa, surrounding a glass-topped coffee table. The floor was tiled and there were several large paintings of the Panamanian countryside adorning the walls. But I quickly saw that John hadn't done at all well living on his own and asked how he had survived without some essentials that were desperately needed, such as crockery, pots and pans and even a loo brush.

I found most of what I needed in a supermarket-cum-general store a short stroll from our new home. I was an avid window-shopper and loved to spend hours wandering along Avenida Central, a pedestrianised street covering six blocks, lined with countless restaurants and stores of varying sizes, where you could buy just about everything imaginable at dirt-cheap prices. On an outing with John, we even picked up a machete, which we had been told would come in extremely useful when hacking our way through the land we had now set our hearts on buying.

We soon settled into our new way of life, usually rising early, around 6.30am, and starting our day on the patio with a leisurely breakfast of yoghurt and fresh fruit – peaches, melons, mangoes, papaya – my favourite – and bananas. I would potter around the apartment, usually in my bikini, tidying up as we went, then make the most of the tropical climate by sunbathing on the terrace overlooking the city for an hour or so, before the heat of the morning sun became too unbearable. John would either sit and read or move inside and beaver away on his computer. We even started to try and establish new friends, attending a buffet dinner and cocktail night for local expats at Siciliano's Cafe, in the heart of the financial district.

Back at the apartment, I marvelled at the exotic, brightly coloured birds I saw from the terrace: parakeets and tiny hummingbirds – all very different from Seaton's dull grey pigeons, which were forever leaving their mark on The Cliffe. I jumped out of my skin the first time one came through the open kitchen window, but I quickly got used to the little green or bluey-grey geckos – small lizards, with sucker-like feet that hopped around the patio and even in and out of the kitchen window. They were totally harmless and ate mosquitoes and other pests, so were actually good to have around. I could sit and watch them for ages. It was like having your own wildlife show in your back yard.

Not that the show from our balcony was anything compared with what was in store at Escobal, the rugged land we had now agreed to buy at a cost of $389,000 after four further visits between us. In time, we planned to spend a further $100,000 building a villa – Jaguar Lodge (John's idea) – where we could live while developing our eco-resort. The land was home to howler monkeys, wild boar, toucans, tapirs, butterflies and birds galore. There were numerous different varieties of palm and fruit trees, bamboo and hundreds of other trees we simply didn't recognise. We were warned to watch out for deadly rattlesnakes, which scared the living daylights out of me but didn't seem to deter John. On one visit, for the first time in years, we felt able to pose for photographs. At last, we thought, we really were anonymous.

While I'd been in England, John had started his 'master plan'. My husband, John Darwin, had opened a laptop he'd bought as John Jones and logged on using the name Peter Fenwick. Having become an expert at living his life as somebody else, John had created a fake identity for his own fake identity. And now he was creating a blueprint to secure the prosperous future he'd always believed was rightfully his. I'm sure he felt a little smug as he sat poised at his laptop. After all, he felt, if the police hadn't been able to work out what happened to the missing/presumed dead John Darwin, how on earth would they ever catch up with John Jones, the man he'd secretly become, let alone his latest new identity, Peter Fenwick? Not that they were John's only pseudonyms. He had used John Allen after he first disappeared and, more recently, he often signed off on emails as Panama Jack, or, a little cringingly, Sexy Beast!

John's addiction to false identities was undoubtedly the reason his frauds – our frauds – went undetected for so many years. But his fascination for fake names and a fantasy life wasn't initially something borne out of his need to disappear, it was down to his love of computer games. Long before he even thought about doing his vanishing act, John honed his skills at living in a fantasy world playing on his computer. Shortly after moving to Seaton Carew, he'd begun playing an online game called Asheron's Call, fighting virtual 3D monsters in a heroic, fantasy world on a fictional planet. The games quickly became an obsession: every spare moment was spent lost in a world of make-believe, pitting his wits against thousands of other online players, pretending to be people they weren't. That reality world would be the perfect training for what was to follow in real life. For when the time came to fake his own disappearance, one of his first acts was to carefully create a false identity so robust it would give him access to credit cards that would never need to be paid back, and a passport that gave him the freedom to travel and disappear.

John's master plan was complex and intricate down to every last detail. It was designed to guarantee the most important things in his life: the security of the fraudulently obtained cash we had stockpiled and a safe and prosperous retirement in Central America, a place we could live out the remainder of our days in sunshine and luxury. Meticulous in its preparation over many months, the project to re-invent his whole life was laid out lovingly in full colour and even included computer-generated graphics, a flow chart, marked with explanatory notes and a detailed business plan, which plotted every penny of our illicit cash and future expenditure. Arrows pointed out important sections and carefully pasted links could be clicked on for more information from relevant websites. Different colours were used to plot the best options – green being the best, red the worst. There were always alternatives in case Plan A didn't work out.

On 14 May 2007, John opened a new workbook in Excel, clicked on 'Save As' and typed out, 'Jaguar Lodge,' the name of both his master plan and the home he was going to build for us in Colon that was to be the centre-piece of all his dreams. He listed the anticipated cost of everything, from utilities such as water and electricity, hiring staff, and everyday living necessities, to how he would invest every penny of the fraudulently claimed money, even down to his teacher and prison pensions.

As for Jaguar Lodge itself, he planned a 'magnificent house' set in hundreds of acres on the edge of the rainforest, with plenty of accommodation for all the family, including room for not one, but two, maids. After all, John felt he had reached the time in his life when he should be waited on hand and foot. He designed graphics for how the extensive two-storey building would look, complete with doors to a rooftop terrace, with its own outdoor kitchen and high, arched windows from all rooms. There would be mosquito nets on all the windows, security grills, a TV and games room, a library and office... the list went on and on. The spreadsheet was so detailed, he even made a list of the animals we'd need to get his eco-centre up and running: six horses, twenty cows and twenty sheep to start with, with money set aside for veterinary bills. We'd need fruit trees to ensure our guests enjoyed the freshest of produce every day. Initially, he wanted five banana, three lemon, ten mango, five pejibaye (or peach palm), one fig and, for some reason, a hundred guava, plus many other varieties – coconut, melon, passion fruit and avocado to name but a few. He wasn't even sure what trees were already there on our land.

When he showed me the spreadsheet after I'd joined him again in Panama, it was obvious that John had pored over it for hours on end, adding diagrams, maps and costings. It included links to relevant websites, legal advice and the interest and exchange rates that were so important for the efficient laundering of our stolen cash. I wasn't entirely convinced he had thought of *everything* – after all, most of his plans to date hadn't ended well – but I was bowled over by the idea of being able to start again, and by the beautiful country of Panama itself. I was, I admit, as enthusiastic as John when we made an offer on the land.

Once we had bought the land, John, true to character, wasted no time in letting the locals know the new British buyers were serious business people and stupidly put it about that we were the 'front men' for a larger consortium, which planned to invest heavily in the area. When he found piles of rubbish tipped illegally on his land, he wrote a letter of complaint, in my name, to Jaime Luna, the municipal chief of Escobal. The letter, signed, rather grandly, 'Anne Darwin, President and legal representative Jaguar Properties Corporation', warned that fly-tipping was endangering my company's investment and the viability of its tourism project, which was going to 'provide a great economic impulse' to Escobal. I couldn't understand why he had to make such a grand show of it.

He could have simply had a quiet word and asked if there was anything that could be done to prevent it happening again.

I returned to England alone, arriving at Newcastle on 31 July, where my brother Michael and his wife Ann were waiting for me. Very soon afterwards, in early October, I found a buyer for No 3, which had been on the market since February.

Mark and his girlfriend, Flick (short for Felicia), and Anthony and Louise travelled north to help clear out and prepare for my move. John and I discussed giving both the boys some of his personal belongings. Mark chose a pair of black oynx cufflinks and his father's watch. Anthony took his wedding ring, pocket watch, passport and ration book. He also selected some books, one of which was *The Shelters of Stone* by Jean M. Auel. It was only several months later that Anthony realised the paperback had been printed in 2003 – long after his dad had 'died'. Another of the books had an American sticker on it and Anthony realised it must have been bought while his 'deceased' dad was on his US travels. But at the time of the handover of their beloved father's personal belongings the boys were grief-stricken. It was a very emotional moment for me to see their reactions. I was happy that they had something of John's but I felt awful because I was, yet again, deceiving them.

It was at that time I first told the boys that, because I was a foreigner, I had needed to set up a company to buy the land, and had therefore decided to make them directors of Jaguar Properties, each getting 15 of the company's 100 shares. The boys were amazed at my resourcefulness and thanked me for my generosity.

It was lovely to spend the weekend with the boys. It was good to be with them. They were so supportive of me, saying they wanted to come and visit. I knew most people thought I must be potty to be selling up in England and starting a new life, seemingly alone, on the other side of the world at my age. But of course I wasn't going to be alone and my new life was born out of lies and deceiving those I loved most.

The sale of No 3, for £295,000, to John Duffield was completed on 19 October. I flew back to Panama on 22 October, this time via New York's Newark Airport with Continental Airlines, but it wasn't long before the reality of my future life began to kick in.

When I got back, things were good between us at first, but then John started pressuring me to open different bank accounts. I had about £280,000 from the sale of No 3 The Cliffe, and John wanted me to put it in different accounts, so we would get decent interest rates, which we would be able to live off.

While he was on his own in Panama he had been

around all the different banks to find out about the best accounts, but I really didn't want to go through all the hassle of trying to open more accounts. Even the talk of new bank accounts terrified me – I was always worried about something going wrong and history repeating itself. It was not easy to open bank accounts in Panama and I hated the thought of having to do it. I just used to get flustered with all that official stuff. And as far as John was concerned, I could never get things right.

Using a Panamanian bank for the simplest transaction could take quite a long time. There was always an armed guard on the door and others situated at various points inside the banking hall. The queues were lengthy, no matter what the time of day. I had to queue to state the nature of my business and then was directed to a waiting area, with easy chairs; it wasn't unusual to wait 20 to 30 minutes before being called to the desk. It was fortunate for me that most people in business spoke English.

John had researched the various accounts and had already decided on the one that I should request to open. It should have been a fairly straightforward exercise, but then the account advisor began offering different accounts and I became confused and didn't know which one to choose.

I asked 'Which account do you recommend?' A question I later came to regret as that led me to open the 'wrong account' according to John. He got so cross with me. He didn't want to invest all the money in one bank anyway so the next time he accompanied me, as my advisor, to ensure he got the correct outcome.

This was meant to be a happy new start for me but I was worrying about everything again. It worried me that I was still on a widow's pension in England and if I returned on my own I wouldn't be able to support myself. I didn't really know if I was even going to stay in Panama. I didn't even have a Panamanian visa, although I was going to apply for one. We spent an entire fortnight, it seemed, trying to sort out the bank accounts. It was not a happy two weeks. The honeymoon period was over and John returned to his old self. I had been naive to think it would be any different.

Then John told me, for the first time, about a change in the law for permanent residency visas. The Panamanian government was bringing in changes to visa requirements for foreign nationals wanting to emigrate there. Anyone wanting to be granted 'permanent resident status', without exception, would need a letter from the police force in their home country, stating that they were a person 'of good character'. Without that, foreigners would only be able to visit on a tourist visa, like the one John currently held, allowing a stay of only three months at a time. John knew getting a reference letter from Cleveland Police would be an impossibility for John Jones – he didn't actually exist, and the kind of checks needed for a reference would reveal this. What's more, the Panamanian government was planning a crackdown on foreign nationals overstaying their welcome, and anyone found to be repeatedly renewing their tourist visa to stay in the country illegally would face arrest. John simply wouldn't be able to pop over the border to neighbouring Costa Rica every three months to renew his visa anymore. He couldn't actually remain in Panama 'legally' for more than three months and could easily face arrest if he was found to have flouted the new laws, as the government had ordered a crackdown.

I was astonished to learn John had known about this for four months, while we had been buying the land in Colon, and he hadn't said a word. 'It's a huge spanner in the works,' he said.

To say the least! I thought. *What on earth do we do now? If he can't stay in Panama, where will he go? Does this mean we have to sell up and move on again to a different country?* At least in Panama we'd been able to walk around freely without looking over our shoulders, checking to see if the coast is clear, every time we stepped outside. *Now,* I thought, *Do we even have a future here?* I couldn't bear the thought of more upheaval.

That's when John dropped another bombshell on me: he was going to 'come back to life'. He said he'd have to go back to the UK and reinvent himself as John Darwin, so he could return to Panama with his real identity re-established.

I was speechless, but managed to ask, 'How?'

He said he'd come up with a plan to claim he had

amnesia. He thought that if he went back saying he'd lost his memory and remembered nothing for the last seven years it would all be fine. He was convinced he could carry it off and everyone would believe him.

'It's perfectly feasible that if I'd had an accident I could have banged my head and lost my memory. It does happen sometimes.'

'And how would you account for the missing years?'

'I'd say I banged my head again and can't remember how I got to wherever I am or where I've been.'

'How do you account for the suntan?'

'I could have been on holiday.'

'This is crazy, no one will believe you.'

'You think of something better then!'

I thought he'd lost his marbles and couldn't see how he'd ever get away with it. But I also said that if he was intent on doing it, then he should. As far as I was concerned, we'd have to repay all the money we'd fraudulently claimed and start afresh, but that was fine by me. It would actually be a relief.

But then I began thinking of the consequences again. I knew in the back of my mind things couldn't possibly go the way John said they would. They rarely did. I was perplexed as to why he'd bought the land in Colon knowing that the visa rules were about to change. He said the land was a bargain and he couldn't miss out on such an opportunity. The government had been talking about the changes for years and nothing had come of it. Now, without warning, they'd decided to swing into action. It seemed we were doomed whichever way we turned.

Seeing how miserable I was, John suggested we take a holiday and together we travelled to Costa Rica for a week. It was the third week of November and we drove, over the course of two days, to the beach resort of Cahuita, in Limón Province.

I couldn't believe the rickety old bridge we had to cross at the border. Every alternate plank seemed to be missing and it swayed dramatically when heavy lorries drove over. Then we discovered we needed a permit to take the hire car across the border, or risk having it confiscated on our return, so had to drive back some miles to a town we had passed through earlier to find a place we could get one.

I was exhausted by the time we checked into the 38-bedroom Hotel Jaguar on Playa Negra – John undoubtedly choosing the hotel because of its name. The room was fairly basic but comfortable, and just a short stroll from the beach, with its crystal clear water and coral reef. One day we hired horses and went for a ride along the beach, stopping only to cut down some coconuts and enjoy the refreshing milk under the shade of the palm trees. It was a relaxing break, it felt good to be a tourist.

In Costa Rica, we received an email saying our shipment of personal belongings from England would be arriving on 7 December, slightly earlier than had been anticipated. I needed paperwork saying I had applied for a visa in order for the shipment to be allowed into the country, so I knew I would have to get moving with my own visa application.

One evening, we talked about John going back to England and he asked me about the timing. He said the decision was mine, and that if I wanted him to stay in Panama illegally, he would.

I really didn't think he would get away with his reincarnation plan but, in truth, if it wasn't going to work, I would rather it didn't work sooner rather than later. John said he desperately wanted contact with the boys again and thought it might give him the opportunity to pick up the pieces of his family life.

We talked about what he was going to say to the police, to the boys, who we knew would be stunned, and what I would say when he put his plan into action. He decided to say he couldn't remember anything after a holiday we had in Norway in 2000, though why he picked that date I'm not sure. I was worried because John was tanned from more than six months living in Panama and asked how he was going to explain it. He said he didn't want to look like he had been incarcerated indoors all those years, and he felt he could bluff his way through it, then return to Panama as John Darwin, and we would live happily ever after.

We also discussed the possibility of some of John's movements over the last few years coming to light, and came up with a plan for this too. If that part of his lie was exposed, I was to say that I had only found out after the inquest, when he turned up on my doorstep – that way I could still argue all the insurance claims had been made in good faith and we wouldn't necessarily lose everything.

There was no massive row, as was later suggested. It was simply a case that John didn't have a better plan, and nor did I, and so it was agreed. If he was going to try and get away with this latest charade, it was up to him. John had little regard for the police, after all. They hadn't covered themselves in glory when he disappeared and then returned to live in his own home, right under their noses, just over three weeks later. He'd fooled them once already and he was convinced he could do it again. He thought they'd believe his story and would just be glad to get him off their hands as quickly as possible.

As for the boys, he thought they would be so thankful he had returned from the dead they'd barely question him and would welcome him back with open arms. And although he'd have some explaining to do with the insurance and pension companies who'd made payments to me, he believed they too would accept his story and let us off completely. At the very worst, they would accept a deal to maybe repay some of the money over a period of time. Anyway, all his, or rather my, assets, were safely protected in Panama, well away from the reaches of the

British authorities, so no one would get their hands on anything very easily.

As soon as the dust had settled, he would return to Panama as John Darwin, with a new passport and a letter of good conduct from the police – ironic, I know – and he and I could get our visas and settle down for a nice quiet life in Panama, and the boys could come and visit whenever they wanted. We could simply pick up where we left off, developing an eco-retreat that, according to John, would make us wealthy beyond words. One day he'd sell it for a small fortune and be that millionaire he always said he would: it would just have taken a few more years than he'd boasted. In his mind, it was all so simple.

I bought him a single flight to Heathrow for Friday 30 November. It felt very surreal as I drove John to the airport and when he left it was quite emotional. I was going to stay in Panama on my own and he was going home with this story, which I didn't think anyone would believe for one moment. *Here we go again*, I thought.

I also felt that, although it was true John missed his sons, had it not been for the change in visa regulations there's no way he would have rushed back to the UK and gambled on possibly losing everything he'd spent nearly six years working towards. If it went wrong, and the police didn't buy his story, he'd lose everything, be arrested – and be right back where he was at the point of going under in

March 2002. If he could have stayed in Panama, even if it meant he'd never see the boys again, I'm sure he would have done. That was the man John had become.

Chapter 12

'I Think I'm
a Missing Person'

London, Saturday 1 December, 2007

Even among the hordes of Christmas shoppers, the balding, sun-tanned man in his fifties must have looked somewhat out of place as he wandered aimlessly around a Topshop store in Oxford Street in London's West End. He looked confused and when an assistant asked if he was all right, she was taken aback to be told he had lost his wife, his children and his Rottweiler dogs. She called a security guard, who walked him around the corner to the West End Central Police Station. It was about 7.30 p.m.

'Yes sir, how can I help you,' asked the officer on duty.

The man peering through the glass screen shifted uncomfortably from side to side. 'I think I might be a missing person,' he responded, a little shakily. 'My name's John Darwin. I'm from Seaton Carew.'

I'm sure the officer must have raised his eyebrows, thinking, *I've got a right one here*, as John put his ludicrous amnesia plan into action. John, who was wearing walking boots, baggy, dark blue trousers, a blue shirt, still showing the folds from being packed for the flight, a grey, crew-neck jumper and a leather jacket, said he wasn't quite sure where he had come from or how he had arrived at the police station.

'I see, sir,' the officer said. 'John Darwin, you say? Yes, sir. Can you just wait there for a minute?'

It didn't take the policeman long to discover there was indeed a John Darwin who had disappeared off the Cleveland coast in 2002, but he wasn't missing – he was dead. He rang Hartlepool police station to see if anyone there could throw any light on the curious case he now found himself dealing with on a cold December evening. 'He thinks it's still June and asked why all the Christmas decorations are up.'

The officer had already established 'Mr Darwin' had no form of identification on him, simply a wallet containing £140 and a key ring with several keys attached. He claimed not to know what any of the keys were for.

Mark was partying at a friend's wedding in Balham, south London, when his mobile phone rang. It had just gone 9pm and the party was in full swing, making it difficult to hear over the beat of the music, but he could just about make out that the woman was saying she was a police officer from Hartlepool, so he moved outside.

'We have someone who is saying they are your dad in the West End Central Police station in London,' the duty inspector, Helen Eustace, told him. 'He appears to be suffering from amnesia.'

Mark began shaking and was rooted to the spot. *Dad? No, surely, it couldn't be? Could it?* The inspector asked Mark about his father's disappearance and he told her he was presumed to have died at sea in a canoeing tragedy in March 2002.

'Well, this man is saying he's your dad,' the inspector repeated.

Mark was absolutely stunned. 'My whole world stopped,' he said later 'My heart was pumping. I couldn't believe it. I was overjoyed.'

He rushed back inside to tell his girlfriend, Flick, and they hastily left the wedding and headed to the West End, not really daring to believe it could be true.

Anthony, meanwhile, was at home in Basingstoke with Louise when the police got hold of him. Like his brother, he could barely believe what he was hearing. He tried to call Mark but couldn't get through because his brother was on the Tube, so he rang the London police station directly and was talking to an officer when Mark and Flick walked in. Over the phone, Mark told his younger brother to stay put until he had seen the man purporting to be their father, to see if it really was him.

Mark and Flick were taken into a room where an officer talked him through what they knew, then asked if he wanted to see the man claiming to be his dad. After being briefed by the station sergeant and told his father had seen a psychiatrist and been arrested under the Mental Health Act, for his own safety, Mark braced himself for the meeting, terrified it would be some cruel hoax or a man who had simply assumed his father's identity – but, of course, it wasn't. Standing there in front of him, looking older, with a little less hair and thinner than the man he remembered, was the dad who had disappeared from his life more than five years earlier.

'It was as if everything was stopped in the room,' said Mark. 'I remember us looking at each other as he walked in and I said, "I didn't believe it was you."'

Mark was in tears as he hugged his dad, who asked where his Mam and the dogs were. Mark said the dogs had long since died but Mam was fine – and living in Panama.

Mark called Anthony, who had by then been anxiously waiting at home for nearly half an hour, and told him the man was indeed their long-lost dad and said he'd better get to the police station as quickly as he could. Anthony and Louise jumped in their car and headed towards the city but Anthony was in such a state that he was soon lost. He ended up having to call the police and, after explaining his predicament, was obliged with an escort to the station.

Anthony was as stunned as his brother when he first set eyes on his father, telling me later, 'When I first saw him he called my name and we hugged. I just sat and stared at

him for about ten minutes and didn't say a word. I felt
overwhelming joy that he was there.'

Mark rang me before Anthony got there. He couldn't wait
to let me know that his dad had returned from the dead.
His fingers shook as he punched in the phone number to
my Panama apartment. He rambled on before finally
saying, 'Brace yourself – I am sitting here next to Dad.'

Of course, I had been waiting, dreading, this call since
the moment John left the previous day. I had played it out
in my mind a thousand times, trying to work out what best
to say in order to feign complete surprise. Mark said,
'Would you like to speak to him?' and of course I said I
would.

It was a very strange conversation to have. I said
something along the lines of 'Is that really you, John?
Where have you been? Are you OK?' We had a fairly
brief stilted conversation and then he handed the phone
back to Mark, who said his dad was confused and couldn't
remember anything. He said John looked as if he'd had a
stroke or something similar and, his top lip in particular
looked peculiar. His hair had receded a bit and he was
slightly thinner than when he went missing, especially in
the face. He was well dressed and appeared to have lost
some of his north-east accent. It was an incredible
emotional moment for me. Mark and Anthony were
reunited with their dad after nearly six years, and now

everything, I thought to myself, would surely come to a head.

I sat for a while, unable to move, then I started to pace the floor not really knowing what I was supposed to do now. Think, Anne, think. I was about to call Mam and Dad but remembering the time difference, with the UK being five hours ahead of Panama, it would have been around midnight and they'd be asleep. I decided to wait until morning.

I couldn't settle to do anything. The flat was so quiet and I was all alone with just my thoughts for company. My thoughts were in that London police station, but I had no idea what was happening. *Will John be arrested? Will the police see right through his story? How are the boys feeling? Do they believe him? What happens next?* I couldn't sleep, I couldn't read, I tossed and turned all night long.

As far as the police were concerned, John was free to go. He wasn't a wanted man, and although it was certainly a strange old case, there was nothing to stop him leaving with the boys. Officers said they would be in touch the next day and advised them to keep a very close eye on their father.

It was decided that John would stay with Anthony and Louise in Basingstoke, as they had more room at home than Mark, so all five headed off to Hampshire together in Anthony's car. When they arrived, they sat chatting and looking at old family photographs until the early hours, hoping something would jog John's memory. He told them he did recall that he worked as a teacher, a job he'd left many years earlier, and he quite liked hunting rabbits (which he didn't – the closest he came to rabbits was with our pet ones when the boys were young), but he couldn't recall much more than that. Anthony took a photograph of his dad sitting on his sofa, looking slightly dishevelled and emailed it to me. I sent back a picture of myself taken, a few weeks earlier, of me riding a horse in Costa Rica. The boys simply assumed the photograph must have been taken by a fellow holidaymaker – little did they know the picture was really taken by the man they were sitting with. Anthony showed John to the spare room and Mark and Flick decided to stay over, but no one got much sleep that night.

The next morning, Anthony drove his dad to the nearby Asda supermarket, as the only clothes he appeared to have were the ones he was wearing. He bought John some jeans, several T-shirts, three pairs of underpants and some socks. John said he wanted to pay for them but Anthony wouldn't hear of it. There was one brief moment of panic for Anthony when he suddenly turned round and couldn't see his dad, who had wandered off into another aisle. Anthony was terrified he had disappeared again and ran from aisle to aisle looking for him before eventually finding him.

Later that day, Mark and Flick left to return to

London, as Mark was starting a new job the following morning. It was left to Anthony and Louise to continue gently trying to coax information from John as he carried on his charade of not being able to remember anything after the year 2000. He said he didn't know what baked beans were and couldn't recall whether he took sugar in his coffee, yet he remembered Mark and Anthony's dates of birth. I spoke regularly on the phone to John but we were obviously very careful what we said to each other. The boys seemed slightly puzzled when I said I couldn't return straightaway because I was sorting out some problems with my visa, but they didn't press me. They were just thrilled to have their dad back.

That evening, (Sunday, 2 December) Simon Walton, a reporter on the Evening Gazette in Middlesbrough, was making one last round of calls to his local police force, checking for any late-breaking stories before finishing his shift. He was checking some details with a duty inspector at Cleveland Police, when she mentioned she had another story which may be of interest. A local man named John Darwin had mysteriously turned up in London, apparently suffering from memory loss. He had been missing for five years. There was going to be an announcement in the morning, but seeing as he had rung she decided to give him the details. For a few moments, the name rattled round the journalist's brain — then it hit him. More than five years earlier, Walton had been a junior reporter in Hartlepool when he had covered the story of a canoeist who went missing off Seaton Carew. The man's body was never found and he was presumed to have drowned: his name was... John Darwin. Walton nearly dropped the phone in amazement, knowing he had a front-page story on his hands. Sure enough, the astonishing tale was the main story in the following day's paper and it wasn't long before the story was being followed up by just about every news organisation in the country. The press interest was something John and I simply hadn't bargained on. We naively had no idea his reappearance would be such big news.

It wasn't long before journalists tracked down Anthony's address and reporters and photographers started turning up on the doorstep inquiring about his father's incredible return from the dead. Anthony, still in shock and overwhelmed by the situation, contacted his local police station for help, begging them to keep the reporters at bay. The amazing 'canoe story' quickly gathered steam, with journalists desperate for more information. The two questions on everyone's lips were: where had he been for all those years, and where was his wife? The race to find me was well and truly on.

Chapter 13

'I Need to Speak to You about Your Husband...'

Panama City, Monday 3 December, 2007

For newspapers and broadcasters across the country, the
'Canoe Man's' incredible return from the dead was
one of the most intriguing stories of the day. And while the
Metropolitan Police seemed in no hurry to follow up on
the man who had walked into one of its police stations
nearly six years after he was presumed drowned at sea in
his red canoe, journalists most certainly were. They
thought there simply has to be more to this story than
meets the eye. Newspapers and broadcasters went into
overdrive, desperate to discover the truth behind John's
reincarnation.

I spent most of the time sitting anxiously in my
apartment. I had to stay in Panama to receive the
shipment of my personal belongings arriving in a few
days, 7 December. I wasn't internet savvy at the time, so
could only hear the latest developments from John and the
boys over the phone. Little did I know teams of journalists
were already hotfooting it to Panama to find me.

It was dark that night, 3 December, when the outside buzzer rang. Strange, I thought, it rarely rang at all and never at night, so I ignored it. Then it rang again, and again, and again, but each time I ignored it, thinking maybe it was children playing games or someone calling the wrong apartment. All went quiet.

Fifteen minutes later, I jumped when the bell of my actual apartment rang, then someone was knocking on the front door, and asking repeatedly, 'Mrs Darwin, are you there?' Silence, but not for long. 'Mrs Darwin, I need to speak to you about your husband, are you there?' More knocks and more questions. 'Mrs Darwin, I've come with news about your husband. I need to speak with you.'

For 30 minutes or more, I sat there, terrified, not daring to move or knowing what to do. You couldn't even get into the building without being buzzed in by intercom, so I felt extremely panicked. Whoever it was wasn't going away, and every five minutes there was another knock on the door and yet more questions. Finally, I decided I couldn't ignore it any longer.

'What do you want?' I asked, after looking through the peep hole and seeing two men outside my apartment. I knew they were English by their accents.

'I've come about your husband, John. I thought you'd be relieved that he's turned up safe and well in England?' said the man asking all the questions. 'Presumably you know about it?'

I wasn't at all sure what to say, so said nothing.

'Aren't you pleased your husband is alive and well?' he asked. 'Perhaps I can help you in some way?'

'You can't, nobody can,' I responded eventually. They were not the cleverest words I could have chosen, as I knew immediately there was an implication that I was somehow in trouble.

We struck up a strained conversation and I asked who they were and where they were from. The man said his name was David Leigh, he was a reporter, and his colleague, Steve Dennett, a photographer. They were journalists employed by a news agency, Splash News, and had come to Panama seeking my reaction to John's mysterious reappearance.

I said I didn't want any pictures, so David said Steve could wait in their car outside. 'How do I even know who you really are?' I asked, so David slipped his press identification card under the door. He told me he lived in Miami, with his wife and two young daughters, and that other journalists were already on their way and perhaps he'd be able to help me in some way.

I slid the chain from the latch and slowly opened the door. 'I suppose you'd better come in,' I said. 'You can call me Anne.'

I showed David into the reception room and offered him a glass of water.

'You must be incredibly relieved about your husband?'

he asked.

'Of course I am, yes,' I responded.

'But I have to ask,' he continued, 'lots of people are wondering why you haven't dashed back home to see him?'

I felt incredibly flustered and didn't really know what to do or say. I think, more than anything, I was intrigued to find out what David knew about what was going on at home with John. I'd been in touch with family in England and they'd told me Sky News and the BBC were already reporting that I was in Panama. But I was still astonished anyone had been able to find me quite so quickly. David explained that he'd been sent to Panama by the *Daily Mail* foreign desk but the *Daily Mirror* had come up with my address, he believed from the person who'd bought my old home in Seaton Carew, so he was working for both papers. I wasn't really taking in everything he was saying, my mind was racing.

I said of course I'd wanted to rush home but couldn't leave Panama immediately because there was urgent paperwork I needed to sign regarding my visa application and, in three days' time, my entire lifetime's belongings were due to arrive on a cargo ship from the UK, and I had to be at the port in Colon to sign for my container. Once I'd sorted that, I would of course be flying home.

As we talked, I relaxed a little. David said everyone at home was amazed by the story, and at John's remarkable reappearance, and was desperate to hear my reaction.

'Yes, I can understand why everyone could be so curious,' I said, cautiously. 'I'm finding it pretty hard to take in myself.' I said John's return was a mixture of shock, joy, disbelief and confusion.

I didn't know at the time but David was under immense pressure to get me away from the apartment – and his rival journalists. He told me it wouldn't be long before I'd be besieged by other British reporters and TV crews, some of whom were already in Panama and others on a flight from New York. I didn't believe him. I couldn't understand why there should be so much interest. But if it was true, I didn't want to take the risk of being caught in the middle of a scrum. He suggested that while I worked out what to do next, I might perhaps be better off leaving the apartment and moving to a hotel away from the area, where I wouldn't be found or bothered and he could help me with whatever arrangements I needed to make. He said journalists would be camped outside the apartment around the clock, making life pretty miserable for me, and I wouldn't be able to go anywhere without being followed and having television cameras pushed in my face.

'I promise you I'll look after you and keep those nasty journalists away from you,' he said with a smile, well aware I knew he was one of the very people he was promising to protect me from.

I said I needed to make a phone call to England to get

some advice, which I'm sure was the last thing David wanted to hear. I went into my bedroom, closing the door behind me, and spoke to a good friend who had been in touch since the news about John had broken. He felt getting away from the apartment was probably a good idea. I was advised to be careful and if I wished to make a statement I should do it through my lawyer. Feeling happy that someone at least knew who I was with, gave me the confidence in my decision to go with David. So I quickly packed a small case, put my important letters and files in a brown leather document case and opened the door of my bedroom.

'Are we going?' asked David, who looked amazed, and when I said yes, he quickly called Steve, telling him to pull the car up to the front of the building.

I felt incredibly nervous as David opened the back door of their small rental car for me to climb in. I had no idea where we were going or what the likely outcome of my journey might be. But I knew that I didn't want to be alone in the apartment if what he was telling me about more reporters was true. Getting into a car with not one, but two strange men went against my natural instinct but I considered it to be the lesser of two evils.

It was dark and the roads were choked with traffic as we drove to the nearby El Panama Hotel, where David and Steve had earlier checked in and dumped their bags.

'We can't stay here, it's too close to your apartment,' David said, so while Steve sat in the car with me, he dashed up to their room, grabbed their luggage, paid the bill for a night he wouldn't be having, and we headed out of town.

'Where to?' said Steve.

'No idea,' David replied. 'Just drive. Let's just get as far away from here as we can.'

He knew rival journalists would be hot on our heels, so getting as far away from my home was the most pressing objective. I tried to assist, saying I vaguely recognised one of the main roads out of town, so with no better plan of their own, we took that and headed off into the unknown. Using my very limited Spanish, I asked for directions to a town on David's map at the first motorway toll booth we arrived at, but the response was a completely incomprehensible series of rapid gestures and instructions. I smiled politely, thanked the man kindly and we cluelessly drove on into the night.

We were still on the road as the hour approached 2am. Everyone was shattered and I was beginning to wish I hadn't been so quick to accept the offer of escape. What had earlier been a busy dual carriageway was now a totally deserted single-track road, so when we spotted a brightly lit backpackers' hostel on the other side of the road, we decided to pull over and seek a bed for the night. David rang the bell and eventually a sleepy receptionist, who we'd obviously woken, opened the door and grasped that we needed two rooms for the night. She led us up a flight of stairs to what resembled a school dormitory. If I'd been expecting a stay in luxury accommodation when I accepted David's offer of a hotel for the night, I would have been sorely disappointed. What we got was the most basic of hostels costing £12.50 for both rooms, one for me and one for David and Steve.

The rooms were small but clean and the beds rock solid. It was like lying on concrete blocks. As I lay back wondering what might happen tomorrow, next door David was busy writing emails for the papers he was working for, telling them what had happened and that he had me – the prized catch – in the hotel room next door. Once again I questioned my judgement. I should have stayed put and spoken to my lawyer. We couldn't stay where we were, so where to next? I really had no idea what lay ahead. After a restless night it was time to move on.

It was a warm, sunny morning, with cloudless blue skies as we set off, heading north-west, away from the hostel and further still from Panama City, on the Inter-American Highway. The landscape was breathtaking, with wide-open plains disappearing into the distance and a mountainous backdrop, but I was lost in thought and wondering, among other things, what on earth I had got myself into. No one seemed to have any idea where we were even going as overnight the journalists escorting me had somehow managed to lose their map. 'Just keep driving,' David told Steve.

What didn't concern me at the time was whether they had hit on the truth. As far as I had considered it, I thought the police solve crimes, not journalists.

After about an hour on the road, we pulled up at the first decent-looking hotel we came across – the Hotel Coronado and Beach Resort, just outside the small town of La Chorrera, 60 miles from Panama City. The hotel was quiet, save for a few American holidaymakers. David booked two rooms using false names, something that was becoming an increasingly familiar part of my life. He explained that other journalists would be desperately trying to find us and calling round hotels in the area was a trick of the trade they were bound to use.

Now David had put some distance between ourselves and his journalistic rivals, and he had a story to file that would almost certainly be on the front pages of the following day's papers, but he still needed a new photograph of me. England is five hours ahead of Panama, and time was ticking. David explained he also had a deadline to meet to get copy to press and a new picture would confirm that I was indeed in his presence. I felt obliged to have a brief chat – after all he had 'rescued' me, I felt I had to offer something in return. If I didn't, would he simply walk away and leave me stranded?

First we had breakfast, but I just picked at a fruit plate while drinking a cup of strong local coffee. I said I wanted to freshen up a bit and change out of my shorts and T-shirt and into something a little less casual for the photographs. David sensed I was incredibly nervous and assured me he would run through whatever quotes I gave him before hitting the send button on his story. The reassurance steadied my nerves and I finally said I was ready to proceed.

They found a spot to take photographs on the hotel terrace, and I sat in a wicker chair, feeling smarter in a blue-patterned top, khaki trousers and brown sandals. Steve snapped away as I began to open up about my remarkable – and mostly fictional – story.

'You've got to understand, this is all so amazing and hard for me to take in,' I said. 'This is the moment I always prayed for.'

I said the timing of John's reappearance was incredible as I had moved to Panama just six weeks earlier, having sold my home in the UK after years of agonising over how best to pick up the pieces of my life after John's 'death'. Now, just as I was starting out afresh, my whole world had again been turned upside down and I was struggling to take everything in. 'But it is the most wonderful news, it really is,' I tried to emphasise.

David asked about the precise moment I found out John was still alive and how I had felt. So I explained how Mark had called me three days earlier from the police station, told me John had miraculously come back from the dead and asked if I'd like to speak to him, which of course I did. I was overwhelmed. We said goodbye and Mark said they'd call again in the morning. Eventually I went to bed but, of course, I couldn't sleep. I just lay there wondering if it was really true or if I was imagining it all.

Well, that was what I told the journalists. What I actually wondered was how long it would be before John was found out and we'd both be arrested.

I said we had spoken again the following day and again after that, and the more we spoke, the more normal John's voice became. 'But what happened, I just don't know,' I said. 'I can't make any sense of it all. I know there must have been an accident that day he went out on the canoe and he must have hit his head or something. But I know there are so many unanswered questions. It is a complete mystery to me.'

David listened intently, taking down every word I spoke, but when I had finished, he said it was very difficult for him and everyone else to comprehend why I hadn't caught the first flight home. 'I want to get back as soon as possible, but I have some issues with my visa that I need to address. I also have to oversee the arrival of all my belongings, which had been shipped from the UK and are due here this week,' I said, repeating the story from the previous evening. 'I have to be here to clear everything through customs. As soon as everything is sorted out, of course I'll be straight back. We have so much to talk about, so many things to try and sort out. I want to see John and my family and try and see if I can put the pieces of my life back together again.'

Then David asked outright if I had known all along that John had been alive. 'No, I did not,' I responded, alarmed, but hoping to sound shocked. 'I'm as amazed as anyone.'

David said it was already being suggested that John may have faked his death because of some financial problems and even that I may have been in cahoots with him. Feeling on the back foot, I quickly replied, 'People can think what they want, I know the truth.'

He again asked if it was possible that John might have planned his disappearance, even if I hadn't known about it, but I shook my head. 'John just wouldn't have done that,' I said. 'If there were problems, we talked about them.'

The brief chat soon felt more like an in-depth interview. Then the questions turned to the prickly subject of our finances and I was asked if we'd been in debt at the time of his disappearance. This was the last thing I wanted to discuss, and what gave a journalist the right to ask such questions? I insisted that was nobody else's business. But I did acknowledge that I'd received some money from life insurance policies paid out after the coroner had declared John dead the year after he vanished, and said I knew it might now have to be repaid. I admitted the money had been playing on my mind, adding: 'It is one of the many things I am struggling to come to terms with. They were claimed in good faith when I believed I had lost my husband and now he has come back from the dead. If that happens, of course it won't be easy, but I'll deal with it. It is not the money I ever wanted – it was having my husband back. It took a long time for the insurance companies to pay me and I'm sure they'll be looking closely at the situation.'

Asked if I would be able to repay the money or if I had already spent it, I replied with my now stock answer, 'My finances are of no one's concern. It's a private matter.'

David did apologise for having to ask such tough questions but explained it was what everyone at home was asking.

'I can understand everyone wants to know,' I said, a little calmer – I didn't want to appear hostile. 'Maybe all the speculation is to be expected. There was a lot of speculation after he disappeared. People speculated about our finances, all sorts of things, but that's all it was, speculation.'

It felt like this 'brief chat' would never end. Next David asked why I had moved to Panama, so far away from my loved ones?

The answer to this question came much easier, as I'd been using it on friends and family for a long time. 'I'm sure it came as a surprise to many people that I decided to move here to Panama and start a new life for myself,' I said. 'But I moved here for me, to try and start afresh. I came here two years ago for a holiday by myself, as I had always wanted to see the Panama Canal. It was breathtaking and I fell in love with the country and its people straightaway. I came back a couple of times after that and decided it was where I wanted to live. I love the climate, everything about the place. I've been learning Spanish and starting my life again.'

I said by the time I returned to Seaton Carew, I already knew in my heart that I needed to make some drastic changes to my life and, over the next 18 months, I flew back to Panama for several more visits before taking the plunge and deciding to start life afresh on the other side of the world. I told the family I'd bought an apartment and that 'I felt, in some way, like I had been reborn.'

About John's reappearance, I said, just like our script, 'Now I really don't know what the future holds. I will fly back and see John and hopefully he will be able to move back over here with me and we can start afresh. I really don't want to live in England any more, I don't like the cold, but whether John will want to come here remains to be seen. There are many, many things we have to talk about. I know it's not going to be easy.'

Over the next hour, David asked me about my life and marriage to the boy I met on the school bus in our little mining village in the north east of England. And about how my life had changed forever on that fateful day, 21 March 2002, when John disappeared.

Finally, and much to my relief, it was over. David said he needed to file his story and, as promised, he first told me the quotes that would be attributed to me. What I had no idea at the time was that there were large parts of the story that David simply hadn't believed, and on top of the story he filed that afternoon was a note, marked 'Not for publication: This is what Mrs Darwin is claiming – but she's obviously lying through her teeth.'

The next morning my story was on the front page of both papers. The *Mirror* carried the front-page headline, in bold capital letters, 'SECRET LIFE OF MR CANOE', while the *Mail*'s, again in capitals, was 'YES, I *DID* POCKET THE LIFE INSURANCE'. Both carried Steve's pictures of my smiling face.

But there was worse to come the night before the stories were even published, when another very dramatic development came to light.

Chapter 14

'The Game's Up, Anne'

La Chorrera, Panama, Tuesday 4 December, 2007

While the following day's papers were going to press with front-page headlines revealing my reaction to John's dramatic return from the dead, it was still only lunchtime in Panama. After the interview was over and Steve had put away his cameras, I felt a lot more at ease. I was relieved to have given my side of the story and was blissfully unaware that the journalist hadn't believed most of what I was saying. I felt that all 'the fuss' would now start to die down. I had no real grasp of what a big deal the story had become or the headlines it was making at home in England. If I thought it was now about to go quietly away, I couldn't have been more wrong.

With my 'photo session' over, I changed back into shorts and a T-shirt and the three of us drove off in search of food. We were about 15 minutes from the town of La Chorrera, on the Gulf of Panama, which I knew from our property searches. A little agricultural community known for its cattle, oranges and coffee, and for the spectacular waterfalls along the Caimito River, many ex-pats had purchased cheap second homes in and around the town.

Steve spotted a restaurant and villa complex and was about to turn in when I suddenly recognised it as a place I had visited with John. I quickly said I'd rather not go there and could we find somewhere else, which must have puzzled the journalists, although they said nothing.

We drove on and found another restaurant, which was little more than a wooden shack and completely deserted, and after lunch I said I'd like to stretch my legs. We followed a winding lane towards the coast and took a short stroll on the first beach we came across, which turned out to be in a picturesque bay. It was pebbled and not the easiest to walk on but when I stopped to look out over the sea and towards the mountains in the distance, I was reminded again about just what a beautiful country it was, so peaceful and unspoiled. 'I do love it here,' I said to David and Steve.

Back at the hotel I returned to my room; I was exhausted and needed a lie down. I hadn't had a proper night's sleep in days. At about seven o'clock, David knocked on my door to see if I wanted dinner. Fifteen minutes later, with my hair still wet from the shower, we headed down to the hotel's La Caretta courtyard restaurant. David said Steve wasn't hungry and was tired from driving, so was taking a nap and wouldn't be joining us. I found out later, he had returned to the restaurant I had not wanted to visit earlier that day to see if he could establish exactly why I had been afraid to show my face.

During dinner, David questioned me further, asking why I had upped sticks and relocated to the other side of the world, thousands of miles from my beloved sons, elderly parents and lifelong friends. He said he was finding it hard to comprehend my story. But I felt I'd said more than enough that day already, and concentrated on my dinner, trying to skirt around any probing questions. David was relentless and I was weary. I repeated how keen I was to get back home and be reunited with John, and talked about how hard it was going to be to pick up the pieces of my life, stressing that I really didn't want to live in England anymore.

'Surely,' David said, 'with your husband back from the dead, you should be the happiest person alive?'

I said that was true but Panama was my home now and whether John would want to come and live here with me I really didn't know. 'I don't even know where he's been all this time,' I said. 'Everything is so confusing. I really don't know what I'm going to do.' I really just wanted the questions to stop now. More than anything else, I wanted time to clear my head, so I didn't say something I'd later regret. Like the truth. We'd had our 'brief chat' and he had got the pictures he wanted. There really was nothing more to say or, at least, nothing more that I wanted to say.

Towards the end of dinner, David's mobile phone rang. He excused himself, moved away from the table and spoke for ten minutes or so before returning. He said one of the papers had sent him something, an email, that he needed me to have a quick look at before turning in for the night. I didn't have the foggiest idea of the ticking time bomb that was about to blow up in my face.

We went back to the bedrooms, and I was a little baffled, but not unduly concerned, as I sat down opposite David and he turned on his laptop, looking for the email he'd been sent.

'I've got something to show you, Anne, a picture, and I'm afraid it's not going to be very easy for you,' he said.

I could feel the colour draining from my face, even before I fully focused on the photograph on the screen in front of me: *that* photograph of John and I with estate agent Mario Vilar, smiling into the camera, taken in Panama the summer before last.

'The game's up, Anne, I'm sorry,' said David. 'We know you've been lying.'

It was the moment my secret double life was finally exposed. It was the moment I'd known would happen eventually, the moment I'd dreaded. I couldn't deny it any longer. The truth was there in front of me, for all the world to see. I was broken, ashamed, relieved and worried, all at the same time. In the back of my mind, I'd always worried about that picture and had expressed concerns to John. To have it revealed like this was numbing.

It turned out the phone call at dinner had been from one

TOP LEFT Anne aged five with the family's pet dog

TOP RIGHT Anne's wedding day with Dad Harry and Mam Kathleen, Blackhall Colliery, December 22, 1973

ABOVE Crowned Miss Blackhall, aged 17, in 1969

RIGHT Wedding day in Blackhall Colliery with husband John Darwin, December 22, 1973

OPPOSITE TOP Anne with husband John and sons Mark and Anthony at a family wedding in 1997

OPPOSITE BOTTOM Anne and John in 1997 with his cherished Jaguar, displaying private number plate B9 JRD, for John Ronald Darwin

ABOVE Nos 3 and 4 The Cliffe in Seaton Carew – the houses that would ultimately lead to the Darwins' downfall

RIGHT The view of the North Sea from the drawing-room window at 3 The Cliffe

TOP LEFT The bricked-up passageway between Nos 3 and 4 The Cliffe

ABOVE RIGHT A copy of *The Day of the Jackal*, from which John had the idea to create his fake identity, John Jones. The book was found in one of his secret hideouts

ABOVE LEFT John Darwin's death certificate, which allowed Anne to claim his life insurance and pension payouts

RIGHT New owner of No 3 The Cliffe, John Duffield, shows the entrance to John Darwin's secret passageway to his hideaway in the rental house next door

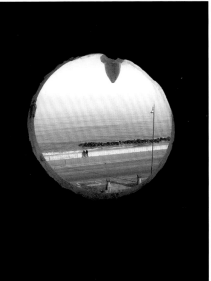

TOP LEFT A pamphlet on emigrating sent to Anne at the Darwins' home in Seaton Carew

ABOVE LEFT A letter sent to John's fake persona, Mr J Jones, at his own home, 3 The Cliffe, Seaton Carew

TOP RIGHT A view of the North Sea from a port hole in the roof space of No 3 The Cliffe

ABOVE A Cleveland Police photo of John's battered red canoe after it was washed ashore six weeks after he 'vanished'

RIGHT The 60ft catamaran *Boonara*, which in November 2005 John looked at buying to sail round the world

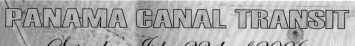

PANAMA CANAL TRANSIT

Saturday, July 22th of 2006

Let it be known to all Ditch Diggers, Mosquito Swatters and Adventure Lovers, that I have transited the Panama Canal aboard the good ship M/V Pacific Queen.

**Been There.....
Done That!**

ABOVE Anne visits the Panama Canal, July 22, 2006

LEFT Anne gets the keys to the Darwins' new Jeep in 2007

BOTTOM LEFT The Darwins' fourth-storey Pamana City apartment

BELOW Heart in the sand drawn by John on a trip to Costa Rica in 2007

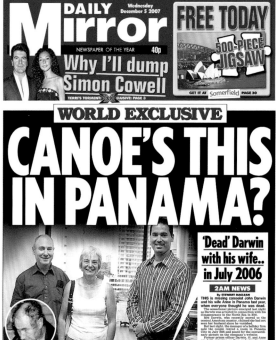

ABOVE The dramatic picture that ended the lies: Anne and John with realtor Mario Vilar in Panama on July 14, 2006 – proving she'd known her 'back-from-the-dead' husband had been alive the whole time

LEFT The *Mirror*'s dramatic exclusive front-page exposing the Darwins' lies

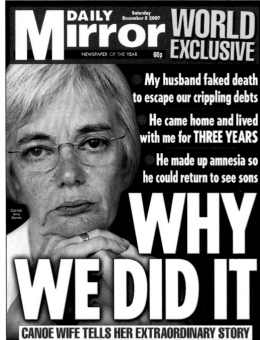

ABOVE Anne holds her head in her hands after her lies were exposed in Panama, December 4, 2007

RIGHT The *Mirror*'s front page story on Anne's dramatic confession, December 8, 2007

5

LEFT John is arrested at son Anthony's Basingstoke home in the early hours of December 5, 2007

BELOW RIGHT Detective Superintendent Tony Hutchinson shows the press a picture of John in his disguise as John Jones

BELOW LEFT A police mugshot of John

BOTTOM John about to be quizzed by Cleveland detectives

EXCLUSIVE: CANOE WIFE ARREST

DAILY Monday December 10 2007
Mirror
NEWSPAPER OF THE YEAR 40p

RICKY I'M NOT QUITTING
HATTON VOW: SEE SPORT

- ● Armed cops hold her on jet
- ● She suffers a panic attack
- ● My 'dream life' is in ruins

By DAVID LEIGH

DISTRAUGHT canoe wife Anne Darwin was arrested by police yesterday as she landed back in Britain.

Tearful Anne, 55, was met by six armed officers when her plane touched down at 5am.

And she suffered a panic attack as she spotted them boarding the packed jet at Manchester International Airport - admitting "I'm absolutely terrified.

During her seven-hour flight from Miami Anne had told of her and husband John's doomed attempt to start a new life in Panama.

She said: "My dream is over. I don't know what is going to happen now."

Anne and John have both been arrested on suspicion of insurance and pensions fraud.

HELD John

HER FULL SENSATIONAL INTERVIEW: PAGES 4 & 5

IT'S ALL OVER: Anne is held on plane yesterday

I'M TERRIFIED

OPPOSITE Anne flies home to Manchester, facing arrest and jail, Sunday December 9, 2007

LEFT *Mirror* front page capturing Anne's arrest at Manchester airport after her flight

BELOW Anne's police mugshot

BOTTOM Anne is led out of Manchester Airport's police station to be driven back to Cleveland for questioning

LEFT *Mirror* article showing betrayed sons Anthony (left in glasses) and Mark Darwin leaving Teesside Crown Court in Middlesbrough during Anne's trial in July 2008

BELOW Anthony and wife Louise (front) and Mark and future wife Flick, leaving Teesside Crown Court during Anne's trial

ABOVE Anne leaves Hartlepool Magistrates' Court by prison van

RIGHT John Darwin appears at Teesside Crown Court for a proceeds of crime hearing

BELOW *Mirror* front page depicting Anne as the 'mother of all liars' during her ill-fated trial

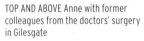

TOP AND ABOVE Anne with former colleagues from the doctors' surgery in Gilesgate

RIGHT Anne at the York and district RSPCA charity shop

Anne Stephenson, as she is known today, at a Yorkshire beach on a blustery winter morning

BEWARE
DANGER FROM
HIGH TIDES
BEYOND

Anne today, happily single after her divorce from John

of David's old colleagues, Martin Newman, night news editor of the *Mirror*. He had explained how a reader, trawling the internet, had quite incredibly found the photograph of John and I, taken in Panama City in July 2006 – more than four years after John's 'death' and nearly 18 months before he had mysteriously reappeared. The picture proved beyond doubt that both our stories were a pack of lies and that I knew full well John was alive and well long before getting the phone call from Mark.

The *Mirror* had called at about 8.30pm in Panama, 1.30am in London, and apparently the editor, Richard Wallace, had decided to replace the paper's original front page with a new 'world exclusive' story revealing our lies and showing the dramatic photograph of me and John in Panama. The reader had outdone the police and the press and incredibly found the picture by simply entering the words 'John' 'Anne' and 'Panama' into Google. That is how easily John's years of scheming, and my lying, came undone.

Whoever found the picture also passed it to Cleveland Police, sending senior detectives into a spin. Concerned that John might do another disappearing act once he realised the game was up, the police knew they had to act quickly and immediately sought an arrest warrant, while at the same time alerting their colleagues in Hampshire, hundreds of miles away, where John was staying with Anthony. Officers dashed to the address and, as soon as they had confirmation the warrant was signed by a judge, at about 11.50pm, they rang the bell, barged past a stunned Anthony, who had only minutes earlier been happily chatting to his dad, and arrested John on suspicion of fraud. He had been back from the dead for just three days.

As John was driven away, Anthony immediately called Mark and told him what had happened. The boys were stunned. How could this all be happening?

Back in Panama, David asked if I was OK, if that really was my husband in the picture and if there was anything I wanted to say.

Steeling myself, I shook my head, and still staring at the screen, said: 'Well, I guess that picture answers a lot of questions. Yes, that's John, that's my husband. My sons are never going to forgive me.'

It looked as if I was going to be left without a husband, a home or a family. To all intents and purposes, I did indeed know 'the game' was well and truly up.

But – and, yet again, I deeply regret this now – instead of coming entirely clean, I stuck to John's back-up story. I insisted I had initially believed he had died after paddling out into the North Sea. I said it was 'quite some time' before I discovered he was really still alive. Not knowing what was happening with John, I didn't want to be the one to end his dream. If I told the truth it would all be over for him and he would never forgive me. I had lived this lie for so many years it had almost become reality and the words just tumbled out of my mouth.

I had to choke back the tears as I answered yet another question from David. He asked me if I still loved John. 'Yes, I do,' I said, 'and that's probably what got me into this situation. When you love someone, all you want to do is protect them.' And that was the truth. As infuriating and as selfish as John could be, I was his wife and I loved him. I really did want to protect him from himself.

Just six weeks after leaving England to begin a new life in the sun, I would soon be heading back to face a very bleak and uncertain future. I didn't want to live my life as a fugitive, but I knew my family would be absolutely devastated by all the lies. My sons had known nothing of our deceit and would be mortified. I had let them think their dad was dead. They had grieved for him for nearly six years. Now they would detest me, probably forever. I felt completely broken, but when David gently pressed me on whether I was really telling the truth about not being party to John's disappearance plot, I still insisted I wasn't involved. The lies had not yet ended.

The following day things got even worse. Mark and

Anthony were now well aware they had been deceived in the most heartless way possible by their own parents. They had both seen 'the' picture of us on the morning TV news and plastered across the front pages of the newspapers. Their dad had faked his death and I, their mother, had repeatedly lied to them and let them believe he was dead for nearly six long years.

Not surprisingly, although the 'death' of their father had crushed my sons' worlds, this news – this betrayal by both their parents – left them devastated beyond belief for a second time. Anthony was in a terrible state: angered, heartbroken, bewildered. Questions were being asked in the press and, no doubt, by police, about the boys' possible involvement – it was reported that they were directors of the company we had established in Panama to buy property. Surely they must have known?

Anthony spoke to Cleveland Police to see what he could find out, but it was an active criminal investigation so there was little they could divulge. He was told detectives would like to speak to him. In tears, he rang relatives, asking what he should do. He didn't want to stay at home because journalists were camped outside, so the police arranged for him to check into a London hotel. He went to work at his insurance brokerage firm in Reading, where he was employed as a service advisor, and explained to his bosses what was going on. They were sympathetic and told him to go and get things straightened out. But Anthony was struggling to cope with anything. His life had rapidly descended into a crazy blur in which nothing made sense any more.

As the realisation that they had been so cruelly lied to began to set in, the boys issued a statement through Cleveland Police. This said that if reports of my confession were true, they felt the victims of a terrible and heartless scam and wanted nothing more to do with either of their parents. These were words I never expected to hear, we had always had a close relationship. But I knew I had completely shattered their lives and had probably lost them forever.

David read their devastating words to me as I held my head in my hands. 'What sort of mother am I?' I sobbed, distraught. 'Who can blame them? How can they ever forgive me for what I've done to them?'

I insisted to David they were innocent, and tears streamed down my face as I kept repeating, 'What have I done? What have I done?'

David told me Cleveland Police were continuing to quiz John and I knew it would be me before long. I was patently aware we could both go to jail if found to have committed fraud, which now seemed very likely. The prospect was terrifying.

Chapter 15

Escape from Panama

Panama City, Thursday 6 December

Since Tuesday morning, I had been trying to get hold of my Panamanian immigration lawyer, Beth Anne Gray. On Wednesday afternoon, I finally tracked her down and made an appointment for the following morning. I'd been told that the papers David was working for had been keeping Cleveland Police abreast of our movements, and detectives wanted to speak to me on my return. This was only to be expected but was nevertheless a frightening prospect. I urgently needed to speak to Beth Anne, to see what advice she could give me as well as discuss my visa situation and the imminent arrival of all my possessions.

With the world – and most importantly, my sons – now knowing I had told some beyond-terrible lies about John being dead, my mind was awash with questions. *Would I ever see them again? Could I ever face family and friends and look them in the eye again?* I was in complete turmoil, my entire body ached with the tension. On one occasion I caught my reflection in a mirror – my eyes were heavy, my nose crimson and my skin pale and blotchy, all through crying and lack of sleep.

So now we had to head back into the heart of the bustling Panama City – the 'lions' den', as the journalists put it, where all their rivals were looking for us. We rose early and, the closer we got, the more apprehensive David and Steve became. As we approached the offices of Gray & Co, they were craning their necks in all directions. We drove past and circled the office twice, even pulling up a little further down the road, where Steve used binoculars to see if he could spot anyone lurking with a camera in a nearby window or doorway. I felt a bit like a character from a spy movie. The coast appeared to be clear so we pulled up outside.

'What on earth are you expecting to happen?' I asked.

'I just don't want anyone else getting to you,' David responded, and I thought, *Well that's for your sake as much as mine.*

I said I wanted to see Beth Anne on my own. Clutching my document folder I got out of the car and walked up the iron stairs to the main door. I had a mobile phone and David said to call if I needed anything, and to let him know the minute I was through so he and Steve could be there to pick me up. They were off to the internet café down the street to grab a coffee and see if there were any updates on the story.

Beth Anne was great. She was in her late thirties, very pretty, with long flowing blonde hair. She was always upbeat and smiling, and despite my telling her about the difficult situation I found myself in, seemed totally unfazed.

First, she said she would be able to sign for my shipment of goods from England when it arrived, which was reassuring. She explained that it was vital that I formally applied for a visa before returning to the UK. As long as I had the visa, there would be nothing preventing me from returning to Panama, even if, God forbid, I was convicted of a crime and served time in jail. All that was needed for me to be welcomed back with open arms was to have the visa and to declare any convictions on the immigration form.

At least I still have a home here, I thought. I had betrayed everyone, and returning to Panama might be my only option if I was disowned by my family.

I'd been with Beth Anne in the glass-fronted interview room for about 30 minutes when I became aware of a man in reception, who seemed to be staring at me. When Beth Anne got up and left briefly, saying she needed to get something from her office, the man, who I quickly realised was a journalist, burst in and started asking questions. A colleague of his was trying to take pictures of me. There was a right old commotion before Beth Anne and her team managed to shoo them outside.

When I tried calling David, there was absolutely no service and I couldn't get through. When I still couldn't reach him after another 15 minutes, Beth Anne asked a member of her staff to call the British Consul, to see if anyone there had any advice. When they got the distinct impression that the British Consul didn't really want to get involved, I was greatly relieved, as it probably meant there was no warrant for my arrest. Although I was on my way back to the UK, I wanted to return of my own free will. I tried David one last time. This time, his mobile rang and he answered.

'I've been trying to get through to you for ages,' I said, and explained what had happened. David sounded frantic and said he'd be at the offices in less than five minutes. He and Steve dashed around the corner, only to have their worst fears realised as they were greeted by the sight of a smiling colleague from a rival newspaper, someone they knew well, standing right outside Beth Anne's office with a photographer.

They walked up the stairs to the solicitor's door and rang the bell, and were warmly greeted by Beth Anne, who shook their hands and said, 'Ah, so you're David, we've been trying to get hold of you. Where have you been?'

David shook his head. 'I'm sorry,' he said. 'I didn't realise the reception around here was quite so bad. What on earth has been going on?'

Beth Anne led David and Steve through to a small

conference room, where I was sitting, feeling rather shell-shocked after the journalist's visit and the British Consul's news.

'We had some visitors, didn't we, Anne?' Beth Anne said, and she explained what had been going on. They were, she said, now making checks to see if there was an international arrest warrant out for me.

David peeked through the conference room's slatted blinds and said he could see several other journalists had already joined the reporter and photographer they'd met on their way in. He said he had no doubts the 'pack' – now working together and with me firmly in their sights – would grow as time wore on, and getting away from everyone was going to be nigh impossible. Some of the journalists had already driven their cars up to the street entrance of Beth Anne's offices, there were photographers walking about with their cameras slung over their shoulders, and one guy even had a TV camera. Everyone was sitting and waiting for us to make our move.

For several hours, I just sat there in the corner in a daze. My mind was thousands of miles away in England, worrying about what I was going back to, whether my beloved sons would ever forgive me and if I was headed for jail. The predicament in which I now found myself in Panama really was the least of my concerns: that was David's problem.

I suppose, in some ways, I was actually relieved it was all coming to a head. The boys, and how they must be feeling, were constantly on my mind. What they must have thought of me, God only knows. I had let them down so terribly badly. Both their parents had. I knew very well that if I'd had an ounce of sense in my body, I'd have walked away from the whole absurd scheme at the very start. Why hadn't I just told the boys at the very beginning? I wanted to and kept telling myself, 'Talk to the boys, Anne, stop being so stupid,' but I didn't. They would have talked me out of it, I know, and put an end to all the foolishness there and then. They're both very sensible – certainly a lot more sensible than their parents. Maybe it was because I knew what they would say, or maybe it was because I didn't want to risk implicating them in what I knew to be a pretty serious crime? Whatever the reason, I had kept shtum and very soon now I would have to pay the price for my dishonesty.

Once I had started lying, I felt I was almost immediately in too deep to go back and simply didn't have the guts to undo the considerable damage I had already done. One lie immediately led to another and another and everything rapidly escalated from there. I had no idea how quickly things would spiral out of control after making that initial phone call to the police saying John was missing and within days, I was lying to every single person I knew and loved. Yet one telephone call could have ended it. Yes, there would have been public humiliation and

shame and John would have been incandescent. But it
would have been over and the consequences nowhere near
as serious as they had now become. I knew there was a
very real chance I could end up going to jail and was
absolutely terrified at the prospect. I couldn't even really
bring myself to think about it. It was the most frightening
thing imaginable. It was the fear of the unknown that was
haunting me. There was also the shame, the
embarrassment – and the disgrace for my sons that both
their parents might end up behind bars. I felt I had been
living a kind of prison sentence for the last five years, but
that had been my own private sentence – now the public
one would soon follow. It was John's fault, I did believe
that, but I knew I had to accept my share of the blame.

John was a clever man, very well read and he'd been a
very good teacher and was well respected. The problem
was, he was never satisfied with what he had. He always
had ideas above his station and wanted to be grander than
he was. He wanted people to look up to him but I wasn't
interested in any of that and never really cared what other
people thought. All I ever wanted was a nice quiet life. But
John was always very materialistic. In the early years of
our marriage, he'd bought an old Jag we didn't need and
certainly couldn't afford. And at one stage, he bought a
sporty little kit car, the sort of car a normal person might
drive on a Sunday afternoon. But not John – he'd drive it
in the snow with the roof off if there was a chance of
someone seeing him.

I knew my entire life for the last five-and-a-half years had been a tissue of lies and it was time for that to end. But, even as I prepared to fly home, the lying wasn't over and I still wondered whether I could get away with convincing the police that I hadn't been part of the plot from the start. I knew I'd be in a lot more trouble if they worked out I had. John had warned me that if this day ever came, it was vital we both stuck to the story that I had only found out many months later, when he turned up on my doorstep. That way, I could still argue all the insurance claims had been made in good faith and we wouldn't necessarily lose everything.

As usual, I wasn't optimistic we'd get away with it, unlike John, who always knew best. He could be so pig-headed at times. I told him he was a complete fool. He had such a good memory and was always very good with dates, which is one of the things that made him such a good teacher. Anyone who knew John knew what a good memory he had.

My mind and emotions were in chaos. John was my husband, the father of our sons, and I didn't want him to go to jail, for his sake, or the boys' sake, so I supposed I was prepared to do anything I could to prevent that from happening. I very much doubted that the boys would want anything to do with him, or me, again. And although I wanted to help John, I was furious with him for getting us into this whole wretched mess in the first place. Why hadn't we just done the sensible thing all those years ago?

David was talking regularly to Jeremy Armstrong, the *Mirror*'s north-east correspondent. Jeremy was liaising with Detective Superintendent Tony Hutchinson, who was in overall charge of the police operation. He said the police remained quite calm and were pleased that I had decided to make my own way home, rather than forcing them to seek an extradition order, which they knew would be costly and take time, probably many months.

But before we could fly home, David was still working on the best plan to escape the growing number of journalists camped outside Beth Anne's office. He briefly went outside to talk to his colleagues, to see if there was any way he could work out a deal with them. But he knew that was really a lost cause. They were too hungry to catch up on the story.

He walked round to check out the car park at the back of Beth Anne's office but there was no other escape route. It was surrounded by walls or fences on all sides, all too high to climb. There was only one door out of the office and one driveway by which to leave. The other journalists now had it comfortably covered, waiting for our departure, with several cars ready to follow wherever we went.

At one point, David asked how I felt about being dangled from the second-storey balcony at the back of the offices by my wrists and dropped onto a rusty corrugated tin roof, so I could climb down a ladder, with most of the rungs missing. 'It's the only way we can exit the building from the back, out of sight of the journalists.' Then, he said, I could hop into the boot of a waiting car that would shoot off at high speed through the bustling streets of Panama City, probably with several journalists in hot pursuit.

'What the hell is Plan B?' I asked him.

Beth Anne was amazingly understanding and helpful, and told David that if he needed any assistance to let her know. She even said she'd be able to enlist the help of the local police, if needed, to move the journalists on shortly before we made a run for it. But David said the chances of losing everyone were still slim. One of the main problems was that it was impossible to get me to the car park without being seen, as the only steps down to ground level were clearly visible from where the journalists were waiting outside the front of the building, meaning they would have plenty of warning we were preparing to leave.

'It will have to be something a little more cunning,' said David. Eventually, he decided to take up Beth Anne's offer of help and use most of her staff to assist in putting his plan into effect.

We waited until 4.30pm, which was the time the offices shut and the start of rush hour in Panama City, meaning the streets would be at their busiest. Gleaming new luxury cars would jostle for road positioning with huge, battered old trucks spewing clouds of deadly fumes, as well as former American school buses, brightly painted in psychedelic colours. Noisy put-put motorbikes and mopeds with wire cages precariously strapped to the back, carrying chickens to sell at street corner markets, would weave in and out of the cars, buses and lorries, their riders doing their best to avoid running down the vendors standing in the middle of the road, peddling strange looking fruit, bottles of water and gum. It all added up to traffic chaos and David said for his plan to work, it was as good an opportunity as we'd get.

He enlisted the help of about ten smartly dressed secretaries and legal assistants, and they huddled closely together around me as we went out the door and inched down the wrought-iron staircase, carefully keeping me out of sight from the prying camera lenses. I'm sure we must have looked quite ridiculous as we slowly made our descent, with me just about out of sight in the middle. Naturally, as soon as the waiting journalists saw the huddle of bodies, they knew we were about to make our move and while some jumped in their cars and started their engines, ready to follow, others waited on either side of the automatic gates to the drive – the only way out – with their cameras ready. Everyone was desperate for new photographs of me.

Our huddle headed back into the car park and moved to where we were just about out of sight. David told each of the women assisting in the getaway plan to get in their cars, line up and wait for his order to go. 'Ready? … Go!' he yelled, and with a piercing screech of tyres – these women were good – the convoy tore down the drive and out into the capital's rush-hour traffic. Crouched down on the floor in the back of the last of the six vehicles, I was petrified. 'For Christ's sake keep your head down,' David said from his hiding place alongside me, and my nose instinctively moved to within an inch of a rubber floor mat.

The journalists outside were in a state of utter confusion, helplessly trying to peer into the blacked-out windows of the cars racing past them and out onto the busy one-way circular system. They had almost certainly been expecting just one, or maybe two vehicles at most, and now they were in a blind panic about which of the six to follow. They were trying to take photographs while frantically dashing for their own cars. To make matters even worse for them, each driver in the convoy had been instructed to fan off in different directions as soon as they possibly could, making the ensuing pack's task of picking the right car a nightmare.

I was crouched up like a ball, my face glued to the floor of the car as we raced along the traffic-choked streets, weaving in and out of vehicles, praying we weren't involved in a crash. Our driver, Joe, a burly black guy, seemed to constantly blare the horn. I knew first-hand that driving in Panama was like being in a rat race, and there were very few rules of the road. It's very much a case of who dares wins. It may not have been much fun in the back, but up front, judging from the insane grin on his face, Joe was having a ball. If it wasn't for the seriousness

of the situation I found myself in, it might have been
exciting.

There was a sudden thud as the car swerved violently
to the right and I glanced out of the window and realised
we'd mounted the pavement to steer around a stationary
bus, whose disembarking passengers were now running for
their lives as Joe roared by, furiously yelling and
gesticulating at them to get out of his way. Obviously
delighted with his latest manoeuvre, and without taking
his foot off the gas, he turned round and gave a beaming
gold-toothed smile, convincing me that he really was mad.
David gave him the thumbs up, then turned to look at me,
mouthing, 'Don't worry, he's nuts,' and twirled his finger
next to his head, in case I hadn't grasped what he was
saying.

David's mobile rang. 'Come on, Dave, which one are
you in?' came a voice from the other end. It was one of our
pursuers, working for a rival paper. 'Tell me it's the Merc?'

'Sorry mate, this line is terrible,' he responded. 'I think
I'm losing you…' Click.

It wasn't the Mercedes, or one of the three smart black
BMWs in the convoy, that had been chosen as our
getaway car. David had picked the least likely of the cars
available to us – a battered old heap, which he hoped the
journalists would dismiss as too unlikely an option.
Fortunately, he'd been right. Now out on the open freeway,
and with Joe seemingly doing his best to break the land
speed record while driving with one arm dangling out of

his open window, David decided to pop his head over the parapet, and looked back to see if we were in the clear. The other journalists had obviously chosen to follow the luxury cars, whose drivers, with Beth Anne's blessing, had been instructed to circle the city centre for the next hour, which we hoped would give us just enough time to make our getaway.

Initially, we had been heading directly away from the airport – the most obvious destination. Now David asked Joe to double back and head there as quickly as possible. Joe repeatedly nodded his head and grinned but said nothing, jerking the steering wheel to make the latest in a series of highly illegal turns.

Steve, who had initially stayed behind at Beth Anne's offices, was already at Tocumen International Airport, 15 miles to the east of Panama City, having quietly made his way there as soon as the other journalists had left. He sent David a text saying simply: 'Coast is clear.' David had checked possible 'escape flights' before setting off and the best bet was a Copa Airlines flight to Miami, leaving in just over an hour's time. Joe screeched to a halt outside the terminal and we jumped out, grabbed our bags from the boot, and dashed inside to where Steve was waiting. Joe was still smiling but said nothing as David thrust a wad of crumpled notes into his enormous palm and shook his hand. He just kept on grinning.

Seeing there was no unwanted welcoming party, we quickly checked in and went through security to an airside lounge, where we huddled tightly together in the corner. Finally, the flight was called, and we went to the gate, boarded and took our seats. And everyone let out a huge sigh of relief as the Miami-bound plane took to the skies. I was relieved to be on the way home, whatever lay ahead.

Chapter 16

'We Would Like to Speak to a Mrs Anne Darwin'

Miami, Florida, Friday 7 December

Our arrival at Miami International Airport the previous evening had, unlike the mad scramble out of Panama, been undramatic, with none of the expected newsmen waiting for us. The night air was hot and humid as we walked through the virtually deserted airport. After collecting our luggage from baggage claim, we took a yellow cab for the 20-minute journey to the hotel in the business area of the city. Reservations, as usual, had been made in false names and when we checked in, David instructed the receptionist that absolutely no calls were to be put through to our suite. He and Steve also decided to turn off their American mobile phones to prevent other journalists, who were still constantly calling for information, from being able to hear from the change in dialling tones that we had left Panama. Somehow, we had managed to slip into Miami unnoticed and now no one could know for sure exactly where we were.

Early the next morning, Steve bought two pay-as-you-go phones and David emailed the numbers to the select few executives who had been running the story on the Mail and the Mirror. No one else had a clue where we were – but speculation was rife. I felt like the world's most wanted woman! I was both bemused and terrified.

We were joined in Miami by one of the Daily Mail's senior feature writers, Natalie Clarke, who had flown in from London. Senior executives at the paper had apparently decided they wanted their own member of staff on the ground to help out, so she was given our address at the Conrad. For days, David had been asking me about doing a full interview, to set the record straight, and it had been weighing on my mind. That afternoon, at about 3pm, I finally agreed. I felt more relaxed for the first time in what seemed a very long week, and I was beginning to feel more at ease in the company of David and Steve. They were intent on doing their jobs, and although they may not have believed me, they treated me with courtesy and respect, which was more than I deserved. If I gave him the interview he wanted so badly, it may perhaps put an end to his questions once and for all.

'Well, what do you want to know then?' I asked. We were sat in a semi-circle in the hotel suite, sipping sparkling mineral water that had been delivered by room service. Steve was taking pictures, which I had agreed to. 'First question is easy,' said David. 'Where on earth was John all this time? And please don't tell me he was hiding in the garden shed!'

Obviously, with the journalists at that stage having no idea of what had actually happened, I don't think anything could have prepared them for my answer or the (partial) confession that poured out of my mouth over the course of the following four hours.

'Well, almost,' I said. 'For three years, while virtually everyone close to us believed he was missing, presumed dead, John was actually at home with me.' I could see the look of astonishment on the reporters' faces. 'Yes, I know it seems too incredible to be true, but it is. We were living as man and wife, although it was far from a conventional life we were leading.' I explained how John had the secret bolthole, the bedsit in the adjoining house we owned. And it was to there that he scurried off through the adjoining passageways whenever I had visitors, or when family came to stay. All that separated his secret existence from my house was a single bolt, and we both knew he could have been rumbled in an instant.

Once I'd started talking, it was as if a cork had burst out of a champagne bottle and my confession came flooding out. I probably said far more than I had intended. I admitted John had carefully planned his disappearing act for the exact reason everyone suspected – crippling debts.

'Yes, John planned it all,' I said. 'We had a lot of debt – in the tens of thousands – and he told me this was the only way out. I tried desperately to get him to change his mind but he said there was only one way out of the situation and that was to fake his death. I pleaded with him and said it was the wrong thing to do and I could not go along with it but he badgered away at it.'

But I continued to lie about when I first found out that he had faked his death. 'Whether people believe me or not, I genuinely thought John had had an accident in the sea, and drowned, having had his canoe out the previous week. I guess it was in the back of my mind, but I just didn't think it was possible that he might have done that. I suppose I didn't want to believe he would do that, but he did. Where he went initially I do not know.' I retold the story of his reappearance, and how I hadn't initially recognised him – I just made out that it was many months later, after the inquest, that he had mysteriously turned up on my doorstep one day.

I recounted how we had got into so much debt after John started his doomed buy-to-let housing venture, how we were struggling to make payments on his growing number of credit cards and were being crippled by late fees and bank charges. And how the move to Seaton Carew, to the big house that John had always dreamed of, had been the final nail in the coffin as far as our spiralling debts were concerned.

I told how I lived in fear of being found out and how, at first, I was too frightened to even open the front door. By far the worst thing was deceiving the family. 'I said to John many times, "You know I can't lie, I hate to lie," and I so wish I hadn't because I would not have got myself into the mess I did,' I said. 'You tell one lie and you had to tell another one to cover up for the first one and it all just snowballed. I absolutely hate myself for having done it. There were many times I was tempted to come clean, many times. The boys missed their dad and I know deep down he missed them as well and he always wanted to find a way back so he could be reunited with them. I am sure both boys did believe he was dead. But there was never a body.

'I do not know how long it took for them to come to terms with the fact that he might be dead and not just missing, which was very difficult for them. They used to look at newspapers and the internet and scour the reports of missing persons and reports of bodies that were found. They were tortured. And yes, it was hard to keep up the front. Sometimes the boys would ring up wanting to talk about all manner of things and they would say, "If only Dad was here to advise us." Sometimes John was sitting there next to me and I would put the telephone onto loudspeaker so that he could hear them. If I did not have an answer to one of their questions, John used to write it down. I deceived so many people.'

I got an awful lot of things off my chest, and when the interview was finally over I felt exhausted but relieved. I knew it was a confession that would have serious consequences for both me and John, but I was glad I'd done it. David said it was an astonishing story and he now needed to start writing his copy for the following day's papers. I watched as he sat at a table in the corner and started frantically tapping away on his laptop with two fingers.

'You know I can touch type?' I said after a few minutes.

David turned to look at me, somewhat aghast by the offer he presumed I was making. 'Are you saying what I think you're saying?' he asked.

'Yes, why not?' I said. 'It will give me something to do.'

So for the next hour and a half, I typed my own confession as David dictated my words from his notebook.

It was gone midnight when I decided to turn in, leaving David at his laptop, feverishly tapping away. He said he had to break the back of filing his story that night, so the papers – five hours ahead of us in London – had it first thing the next day. I woke early and at 7am walked into the room where David was still beavering away. 'Surely you haven't been there all night?' I asked.

'Not quite,' David said, stifling a yawn, 'but almost.'

I walked over. 'Move over,' I said. 'I'll finish it off for you.' And with that, I sat down and rattled off the last few hundred words of the story, adding quotes and expanding my thoughts as I went.

'I am just so sorry for all the upset I have caused my family and friends but most particularly my boys,' I wrote. 'All I can say to them at this stage is that I am really, really sorry, and I hope one day they will realise that what I did was not easy. And misguided though it was, it was done out of love for their father. I am just so sorry that it went on for as long as it did and that they have suffered so much. I do not just mean this week, I mean over the last five years. I would just like to say sorry to the rest of the family and all the friends I have hurt and deceived along the way. I know there are going to be many difficult times ahead but I will just have to try to deal with it as best I can.'

And, speaking directly to Mark and Anthony, I added: 'Boys, please believe your Mam when I say, I am truly very sorry and I still love you and hope you can find it in your hearts to one day forgive me.'

After one last spellcheck, David filed his story and shortly afterwards said the Mirror and the Mail were delighted with the copy, and each had cleared seven entire pages of the following day's papers to run every word of the interview. I was totally shocked. Had I really spoken for so long that it would take seven pages to report it? And who would want to read it? It sickened me to think Mark and Anthony would be reading it. Naturally, my boys would want the details but I could not believe anyone else would be remotely interested in two ordinary, middle-aged people committing a crime. The Mirror's front-page headline was, 'WHY WE DID IT', while the Mail's was simply, 'I CONFESS'. Both carried large pictures of me, staring out into the abyss.

The fact that we were no longer in Panama had leaked

out and there was lots of speculation in the press that we had flown to Miami, where David lived, and were making plans to return to the UK. Some reports said we were in Paris, planning to return to London via the Eurostar. There were continued references in the broadsheet newspapers to me having been 'bought up', that is paid thousands of pounds for my story by tabloid journalists, but they were completely untrue. I never asked for, nor was offered, a single penny by David or either of the papers he was working for. Reporters from lots of other papers, however, had pushed letters under the door of my Panama apartment promising untold fortunes for my story.

Back in England, things were heating up for John, who was still being interviewed about mortgage and endowment policies, pension funds and property deals relating to his estate. All in all, police believed the deception involved money totalling more than £1million.

Detective Inspector Andy Greenwood, who was in charge of the day-to-day investigation, called a press conference and revealed police had been granted a further 36 hours to quiz John. He said the investigation into alleged fraud was 'ongoing' and told journalists John had now suddenly started to regain his memory by giving 'an account' of his activities since his disappearance in March 2002.

Asked whether police considered Mark and Anthony part of the investigation, he said: 'I am in contact with their sons. I spoke to them yesterday. They are keeping their heads down at the moment because of the publicity and the trauma they have been through. They have been affected by the publicity but time is a great healer.' Asked outright if they were witnesses or suspects he said: 'That's for me to decide at a later date. But at the moment they are witnesses.'

The following afternoon (Saturday 8 December), after reading my confession in the papers, police felt they had enough evidence to press the first charges. Detective Sergeant Iain Henderson, of Cleveland Police's major investigation team, said: 'The Crown Prosecution service this afternoon has authorised Cleveland Police to charge 57-year-old John Ronald Darwin with offences of obtaining a money transfer by deception and making an untrue statement to procure a passport. He will remain in police custody until he appears at Hartlepool Magistrates' Court on Monday, December 10, where a remand application will be made. Inquiries are still ongoing and as you will appreciate legal proceedings are now active and we cannot go into further details.'

Despite me being responsible for what had happened, I was still shocked when I heard about the charges. 'What's everyone saying?' I asked David.

'People are asking if you were involved from the start, Anne,' he said. 'It's only natural.'

I didn't respond but my mind was racing. Exactly how much trouble was I in?

David and I were sitting together in the front row of the plane as we taxied across the runway at Manchester International Airport. It was just after 9am on a bleak Sunday morning, and I suddenly found myself fighting back tears as I looked out at the grey skies and light drizzle welcoming me back to reality.

Our journey home had begun the previous day. After checking out of the Conrad Hotel, we had taken a taxi to Fort Lauderdale-Hollywood International Airport – David decided against using the nearby Miami International Airport because he said it was too obvious an 'escape route' – and had flown to Atlanta, Georgia, from where we would take the final leg of our journey home to Manchester. We travelled either first or business class on every flight, so we could stay out of sight in the VIP lounges. Free food and drink and comfortable seats were new to me but it was certainly the way to travel… if only I had been going somewhere else.

For much of the seven-hour flight home to England I was lost in thought. The fear of never being reconciled with the boys was what terrified me the most. I was sure they must absolutely hate me and I felt totally and utterly ashamed. And then there were my poor parents, elderly and not in the best of health, and the rest of my family and friends, all, no doubt, horrified at the lies I'd told. How could anyone want anything more to do with me ever again? I tried flicking through a magazine to distract myself, or closing my eyes and trying to snatch some sleep, but neither worked.

I think David sensed I was still holding something back. He told me it was vital, if I was ever to have any hope of being reconciled with the boys, that I was totally honest with the police and tell them the entire story. It didn't matter, he said, if I had lied to him, but there was nothing whatsoever to be gained in lying to the police. 'Hold your hands up and take your punishment,' he told me. I was touched by his kind words and a little sad that our adventure was coming to an end. He had been a true gentleman throughout the time we spent together and, strange as it may seem, I was beginning to think of him as a friend.

I said I would. I knew that's what I needed to do. But, of course, I didn't and stupidly continued lying, hoping somehow I could still get away with the worst part of my deceit.

I knew what was coming when we landed, or at least I thought I did. I had been warned that a detective from Cleveland Police would be waiting for me and I would likely be arrested and driven back to Hartlepool Police Station, from where the investigation into our fraud was being spearheaded.

Jeremy from the *Daily Mirror* had been keeping Cleveland Police abreast of our movements, reassuring them I was coming home of my own accord. David had been told that, once we had arrived at the gate, I should stay in my seat until all the other passengers had left, and then a plain-clothed detective would board and escort me from the plane. It was all to be very low key. After all, I wasn't exactly a terrorist threat or a danger to anyone. I remember looking out the window and seeing a police van waiting on the tarmac and thinking, Thank goodness it isn't for me.

As the plane came to a standstill at its gate at Terminal 2, the aircraft doors swung open and it quickly became clear that things were not going to be at all as we had been assured. A towering Greater Manchester police sergeant, uniformed and armed, like the five officers behind him, was the first on board.

'We would like to speak to a Mrs Anne Darwin,' he told the clearly startled flight attendant.

Passengers, already out of their seats and reaching for their bags from the overhead lockers, were instructed over the tannoy to return to their seats. There was a buzz of confusion as I'm sure many began to realise that they had shared their flight home with me, the now infamous 'canoe widow'. All eyes were on me as, ashen-faced and totally panic-stricken, I slowly made my way the few steps forward from seat 1A to make myself known to police.

David jumped up and tried to speak to the sergeant but the officer made it very clear that he wasn't at all interested in what he had to say and told him to sit down and mind his own business. The same was said to Steve, who was now taking photographs of the dramatic scene unfolding in front of everyone on the plane. He just carried on taking photographs regardless.

I said nothing, simply nodding to confirm that yes I was indeed Anne Darwin. I was read my rights and told I was being arrested on suspicion of fraud. Surrounded by my welcoming party of burly policeman, some armed with frightening-looking sub-machine guns, I was led along the air-bridge to a lift, my head bowed down to the floor, as the doors slowly closed behind me. I was totally shocked and unprepared for the speed at which everything was happening. I really hadn't expected to be arrested in such a public way and suddenly found it quite hard to breathe. It's fair to say I was petrified.

I was then driven in the very van I had spotted to the nearby Manchester airport police station, but at least I was given a cup of tea as I sat waiting in the booking area at the reception desk. I was told my lawyer would soon be calling.

Before leaving Miami, David had asked the papers he was working for to help find me a good lawyer and Corker Binning, one of London's leading specialist criminal and fraud firms, had been contacted. They quickly decided it was a good, high-profile case to take on and it was agreed that Nicola Finnerty, one of the senior partners, would be the ideal person to represent me. I was also seen by a doctor, who said I needed some time to rest and recover from the ordeal of my arrest before I would be fit for my onward journey.

After about three hours, I was passed into the custody of two plain-clothed detectives from Cleveland Police. My brown leather handbag containing all my personal belongings, was confiscated, as was my bright red raincoat, because it had a drawstring, and the laces from my shoes – I was later told this was to prevent any attempt at self-harm. I was led out to a waiting unmarked police car in front of dozens of photographers and TV crews, who had been tipped off that I had flown home and was now under arrest. I was told the case wouldn't be discussed en route and I sat in silence as the car, which reeked of tobacco smoke, shot off at high speed on the three-hour journey to Hartlepool. I nearly said something when I saw at one stage that we were travelling at well over 100mph, but then thought better of it. Hardly a word was spoken.

On the outskirts of the town, our car pulled over at a pre-arranged spot, where two marked police cars, with blue lights flashing, were waiting to give us an escort to the police station. It seemed totally unnecessary and all for show, as if the police were trumpeting my return. I felt a bit like a gangster's moll as I was escorted into the station, surrounded by officers.

Inside, I was seen by a woman doctor, who was kind and friendly and said I should be given some decent food and 'not the usual rubbish'. She took saliva samples, saying I was being tested for drugs, which was routine. Then I was led to a cell and told nothing would happen until my solicitor arrived. A shudder ran down my spine, probably with a sense of foreboding, as the door was slammed shut and locked behind me, making every bone in my body shake. The room was small and stark, with a toilet in one corner and a concrete 'bed', on top of which was a thin, navy blue vinyl covered mattress and one blue blanket. I felt exhausted, frightened and very alone.

An hour or so later, I was told my lawyer had arrived and was escorted to an interview room where Nicola was waiting. She explained she was an expert in criminal law, specialising in fraud, business crime, money laundering, financial compliance, asset seizure and confiscation. My case had already attracted an enormous amount of media attention and Nicola was well accustomed to dealing with the press, having acted for entertainer Michael Barrymore at the inquest into the death of Stuart Lubbock, a young man who had died in mysterious circumstances in the swimming pool of the television star's multi-million-pound home. At this point I still had absolutely no idea how big this case was and couldn't understand why I should need a lawyer from London. Nicola did her best to put me at ease, advising me to try to get some sleep before the interviews would begin the next morning. She explained that we would have an opportunity to speak in private before the police started their questions. Nothing would happen without her being present. I felt slightly reassured but my stomach was churning all the while.

Back in my cell, I lay down on the bed and tried to get comfortable. I knew I'd be here for some time. The nightmare had well and truly begun.

Chapter 17

Wet Footprints
on the Stairs

Spending a night in a police cell is a frightening experience. When you have no idea what the future holds, lying awake all night and wondering just how many more similar nights lie ahead consumes your mind. That night, I was exhausted but I couldn't sleep, my head running wild with the same, terrifying thoughts. Would anyone ever forgive me or understand why I did what I did: my beloved sons, my elderly parents, my family, my friends? Would I be able to cope with being cut off from the outside world and the family and loved ones I'd so cruelly deceived? Would being locked away in a cell, disowned and ostracised by all I held dear, simply become my new life? Would I even be safe or might I be attacked by some crazed inmate? There were too many awful things to think about.

I knew being locked up was what I deserved but I was terrified at what the future held. And that's why, admittedly, I would still have done just about anything to save my skin. I knew the situation in which I now found myself was my fault and, other than John, I had no one else to blame. But was that really who I'd become? A pathetic, weak woman, unable to make any of my own decisions in life and able to be bullied into doing things, which I knew were wrong in every respect, by an overbearing husband? Why hadn't I been strong enough to stand up to John and say no to his crackpot scheme? He wasn't a violent man – I knew he would never hurt me. He was manipulative, used to getting his own way and long ago I'd given up trying to stand up to him because I knew I could never win. All I knew was that I'd told him we'd both end up behind bars and I'd been proven right. Not much of a boast, I know.

But, of course, I never really thought it would actually come to this. Who would? Not John, who had simply scoffed at my prophecy and, as usual, rolled his eyes. I know I had a choice. But I admit I simply wasn't strong enough to say no and I couldn't bear the thought of losing my husband, the man I had been with my entire adult life, and the father of my two sons. I had only, very reluctantly, agreed to go along with John's crazy scheme because I felt I simply had no option. I wasn't scared of him, but I was scared of what he might do if I didn't agree to help. I was scared at the prospect of being left on my own – that was my biggest fear. Of losing him, the house and everything I owned. If he had taken the sensible course and agreed to bankruptcy, of course I would have stood by him and supported him. We may have been bankrupt but we could have started again and lived a more simple life. I never wanted a big house or a fancy lifestyle. I was happy with my lot. When the boys were born, all I wanted was to be a good mother. That was by far the most important thing to me.

The boys needed me but I never really felt John did. He always did what he wanted to do and was never dependent on anyone. And then, suddenly, he did need me, more than ever and that was the big mistake I made. Without my help he couldn't have carried out his plan and without me he couldn't have existed. He wouldn't have had a roof over his head and he wouldn't have had any income.

I knew, very soon now, I would pay the price for my very misguided loyalty and weakness. I didn't need anyone to tell me I was a wretched fool. But as I lay there awake all night, I still stupidly believed that maybe I could get away with a big part of the lies that I'd told. Maybe I could still convince everyone that I really believed he had died the day he paddled out to sea in his red canoe. That way, all the claims I made for the life insurance payouts would have been, at the time, 'genuine' and the penalty I would pay for my part in the crimes, and harbouring a man supposed to be dead, would be less severe. That is the script John and I had agreed we should stick to at all costs. After all, how would anyone ever be able to prove otherwise? Yes, it was still a lie, a big lie, but if it meant I would get a much lesser sentence, it was one I still, misguidedly, believed worth telling.

With both John and I now behind bars, Cleveland detectives could start interviewing both 'partners in crime', to try and piece together exactly what role I had played in John's disappearance and the subsequent fraudulent insurance claims. They would liaise with the Crown Prosecution Service, to determine exactly what charges each of us should face.

The morning after I returned, Monday 10 December, Det Supt Hutchinson, held a press conference at Cleveland Police headquarters in Middlesbrough. He said the first of a number of interviews with me had started that morning – at around the same time John was making his first appearance before Hartlepool magistrates, having been formally charged with obtaining a money transfer by deception and making an untrue statement to procure a passport. He said they were what's known as 'holding charges', meaning John could be held in custody at Durham Prison while detectives continued their inquiries and worked on possible further charges. Det Supt Hutchinson said he was well aware of all the stories that had appeared in newspapers and that his officers would be quizzing me about the version of events that had been reported.

After he had thanked the media for their cooperation, he added: 'Although our force has dealt with many wide-ranging and complex investigations, this is the first that has been on such a global scale. It has stretched from the

Mediterranean to the Caribbean and beyond. Media interest in these events has been literally worldwide and the couple's photographs have appeared in newspapers on every Continent. That has resulted in countless calls to us with information. We have had e-mails from Spain and the Caribbean. To get to the full truth of matters, I would like that information to continue.' He appealed for anyone who had information about John's whereabouts over the previous five years to come forward. He then distributed a photograph of John, showing him with a beard. 'People may have seen him when he looked like this. They may have known him as John Jones. We need to know where both Mr and Mrs Darwin have been both in Europe and North and South America. We need to know what they have been saying. We need to know who they have been with and we need to know what they have been doing.'

The two detectives assigned to question me that morning, at Hartlepool Police Station, were detective constables Terry Waterfield and Chris Marchant, both specially trained suspect interviewers. I was accompanied by my lawyer, Nicola, and, as John had been just over a week earlier, I was read my rights and warned anything I said could be used in evidence against me.

Other officers continued to question John and, of course, neither of us knew what the other was saying. The police were looking to both of us to provide the evidence that would trip the other up and prove that we had both been in on the plot from the start. It was only ever going to be a matter of time.

I started by sticking to the story John and I had agreed on – insisting I had initially made the insurance claims when I 'truly and honestly' believed my husband had died. I admitted that John had eventually come back, as far as I was concerned, 'from the dead' – yet I had continued claiming the money I knew I wasn't entitled to.

'He did come back and he'd expected everything to be over and sorted,' I offered as way of an explanation. 'I said, "You have to tell people that you are back," but he wouldn't let me do that. John told me I had to press ahead in claiming the money because we had so much debt – in the tens of thousands – and he was convinced it wouldn't take much longer before the insurance companies paid out and then we could straighten everything out. I said I couldn't, I didn't like to lie, and he said if I didn't, then he would say I'd known all along that he was planning to fake his death.'

I was basically claiming John was blackmailing me into going along with his deceit – but, of course, it was all part of our pre-arranged cover story to lay all the blame on John's shoulders. I told the officers I could see, with hindsight, that it would have been better to have come clean but instead I had simply 'learned to live with it'. I said there had been nothing in John's actions before this that had led me to believe he was planning to disappear

and he was in 'reasonable' health at the time. I described
John as 'mentally bright and intelligent' with a good
memory – inadvertently making a mockery of his
ridiculous amnesia story.

I recited the same story, which had appeared in the
Mail and *Mirror*, about the day of his disappearance, the
massive sea and air search for him, and having to break
the terrible news to my family. John had always loved the
sea, I said, and he had long held ambitions to own his own
boat and sail the seas. I also insisted it was only much later
that I discovered the extent of our debt, about £80,000, in
loans and on more than ten different credit cards, as John
had kept it hidden from me. 'I knew there was some debt
but I hadn't realised the scale of it,' I lied.

I told the detectives the financial burden only began to
ease when a death certificate was issued for John after an
inquest was finally held in April of the following year.
With the insurance payouts, and finally being able to start
selling the 12 rental properties we owned, I was able to
pay off the outstanding £130,000 mortgage on Nos 3 and
4 The Cliffe. When, in 2007, we had decided to sell them,
I received £160,000 in March for No 4 and £295,000 in
October for No 3 – meaning we were sitting on a sizeable
lump sum of £455,000.

I told the detectives that most of that money was in
Panama bank accounts in my name: US$365,000 was in
one and US$220,000 was in a timed deposit account, one
of the requirements for being able to buy property in

Panama. In addition to the money in my accounts, I had bought an apartment in Panama City for $97,000 and a parcel of land in Colon for $360,000. They were paid for with the proceeds of the sale of No 4 The Cliffe, which had been placed in a Jersey-based, offshore account with HSBC, which I had opened the previous summer. In total, I had cash and assets in Panama worth just over $1million.

The detectives then turned their attention to the boys and why both Nos 3 and 4 The Cliffe had been transferred into Mark's name before they were sold. I was very aware that the police probably had strong suspicions that the boys must surely have known about our deception. They were listed as shareholders of Jaguar Properties, Mark was named as the owner of the Seaton Carew houses when they were sold, and he had transferred money to me in both Panama and an off-shore account in Jersey. Referring to transferring the ownership of the houses to Mark, I explained: 'It was something that John had asked me to do. He said that as we were going to be looking for somewhere in Panama, I may not be here in the country to deal with the sales of the houses and if we transferred them into Mark's name, then he would be here to deal with everything. So I bitterly regret having done that now as I know it looks as if he was involved, which he wasn't.'

As I broke down in tears, DC Waterfield told me that, at the present time, the police were not suggesting that Mark was in any way involved in any criminality. But he did say Mark would be spoken to at a later date and added: 'I'm not going to try and pull the wool over your eyes and say we'll just ignore it because you say he wasn't involved, but I'm not looking at that at this time, all right?'

I said the transfer of the deeds for the two houses into Mark's name was an 'actual purchase' because John felt it would look better that way. I said both Mark and Anthony had been given £30,000 to buy Premium Bonds on my behalf and I had asked Mark to cash his in and purchase the houses. To the outside world, it would appear I had sold Mark two houses, together worth nearly half-a-million pounds, for just £30,000. But I insisted Mark hadn't profited from the purchase in any way. When the houses were sold, the proceeds went briefly into his bank account but were then immediately transferred into my accounts. The proceeds from No 3 went into a bank in Panama, while the proceeds from No 4 went into my HSBC offshore account in Jersey. I said Mark had obviously been aware I had bank accounts in those two places but insisted he had absolutely no idea his father was still alive.

Turning to the property I had purchased in Panama, the police said it appeared I was the sole owner. I quickly corrected them, saying they were actually owned by Jaguar Properties – because I knew, or at least John had told me, that properties owned by a Panamanian corporation would be outside the arms of the authorities when they tried to recover assets. Even at this stage, I was continuing to try and protect what I knew were properties bought with fraudulently obtained money. I was continuing to play a role in our deception.

The detectives questioned me in detail about the insurance claims I made and I repeated, dishonestly, that the process was started 'in all honesty' and it was only when John reappeared that 'it then became deception'.

'I wanted to ring everybody and tell them but he wouldn't let me do it,' I said. 'He said he'd expected all the insurance policies to have been paid out by then and all the debts to have been cleared. If I said anything, he would say I was in on the plan from the beginning. I just got too frightened. I said I couldn't do it, I hated to lie and he knew that. We had talked about telling the boys because I knew how much they were suffering but we couldn't, we couldn't do it. We didn't want to implicate them in any way.'

That much, at least, was true. If we had told Mark and Anthony what we had done, it would have been up to the boys to decide whether to say nothing and help cover up some serious crimes, or go to the police, knowing both their parents would be arrested. It was not a choice either of us wanted them to have to make. I said John had persuaded me he just needed time to sort out the debt and, being under so much stress and strain, I went along with it. It was 'somehow easier than telling the truth'. I said, 'I just reached a point where it had all got out of hand and I found myself leading a double life.'

The detective finally questioned me about the crucial pieces of evidence that would ultimately expose John – and my lies – that is, when he had really re-appeared on my doorstep. They had by then uncovered the Hartlepool library membership, taken out in the name of John Jones, on 22 April 2002, just a month after he vanished. The address given was No 4 The Cliffe.

Police had also discovered that the librarian, Susan Garrington, had co-signed a passport application for John Jones, which they had recovered from the passport office in Durham. Attached to it was a photograph, which showed John Jones was very obviously John Darwin, but with the 'long shaggy Saddam Hussein arrest beard'. What's more the home address on the application form was, once again, No 4 The Cliffe. The same was true of the John Jones driving licence.

'Can you see what's happening, Anne?' DC Waterfield asked.

'I can see what you think is happening,' I responded, a little too quickly for my own good.

'Well, he hasn't disappeared has he?' said the detective, adding it was obvious John had been in the area the whole time. 'He's giving your address all the time, he's given the address where he's living on official documents. What has happened here is that this has all been planned.'

And then, the detective summed up what he believed had really happened. 'It's all been planned to enable massive debts to be paid off. We have passport, library membership, driving licence, all in false names, false names that you're aware of. A false name, a false identity that you have travelled with and went on to deceive other people with, and into believing that John Darwin was dead. I believe in the coming weeks we will uncover more evidence, which will lead us to exactly where John was. I also believe that evidence will implicate you in the plan that was devised to make John Darwin disappear, so that insurance monies could be claimed to clear your massive debts.

'Having been involved in this investigation and having listened to the interviews with John, and having been involved in this interview, and having looked at the evidence that's coming to light and has come to light, I believe that when you called the police on the 21st of March, 2002, and when the police attended, I'm surprised that the first officer didn't see wet footsteps going up the stairs…' He was, of course, spot on.

At about the same time, other officers were telling John the same story – that the game was up. 'You haven't lost your memory, John,' said DC McArthur. 'It's a story. It's a story that's unravelled before your very eyes. That you've had to change on the hoof and you've forgotten things that you've said to people. From the evidence, it's clear to me that you're not suffering from amnesia.' He told John the evidence against him was compelling, to say the least. He had attempted to portray himself as a man who'd lost his memory; a man who, because of an accident, had been placed in a situation where in order to protect his family, he'd been forced into a course of action that would appear 'dramatic', to say the least. The reality of the situation was somewhat different, the officer told him.

'Some time in 2000 or 2001, you were in some considerable debt. You, together with your wife, hatched a plan to defraud the insurance companies by claiming life cover and fatal accident benefit by faking your death. You've assumed a false identity and you've lived off the proceeds of the funds that you've illegally obtained. Your downfall really was the media, the media attention the case has generated. You planned to maintain a story, your story, of amnesia but you've been forced to change it and alter your position, as various pieces of evidence have been put to you. What I will say to you, John, is this investigation is still a live inquiry. And it'll continue after today. We will be interviewing your wife and your sons to establish their knowledge of the events. And I have no doubt that if further evidence comes to light, I will be interviewing you again.'

Asked if there was anything he wanted to say, John simply said no, but he – like me – must have known there was no point continuing to lie. The evidence was stacked against us and, putting him under further pressure to come clean, the detective had told him that it was his wife, and his sons – his innocent sons – who would now be the ones under the police spotlight. The net was getting tighter.

Chapter 18

An End to Living a Lie

After a second night in the police cell, I received the news I had been dreading. When the day's interviews were over, I would be transferred to a local prison, where I would stay for the remainder of my time in custody. That afternoon, Tuesday, 11 December, my shame was complete as I was led out of Hartlepool Police Station in handcuffs and chains, locked in an individual cell in the back of a 'sweat box', and driven the 45-minute journey to HMP Low Newton, in the village of Brasside, a few miles outside Durham City Centre.

My new 'home' was to be a maximum-security, all-female, 'Category A' prison, housing notorious murderers, violent offenders and hardened criminals. Before all this, I'd never been in any trouble with the police. In fact, I'd only ever had one parking ticket in my life, so the very thought of being inside a prison was terrifying. As John had worked as a prison officer, I'd heard stories of the sort of awful things that went on inside and I really didn't think I'd be able to cope. Terrible thoughts were racing through my mind. *Will I be safe? Will there be violence? How long will I be incarcerated?*

The jail was just eight miles from my old home at Witton Gilbert and, knowing the area well, I saw familiar places and sites through the small window in the back of the prison van as it wended its way through the winding roads leading to Brasside. We pulled up outside the imposing prison gates, waited for them to open, then drove through and they – and the outside world – slowly closed behind us.

With the other women in the van, I was led into the jail's reception area for the business of entering prison to begin in earnest. I had to provide details for my next of kin, and was told to remove all jewellery containing diamonds or other precious stones, so I slipped off my engagement and eternity rings. I also decided to take off and surrender my wedding ring as I'd lost quite a lot of weight during the last week or so, and it felt loose on my finger. I cherished the ring and didn't want to lose it – or have it taken from me. From now on, I was told, I'd be known as Prisoner KP4801.

Then came the horrific ordeal of being strip searched, which was without doubt the most humiliating experience of my life – but one to which I would soon become accustomed as it was routine procedure each time you entered or left the jail. After being patted down over my clothes, came the order, 'Take off your top and bra, hold up your arms and turn in a full circle.' I felt frightened and ashamed but did what I was told and after I put my top back on, I was ordered to strip from the waist down and, again, turn in a circle and show the soles of my feet. I felt utterly degraded. Afterwards, an officer asked if I wanted a shower in the reception area, or on the wing to which I was being moved.

I asked for one then and there as I felt so dirty and violated. I was also still wearing exactly the same clothes I had on when I left hot and humid Miami three days earlier. I just felt dirty, in every sense of the word.

I was given a grey prison tracksuit, a blue T-shirt, a nightdress, a small bag of toiletries, a notepad, and my prison rations – a food pack containing teabags, sachets of sugar, powdered milk, cereal and long-life milk for the following day's breakfast. There was also a small flask for hot water in case I wanted a hot drink during the night.

We new arrivals were then escorted to our cells on the induction wing. Mine was a single room, with its own shower and toilet. There was a bed, a chest of drawers, a small area to hang clothes and a single wooden chair to sit on. To be honest, it was nowhere near as bad as I had expected. There were even curtains over the small window, giving me a view of the prison gardens – though there were bars in the window, of course.

It was 'association time', meaning all the cells were unlocked and inmates were allowed to wander around freely. I very quickly had a steady stream of visitors wanting to meet the 'celebrity' new arrival. The girls had all watched the TV news and read the papers, so knew all about me and my story and wanted to know all sorts of things about Panama, how I had kept the story from my sons for so long – and did I have a secret stash of money hidden away? Everyone was very intrigued but I did my best to play it all down. I was a private person and didn't really want the intrusion, but I was polite and courteous to everyone who came to say hello.

The inmates were of all ages, though most were much younger than me, in their twenties and thirties, and they were all very nice, despite what they might have done to end up in jail, and told me not to worry, that I'd be OK. Some even told me to ask if there was anything I needed and they'd sort it out. There seemed to be a good sense of camaraderie and there wasn't the intimidating or threatening atmosphere I had expected, which set my mind a lot more at ease.

I had to leave my cell for the first time that day for our evening meal, which was the only time the prisoners from every wing were all together. A huge cheer went up when we walked into the main dining hall – I didn't know why, but days later I discovered the cheer had been for me. It was the prisoners' way of welcoming a notorious or high-profile inmate to Low Newton. I remember nothing else about that meal, or even if I ate anything. Shortly before 7pm we made our way back to our rooms for lock-up. And that's where we would remain until the doors were unlocked at 8am the following morning. And thus my prison routine began.

Each 'standard' or new prisoner received the grand total of £2.50 a week but, after six weeks, if you found work or joined an education programme, the pay rose to £10.00. Each week, a 'canteen list' was circulated, from which you could order tea, coffee, toiletries, washing powder, chocolate bars or sweets. If an inmate was disruptive or found to have been involved in a fight, or caught with smuggled-in drugs, they automatically lost all privileges and earnings, were confined to their cell (meals were brought to them) and they were only allowed out to use the showers – not that that ever happened to me, thankfully. There seemed to be a constant round of roll calls, from early morning until lock-up, and you soon got used to the peep hatch on your cell door being slid open during the night to check you hadn't self-harmed, or worse. One of the girls on the wing was known for repeatedly pushing pens right through her skin and into her stomach and legs.

On the day after my arrival, Wednesday, 12 December, I finally plucked up the courage to put pen to paper and write the letters to Mark and Anthony, which I had written and re-written in my head a thousand times. I told them I couldn't even begin to imagine how they must be feeling after all the trauma of the last few weeks, and that I understood if I was the last person on earth they wanted to hear from. 'But I need to tell you both how sorry I am for the pain and anguish,' I wrote. 'There is no excuse for the pain and heartache you have been caused.'

I also wrote to my parents and other members of my family, saying how sorry I was for the lies I had told and the anguish I had created. I said I hoped one day they would be able to understand what had driven me to do such awful things. I didn't ask for forgiveness – I knew I didn't deserve it. The thought of never hearing from the boys again remained too painful for words and I wondered constantly what they must think of me and the terrible lies I had told. Although I was angry with John, I was also still worried about his wellbeing and wondered whether, as an ex-prison officer, he was getting a hard time on the other side of the bars.

I wasn't interviewed by the police that day but I had lots of visitors: the chaplain; someone regarding housing for when I was released, which seemed a little premature to say the least; legal services representatives; drug-abuse advisers.

I was given a risk assessment interview. I was upset that my medication for high blood pressure had been taken away from me when I was arrested. Although I was given one tablet to take every morning, it still caused me some anxiety not to have them with me. But my request to have the tablets returned was denied, probably because attempted overdoses were not uncommon.

That evening I was summoned to see the wing officer, who, rather unexpectedly, said he was going to transfer me to the healthcare wing, because there were concerns over my state of mind and I seemed much too quiet and subdued.

I suppose I must have been bottling things up inside because I suddenly broke down in tears and begged not to be moved. I was just getting used to the wing, the routine and my fellow inmates, and really didn't want to start all over again somewhere else. But my pleas fell on deaf ears and that evening I was transferred. I was told the staff would be able to keep a closer eye on me and monitor my behaviour. I think because I was so quiet and introverted, always keeping myself to myself, they thought I might do something stupid.

I expected it to be like an NHS hospital ward, but the healthcare wing was clearly for inmates with mental health issues. I felt out of place. It was bad enough finding myself in prison, but there was absolutely no need for me to be locked up with self-harmers. I tried not to stare as I passed girls with heavily bandaged arms or others that looked at me through glazed eyes. Some had marks around their necks where they'd obviously had ligatures in an attempt to end their lives. This was scary.

I was given a room with two beds, although thankfully I didn't have to share. There was a washbasin, a toilet behind a curtain but no shower. The room was absolutely filthy, so I had to clean it from top to bottom, then had to go in search of sheets for my bed, as there weren't any. That night, the screaming and banging started. Someone else felt like me – they didn't want to be there either, they just expressed themselves differently.

The next day, Thursday, 13 December, I was supposed to be starting my induction programme, but that was cancelled because Nicola needed to see me regarding my case and to prepare me for the following day's remand hearing, which was to be done by video link from the court.

This happened at 10.20am on Friday, 14 December. I was escorted to the video-link room, which was divided into small booths where it was possible to have a video link between inmates and legal teams, or inter-prison contact between spouses. They were small, stifling rooms but I was taken into a larger room with a huge TV screen at one end, a large table and a chair for me to sit at with a placard behind me that said 'HMP Low Newton'. The prison officer who accompanied me explained that I would be able to see the magistrate but no one else, and they would see me appear on a screen in the Magistrates' Court. He then stood to one side so that he wasn't seen in court. The hearing was over in a matter of minutes. All I had to do was state my full name and give my address as HMP Low Newton. I was remanded in custody until 11 January, 2008.

On the evening of Saturday 15th, I played bingo for the first time in my life and was thrilled when I won a bottle of shampoo and conditioner – it's amazing how quickly you stop taking the small things in life for granted when you suddenly find yourself with nothing.

As December progressed, I grew more depressed about not hearing from the boys. I was given a psychiatric assessment and, although I was now more depressed than when I arrived, I was asked how I felt about being moved out of healthcare and to one of the main prison wings. Once again, I was just starting to feel settled where I was and asked if I could stay put until after Christmas. I was very relieved when I was told I could. I had got to know some of the girls and, although many had very deep and real psychological issues, I couldn't face being moved again so soon.

Saturday 22 December was my 34th wedding anniversary and I was pleasantly surprised when told I would be getting a call from John. This would be our first contact since he was arrested and I wasn't hopeful of hearing from any other family member. But he was full of a cold and sounded very glum and down, so the brief call, which we both knew was being monitored, did little to lift my spirits. On Christmas Eve, restraining orders, denying us access to our UK bank accounts, were served on us, not that either of us would be popping out to use the cash point any time soon. I just wanted Christmas to be over.

But the day itself was nowhere near as bad as I had been expecting. It started with the prison governor, Paddy Fox, coming round and wishing everyone a happy

Christmas and we were all given extra-large rations in our tea packs – sandwiches, a sausage roll, a piece of fruit, a small packet of biscuits and a few other treats. In the afternoon there was bingo, which always broke the monotony of the day, and a karaoke show, which was really quite fun. Some of the girls were very good, and some were rubbish – and no, I didn't take part – but everyone had a laugh, I even managed to forget about things for a short while and it helped pass the day. We returned to our cells at 7pm and that was that: Christmas Day was over.

On Boxing Day, I was allowed out into the exercise yard for the first time since my arrival. It was a blowy day and being able to taste fresh air and feel the wind on my face for that short spell was really quite intoxicating. The following day I was thrilled to get a letter from my sister, Christine, asking if she could visit at the weekend with Mam and Dad.

I was excited but also extremely apprehensive of what they would all make of me and my new surroundings. Although I had written to Mam and Dad, I hadn't heard back or spoken with them since before leaving Panama. I had lied to them for all those years and I now wondered what must be going through their minds – how could their daughter, who they had raised to be a good Catholic girl, have done something quite so terrible? I felt sure they were probably too ashamed to even talk to their friends about what I had done. They were such good, upstanding members of their community, and the shame must have been terrible for both of them. I knew it would have had a devastating effect on their lives.

I had always been very close to Mam, who was more like a best friend than anything else. We spoke most days when I was in England, and in Panama I called using Skype once or twice a week. Whenever I went to stay, particularly in the years after I married John, the two of us would always sit up talking into the small hours. I knew now they would ask 'How?' and 'Why?' but I didn't really have any answers. I didn't really have any good answers for anyone, not least myself.

Of course, when the day came, they asked those questions and more. They asked how I could have done such a thing, but all I could really say was, 'I'm sorry.' I had hoped, above all else, that they might bring word from Mark and Anthony but they didn't, which was terribly disappointing. It was an incredibly emotional meeting. We all hugged and cried and I could see the pain etched in Mam and Dad's faces, which filled me with terrible guilt. I'm sure seeing me there in a prison environment must have been a terrible shock for them,

The visits hall was set out with three long rows of low, circular tables, with seven or eight tables in a row. Each table had three chairs on one side for visitors and a single chair on the opposite side for the prisoner. There was an elevated desk at one end of the room, near to the visitors' entrance, where an officer sat to survey the room. Three or four more officers were positioned at various points or mingled around the tables. There was a small coffee shop at one end where visitors could buy refreshments for themselves and the person they were visiting. There was also a small play area for youngsters. Once a prisoner was seated we were not allowed to move off the chair. Every prisoner had to carry a key fob at all times, which contained their photograph and a prisoner number. When we entered the visits hall the fob was placed in a box. At the end of visits one fob would be chosen at random and that person was strip searched.

I did my best to reassure Mam, Dad and Christine that I was OK and being treated well, but they seemed totally overwhelmed with the situation. Even coming to the prison and having to go through all the security checks and searches must have been a horrendous ordeal. Just like us prisoners, they had to endure a rub-down search before entering and sometimes there'd be sniffer dogs, looking for drugs being trafficked.

Dad was a quiet man, a kind and gentle but physically strong former welder, and the only time I had ever seen him cry before was when his mother died. But he sobbed that day. To see him sitting there in the visiting room with tears rolling down his cheeks was utterly heartbreaking. He looked so bewildered and sad, as if he couldn't make any sense of what I'd done. They weren't particularly close to John but I knew they both found it extremely hard to comprehend what had happened. Dad was known for his great sense of humour and always had a smile on his face, despite his ill health, and now I had robbed him of that happiness. He appeared a lot frailer than the last time I'd seen him. He'd had a quadruple heart bypass and both knees replaced – we used to jokingly call him the bionic man – he still had heart problems and was also battling cancer. I knew he was a fighter and wouldn't give up, but he was not in a good way and, as I sat there, I seriously wondered if I would ever get to see him again. It really did break my heart.

Dad was such a remarkable and determined man, who had started life as a blacksmith under his father at the mines at Horden Colliery. He later became a welder at Blackhall Colliery and then a plumber for Nimmo's brewery in the village of Castle Eden, where he worked until he retired at 62. He had always been well liked by his friends and colleagues but he wasn't a man's man in that sense of the word. He would never go to the pub alone. He was first and foremost a good family man, who always put his wife and children first. He belonged to the Society of St Vincent de Paul, a Catholic charity that, among other things, kept an eye on families in the community who needed help. That was the kind of man he was – someone who looked out for others less fortunate than himself. He didn't have a selfish bone in his body and I'm sure he must have wondered how his daughter could have turned out the way I had. I felt so ashamed and wondered what affect all the headlines about me must have had on him.

Mam had always been a worrier. She worried about everything, and the older she got, the worse she seemed to get. So how she was coping with what I had done and the fuss I had created, I had no idea. Like the rest of the family, Mam and Dad had suddenly found themselves besieged by journalists, banging on their door and seeking their reactions to John's return from the dead and my subsequent confession in the newspapers. I knew she would be very disappointed in me and shocked at the lies I had told. Lying was just not something that Mam had ever done. She was a typical homemaker, who married her first and only love, went to church every Sunday and, for her entire life, had been involved in lots of different church groups and charities.

She only got a job much later in life, probably when she was approaching retirement age, working in a local bakery. She knew the family and I think initially she had offered to help out when they were short-staffed and it went from there. She'd be up early, helping with the baking of the buns, pies and pasties, but was always back in time to make sure Dad's dinner was on the table when he got home from work. Mam and Dad were simply a decent, honest and hard-working couple who'd done all they could to give their three children the best possible start in life. And look how I had repaid them.

There were more tears all round as Mam, Dad and

Christine left, and I returned to my cell, where I sat with my head in my hands and cried. I asked myself over and over again how I could have done what I had done to my own family. I knew I was a disgrace and felt sick to the stomach. I didn't sleep a wink that night. I just lay there with images and thoughts of Mam and Dad swirling around my mind. And, of course, of the boys.

My induction took place over two weeks, at the end of December and beginning of January. I signed up for work, and was assigned to cleaning duties – starting with the visits hall from 5 January. I put my name down to join an IT course and budgeting and finance course, which I thought a good one to take in light of the crimes I'd committed. I was pleased to learn there was a gym, which I was told I could use every day if I wanted. I was getting my act together, but there was one more thing I needed to do.

Since returning to England, I had continued lying to everyone, including Nicola, about not knowing from the outset that John had faked his death. But one night soon after my visit, I reached the point of knowing it was time for the lying to end.

The next morning I confessed to Nicola. It was not an easy thing to admit to, because the lie had been such a big part of my life for so long, more than five years, and I worried that the boys would now be even more angry with me, if that were even possible.

That morning, Monday, 7 January, 2008, in a sparse police interview room, Nicola told the detectives that I wanted to make a statement and I gave the police exactly what they had been waiting for. I admitted I had been in on John's disappearing act from the very beginning and he had been living with me virtually from the moment he touched dry land. In a taped confession, the interview room silent save for the whirring of the tape machine, I told the officers: 'He went out in his canoe in Seaton Carew, and I waited for him on the shore in the car. I picked him up. Then he moved back in with me, and we pretended he was dead.'

I thought the officers would be pleased with my confession. Instead, they seemed to get very angry and after leaving the room for a while, they returned and asked why it had taken so long to confess and had I really thought I was going to get away with it? They said I had wasted so much time and resources. All I could do was apologise. I was stunned by the outburst but it was to be expected. I had wasted a lot of their time for no good reason. I wished I'd told the truth immediately. Later, when I had time to think, it was a relief knowing I didn't have to lie any more but I knew there'd be more questions ahead.

My confession brought to an end five years and 295 days of living a lie. It gave the police the answers they needed to start to bring to a close what, by their own admission, had been an extraordinary investigation that had gripped the attention of millions of people around the world. It also meant that John now had little choice but to end his ridiculous tale of amnesia: his full and frank confession quickly followed.

Det Supt Hutchinson, who was soon to retire from Cleveland Police after more than 30 years' service, told a press conference: 'Anne told us everything, and I would imagine that was something of a relief for her after all that time. Her husband then had little option but to do the same.'

I knew now that a long stretch behind prison walls was inevitable. There had still been no word from my boys and I didn't know whether I wanted to be with John anymore. I had tried desperately not to be the one to expose the lie. *Where did that get me?* I wondered how he would react. *Will he see my actions as a betrayal? Should I care what he thinks?* I felt confused, I didn't know what to think anymore. Had he simply filed for bankruptcy in 2002, all this would now have been long behind us and we could have picked up the pieces of our lives and started again. John's vanity and the lies I told to make his plot possible had cost us so much more than we could ever have imagined. Exactly how much more it would cost us remained to be seen.

Chapter 19

Questions & Answers

Continuing to lie when I came back from Panama had been a terrible mistake. It was the second biggest mistake I had ever made – the first, of course, was going along with John's scheme in the first place. No doubt it made the police suspicious about what else I wasn't telling them. I'm sure they must have wondered how they could believe a single word I said.

Given the vast amount of evidence I had given the police, I assumed pleading guilty and taking whatever punishment came my way would be my only option. So I was taken aback when Nicola told me there was actually one possible defence to the charges I was facing and it was called 'marital coercion'. The defence, which could only be used by a spouse, was so rarely used that there had been only about five reported cases in the last 100 years. For it to succeed, the burden was on the prosecution to prove one of two things beyond all reasonable doubt: that either John was not physically present (at my side) at the time of each offence being committed; or that John failed to coerce or intimidate me into committing the offence.

The coercion need not be violent but it would be insufficient to say I was simply acting out of loyalty. It had to be proven that my will had been 'overborne' to such an extent that he had total control over my actions.

The defence was far from certain to succeed, Nicola warned me, but if it did I would walk free. The downside, which was considerable, was that there would be a very public trial, played out before my family and everyone else who knew me, and I would face ferocious cross-examination from the prosecution. I had two choices: plead guilty and face a certain prison sentence, which I was told was likely to be up to three years; or plead not guilty, using marital coercion as a defence, and have a glimmer of hope of being freed from custody. However, if I denied the charges and was found guilty, the sentence was likely to be more severe, possibly four to four-and-a-half years.

It was a horrible decision to have to make and for weeks my mind was all over the place, swinging back and forth, not knowing what to do. At that stage, I hadn't even considered that Mark and Anthony could be called by the prosecution to give evidence against me, which indeed they were, a move that would turn out to be one of the most horrendous experiences of my life.

Although my trial was still many months away, Nicola was inundating me with paperwork about my case, including copies of all John's police interviews. It was recorded that he was on heart medication, an angina spray, and was partially deaf – especially when the questions seemed to get a bit tricky! He was being as obstinate as possible, replying 'no comment' to hundreds of questions, although at one stage he did go on a mini-rant about the lenders, who he still blamed for his predicament in the first place.

The interviews were from the time John was still claiming to have amnesia, but it was obvious the detectives weren't buying his story. They also believed it entirely possible our sons had been in on the plot. Perhaps John had spent some of the time hiding out in the home of either Mark or Anthony, the police thought. They both lived in the south, not far from London, which is where he had decided to come back from the dead.

'Were they involved, John?' he was asked.

'Well, the Queen lives in London, too, but I haven't been staying at Buckingham Palace,' he cockily replied. He really didn't seem to be able to help himself, but then he clearly realised his answer was way too flippant, as he quickly added: 'God no. And the reason I replied "God no" is because neither of my sons will speak to me. They, all of the family, won't have anything to do with me. My wife – sorry, it should be my ex-wife, because she won't have anything to do with me now because I created all this mess – so nobody had anything… I've lost everything. Yes, I admit it, it was my fault. I did it. I've got no family left on the outside whatsoever.'

He was asked if he'd had any contact with the boys

during his missing years.

'No,' he responded. 'None whatsoever. I can categorically say that that is correct and I will tell you why. The gunpowder plot failed because too many people knew about it. Myself and my wife knew that I wasn't informing the relevant authorities and that was all. There were two people involved therefore. Two people. Nobody else. Therefore it could be kept in the quiet. More than two people and it certainly wouldn't. That's my explanation.' The police then showed John the photograph of us together in Panama, the damning evidence that had blown apart our concocted stories. Asked to describe himself, John answered: 'An old man, balding, blue eyes.' He was asked to identify the three people in the photograph. 'Well, the ugly one's me,' John replied. 'And which one would you say the ugly one is?' the officer asked, patiently. 'The little one. Little fat fella on the left. The person in the middle's my wife. And the gentleman in the striped shirt is Mario Vilar, from Move to Panama.' Why John had to be so cocky and arrogant I really don't know. I'm sure it must have infuriated the officers interviewing him. But that was him all over and one of the reasons I was still very uncertain if we had any kind of future together.

I had a second visit from Mam and Christine, although Dad didn't come with them this time as he was worried he'd break down and cry again. But he sent his love. I knew I must be such a disappointment to him. It was a much better visit than the first one and there were no tears, until we parted – but Mam did look back as she left the hall, and we both managed a smile.

John bombarded me with letters, so many that I could barely keep up with them, but they were all very repetitive. He would write about how much he loved me, wanted to spend the rest of his life with me, and he'd reminisce about happier times. Then there were questions about where I wanted to live. I should make a decision so that he could apply to live in the same area, preferably in the same house. No one could stop us from living together, we were man and wife. He said we could go back to Hartlepool, perhaps Easington or Blackhall, so I could be close to my family. And he needed to know now. He knew he wouldn't be welcomed by my family but he was willing to go with me to Blackhall, find a park bench to sit on and wait for my visit to end. He'd want to know about my conversations with Nicola and tell me that she was working for me and I should instruct her on how to proceed.

I don't know how he expected me to do any of that when I was feeling totally lost, in a strange environment and unfamiliar circumstances. It was far too early to think about where I wanted to live after release. First of all, I needed an expected date of release and as for living together, well that was the biggest question of all. If I didn't respond immediately, I would receive another letter asking the same questions with more urgency… and so it continued.

On 19 January it had been arranged for him to call at 2pm. He went off at a great rate of knots, hardly pausing for breath in order to get through everything on his list, and then he stunned me by suddenly asking if it would be OK to have a female pen pal. He'd received a Christmas card from a woman and, after writing back to say thank you, she'd asked if they could carry on corresponding.

I was so angry, thinking, Here we go again. 'Make up your own mind,' I told him before hanging up. He didn't usually ask for my approval to do anything, so why now? What could I do to stop him? He'd written reams to me, expressing lifelong love and a desire to be together forever, and then in virtually the same breath had the temerity to ask if he could correspond with another woman.

Police had requested two further days of questioning, in Redcar, so I was driven there in a prison van and seen by a doctor before being handed over into police custody. Nicola was with me for the three short sessions of questioning, and in between there were long periods of waiting around. I was told later that, as they were also questioning John, they probably wanted me on hand to corroborate or deny what he was saying.

John and I were both being kept in police cells

overnight, and he asked if he could see me briefly that evening. I thought it would just be a brief word through the hatch but, without any warning, an officer opened my cell door and John quickly moved towards me and hugged and kissed me.

I was annoyed with the officer for just letting him in like that. It wasn't what I wanted at all. I still had very mixed emotions about John and his request to correspond with another woman. The next day, I refused John's request to speak to me again.

I was driven back to Low Newton in a police van but it was very apparent the officers didn't really know where they were going. 'You're certainly taking the scenic route,' I commented.

The officer driving admitted he was a bit lost and when I heard him on the radio asking for directions, I told him not to bother because I knew exactly where we were and could easily show him. *I must be quite mad*, I thought, *first typing my story for a journalist and now giving police directions to take me back to jail.* But I was actually glad to be back in prison and my, by now, familiar surroundings.

John called again, towards the end of January, and this time he sounded desperate, a broken man, and I felt I had no option but to give him some hope for the future. I was worried he might harm himself, or worse. Maybe it was just emotional blackmail but I didn't want it on my conscience if he did anything stupid. Of course I was angry with him, but I certainly didn't wish any harm on him. I wanted him to be OK.

At the start of February, I was transferred to E (for Elvet) wing, which had its own dining room, laundry, a couple of shower rooms and even a pool table. At times, it seemed a bit like a *Hi-de-Hi!* holiday camp, with regular announcements over the tannoy system – although there was no 'morning campers' announcement. The food in Low Newton wasn't good. It was chips with everything. There was no way we would ever get our five a day. But on E wing I was surprised to find there was a small garden area we could use, with a footpath round the edge. I started walking, gradually building up to a jog. I thought if I could do that every morning, and use the gym a couple of evenings a week to do some weights, I'd be in pretty good shape.

I was delighted at my next health check-up to discover my blood pressure was almost back to normal, so the exercise was obviously paying off. But my morning jogs soon came to an end when I was told there were concerns over the number of drain and manhole covers in the yard, and in future I'd only be permitted to walk. Apparently, a governor had seen me jogging and asked the works' department to perform a risk assessment. From that day onwards, I power-walked around the garden and used the running machine in the gym instead. I was keeping my mind active as well. I took a level-two numeracy test, although I failed miserably, and my IT course was going well. With an exam coming up, I spent what time I could doing revision and practice papers.

Towards the end of February, a prison officer came to my cell one Sunday afternoon and asked that I accompany him to the association room, where a female officer was sat waiting for me. She handed me a page from the *News of the World*, and I knew it could only be bad news. There was a huge picture of John and a letter, in his handwriting, on prison paper. At first I thought it must be one he had written to me, but it was, in fact, one he'd sent to another woman, obviously the woman pen pal he'd told me about.

What really shocked me was the sexual content of the letter – it was disgusting, to say the least. I wondered how he could even write in such a manner. I knew how important sex was to John and how frustrated he must be by now but there was no excuse for the filth he came out with.

The officers were very understanding. They offered support but there was nothing they could do to prevent the paper, which was popular among the women prisoners, from being circulated throughout the prison. What would they all make of me? How much more humiliation did I have to take?

I went back to my cell and quietly sobbed. I felt absolutely devastated and wondered what the poor boys would make of their father writing such horrible, childish, filth. I worried about whether the letter would appear on TV and if it would have an effect on my trial. Will this nightmare ever end?

I knew John would never change. An officer from HMP Durham called Low Newton to see if I would talk to John, but the staff told him it was not appropriate as I was too upset. I had a very restless and unhappy night. Two days later, John called the prison again, asking if I would take a call from him. I didn't want to but knew I would have to face up to him sooner or later, so said he could call me on Saturday at 2pm.

I spent most of the day trying to work out exactly what I'd say, but two o'clock came and went, then it was three, then four, and still no phone call, so I began to wonder if it was going to happen. Finally, shortly after 4pm, I was summoned to the phone.

John was full of all the excuses I had expected. He was depressed, suicidal, but I couldn't believe anything he said anymore. I said I wasn't sure if I could ever forgive him. He asked if he could apply for a prison visit but I said most definitely not. The last thing I wanted was him visiting me and having everyone staring at us and watching our every move – it would be in the papers before you knew it. I said I wouldn't write because I had nothing to say – nothing that he would want to hear, anyway. I didn't really want any contact with him at all. I felt like an inadequate teenager who didn't even know her own mind. I knew I had some very difficult decisions to make but didn't yet feel ready to make them.

I felt miserable and, what was worse, the following Sunday was Mother's Day. How lovely it would be to hear from Mark and Anthony, to simply receive a card, and although I hoped beyond hope, I didn't really expect I would. I knew it would be a very difficult day and wasn't sure if I'd even be able to face going to church, as I'd just spend the entire service sobbing. But I also knew I couldn't get through this ordeal without God's help.

When the day came, there were, understandably, no cards. I just hoped that I would briefly enter their thoughts. The boys were in my thoughts every day. I didn't even have the strength to call Mam, because I knew she'd wish me a happy Mother's Day, and it wasn't. How could it be? I thought about writing to John but couldn't find the right words, so left it.

It had been almost three months since I stepped off the plane at Manchester airport and one morning I woke convinced I should plead 'not guilty' at my upcoming trial. How I should plead had been on my mind constantly, and the thought of a prison sentence of any length was so terrifying that I'd finally decided I should gamble on a fight for my freedom.

I knew what I had done was wrong and I'd hurt many people in the process. *It is not that I am trying to get away with it,* I told myself, *but I certainly didn't do the things I did willingly.*

As the day wore on, all I could think about was having to appear in court and stand there, giving evidence. I wondered what Mark and Anthony would feel about me blaming it all on their dad. It was horrible not having anyone to talk to. And having started the day convinced I should plead not guilty, I ended it thinking I should just plead guilty and have done with it. Facing a trial would be too painful to bear.

There were many similar days when my plea was the only thing I could think about and it stayed that way up to the day I appeared at Leeds Crown Court, for a plea hearing, on Thursday, 13 March. That morning I saw John, as he and several other male prisoners were already inside the prison van that came to Low Newton to take us to court. He looked absolutely dreadful and was very emotional, although there wasn't much opportunity to talk.

In court, he and I stood side by side as the charges were read out and we were asked in turn for our pleas. John pleaded 'guilty', while I, having had a last long conversation about it with Nicola, pleaded 'not guilty'. The hearing lasted less than 20 minutes.

After being debriefed by our legal teams, we were driven back to our respective prisons, again in the same van. John looked visibly relieved. For him, other than sentencing, it was all over. He had seemed surprised at my plea but didn't say anything or appear angry.

I wouldn't see him again until my trial was over. Over the last few months I'd tried to support him, as much as I could, but I knew that I now had to concentrate on what was right for me and distance myself from John, who'd got me into this sorry mess in the first place. I had to do what I could for myself.

At Easter, I was moved to G Wing, where, much to my delight, I found I had a slightly larger cell. There was a television on a wall-mount in the corner, even a remote control; a large writing desk and an easy chair, which was comfortable and much nicer than always having to sit on my bed. Maybe not quite the Ritz, but I wasn't complaining.

There had recently been a big fight on E wing, which culminated with a plate being smashed over a girl's head and her being hit with a sauce bottle, which had required staples in her head. G Wing seemed to have a much better atmosphere. It had a large association room, with a Chesterfield-style three-piece suit, a large TV, phone booth, a toaster and microwave, a pool table, two washing machines and driers, a kitchen sink, and small office in one corner for the officers. Upstairs, there was a music room, a quiet room (however, they were next to each other), another pool table and a table tennis table. We had to report to the office for roll call three times a day, 12.20pm, 4.20pm and 7.20pm. Surprisingly the windows, which were double-glazed, didn't have bars, and looking out you could see the spring crocuses in the prison gardens just starting to bloom. That evening I phoned Mam and Dad to let them know I'd been moved and the surroundings were much nicer. I knew that would make them happy.

Nicola had told me that the money from the Panama bank accounts had successfully been transferred back to England and I was now able to write cheques to pay the maintenance for the apartment in Panama, where our belongings were still, which was also a huge relief.

The following weekend, Christine brought Mam and Dad for another visit. They both looked tired. Mam was quite shocked when I told her my sentence, if found guilty, was likely to be two to three years. It also made me think about the length of time I'd be in jail and it was very depressing. I didn't want to be here that long. I didn't want to be here at all. When they left, I felt very low. I wondered what was even left to look forward to anymore. No home to go to, no sons to talk with, no job, no friends.

As if things couldn't get much worse, I received a letter from Nicola saying the flat in Panama had been broken into and my car, the computer and a suitcase, containing who knows what, had been stolen. *Thank goodness the car is insured*, I thought, *or how would I ever pay back the money the police were trying to recover.* But I knew making a claim wouldn't be easy, it being Panama, and wondered if perhaps I'd never get the money back. I just wanted to cry.

That afternoon, I had my hair cut for the first time since I'd been in prison. The girl did a good job but, although it cheered me up a bit for a while, I still felt miserable.

Every day I prayed I'd hear from the boys, but still there had been no word. On Sunday, 13 April, I decided to write to them both once again. They were only short letters but took ages to write and I had to stop several times as I couldn't see through the tears. I had so much I wanted to tell them but to put it in a letter just didn't seem right, so I simply ended up telling them how much I missed and loved them.

I was struggling badly to cope with prison life and had reached the point when I seriously wondered if I could go on. I had an empty feeling in my stomach that my life had no meaning anymore and that I had nothing to live for. I was struggling to make sense of everything, trying to put John out of my thoughts and the pain I had caused the boys. And I kept hearing stories of my fellow inmates getting far longer sentences than they expected, which terrified me. One girl had recently got five years for an offence involving a similar amount of money to me and another three years for a crime that involved a lot less money. Everything looked very bleak.

I had been given back my medication for high blood pressure and, for the first time, started to wonder what would happen if I just took all the tablets in one go. Maybe

I would just drift off to sleep and never wake up. Then I'd be free from everything: no more pain, no more anguish or humiliation. Or would it be a horrible and painful end? Then I realised I couldn't go through with it, even if I wanted to, as I'd already taken half my tablets and would have to wait another week for my next prescription.

It must take a very courageous person to end their own life, I thought. My mind drifted to the boys and my parents, and what effect it would have on their lives – lives which I had already damaged so much. I thought Mark and Anthony might possibly feel guilty because they hadn't been in touch, and that's the last thing I wanted.

I didn't have anyone with whom to share my thoughts, so I wrote them in a diary. I sometimes felt it helped to clarify things when I wrote them down. I looked at the words I had written and knew I couldn't take my life. I would hurt the people for whom I'd already caused far too much distress. I knew then that I had to face up to everything and try, as best I could, to stay strong.

There was a leaving party that afternoon for one of the girls who was going home the following day. Feeling at rock bottom, I was going to stay in my room, but decided to go and say goodbye and was glad I did. Two of the girls came into the common room wearing dressing gowns and proceeded to do a hilarious striptease. Under the dressing gowns, they were wearing underwear over their clothes. They put on a bit of a show, which had everyone crying with laughter – it was just what I needed. It also made me think that perhaps I was spending too much time on my own and I should make an effort to mix with some of the other women.

Three new girls arrived at the prison the following morning. One was particularly upset, so I was asked to spend some time with her in reception. The guards knew I was quite good at helping new arrivals who were struggling to cope with their new environment. It was the woman's first time in jail and I could relate to exactly how she was feeling. It reminded me of how I was when I first arrived – terrified.

I gave her what encouragement I could and told her not to be afraid of the other women, saying most would actually help her out if she needed anything. I think I was able to reassure her that she'd survive, that she'd be all right, as long as she was sensible and didn't cause any fuss. Back on the wing, the staff were amused at my absence. They wanted to know if I'd been carrying out blessings and, at lunch, one of the girls stopped me in the corridor and asked if I was now carrying out some of the chaplain's duties!

Chapter 20

Life on G Wing

Nicola's flurry of letters and legal documents for me to read was followed up by a visit in April. She started with some good news, saying she'd spoken to Anthony, who'd confirmed he'd received the letters I'd sent and was concerned about whether I was coping. He even said he'd get in touch at some point but just not yet. It was a huge relief to know that he was still thinking of me and hadn't completely shut me out of his life.

But then, as ever, the bad news: Nicola told me it was highly likely the prosecution would call both him and Mark as witnesses at my trial, which took the wind out of my sails. I'm not sure why I hadn't considered it before, as the boys would obviously have a lot of information that would be crucial to the prosecution's case. I told Nicola I still had massive doubts about going to trial and this only made matters a million times worse. She said I should wait on making a final decision until I had spoken to David Waters, the QC who'd be representing me at court. I agreed.

I left the meeting feeling extremely upset and confused,

which must have shown because soon afterwards I was called into the wing office and asked if everything was all right. I shed a few tears, but after a cup of tea said I'd be OK.

I had another full day's meeting with Nicola the following day, which was again stressful as I learned there was a possibility the prosecution may now try to pin the money-laundering charges on me instead of John, as originally planned, because all the transactions were in my name. That increased the possibility of a longer sentence. Things just seemed to go from bad to worse.

On May Day, the prison was buzzing with news that one of the women, Suzanne Holdsworth, had won her appeal and been released on bail, pending a retrial for murder. She had been convicted of murdering a two-year-old boy she was babysitting, and had already served three years of a life sentence, but we all believed in her innocence. We knew she wasn't the kind of person capable of murder, especially not a child, and believed poor young Kyle Fisher had had a fit as Suzanne always said. We watched the TV news – the pictures made her look very hard, when in truth the exact opposite was true. Her partner and family had stood by her throughout, and even the child's grandmother thought Sue was innocent. But although all the women who knew her were overjoyed that she was now released, she still had the retrial to go through, and she would never get back the years she had served.

The following day, at about 6pm, a large note saying 'THIS IS A RIOT' was suddenly put up over one of the windows to the landing. The prison seemed quiet and normal and I just laughed and dismissed it as a joke. But then we saw officers pinning sheets and blankets over the other windows and became aware of raised voices and increased activity, and word soon got out that some of the girls had barricaded themselves in on B2 (the second floor of B Wing).

Then the fire bell sounded and we could see from the windows in reception that girls were throwing meal boxes, scrunched up paper, plastic cutlery, duvets – basically anything they could get their hands on – out of one of the windows, followed by hand-made lighted torches, trying to set fire to them on the ground below. We heard lots of banging and shouting and then screaming, and we were worried that perhaps people were trapped, but there was no sign of any smoke inside the building itself. And all the while, we were supposed to be quietly getting on with making tea for the new arrivals and court returns!

We were told to make up some emergency overnight packs containing nightwear and toiletries, then, an hour later, told to make more packs containing tracksuits and underwear. We established that the rioters were going to be stripped and searched, then given a change of clothes to wear and confined to solitary.

Eventually, at about 9.30pm, we were escorted back to our wing, and on the way we spotted officers in riot gear gathering in the visits hall. We could hear a helicopter circling the perimeter but we didn't know how bad things were or what was going on. Someone shouted out that the riot was being reported on the ten o'clock news, so we all tuned in to see what we could find out. Prison was certainly opening my eyes to a different world. I lay in bed, thankful that I wasn't caught up in the riot in any way.

As the prison got back to normal, I concentrated on my studies and was delighted to get a personal visit from one of the tutors, saying I'd passed an English exam I'd taken a couple of weeks before. My IT classes were progressing well and I'd finally grasped the principles of manipulating databases and producing reports – it was thrilling to see the end results coming off the printer.

We had a spell of absolutely glorious weather. The exercise yard resembled a holiday resort, with beach towels spread around a pool… except of course there was no pool! But we did have the sound of running water from the washing machines' discharge pipes. It was lovely to sit in the sun with my eyes closed and dream. I was amazed at how much flesh some of the girls were able to bare without the use of swimwear. We were all urged to use the sunscreen provided but some didn't bother and ended up looking like beetroots. I'd have been grateful for a pair of shorts.

It was towards the middle of May that I first met the counsel charged with defending me in court, David Waters. He seemed nice and did his best to put me at ease. Both he and Nicola advised me to think carefully before making a final plea decision but said I should act sooner, rather than later, as it would affect how my evidence was presented. They stressed how important it was to make the right decision, and not to plead 'guilty' just to avoid a trial. They both said they felt I had a good chance of a positive outcome.

I left the meeting feeling drained and confused. Everyone had been telling me that I didn't have to deal with things on my own but, in reality, that's exactly what I had to do. I had no one to trust, and all letters and phone calls I made were either read or listened in on. I was alone and I had to make this monumental decision on my own. It played on my mind the entire time, particularly at night, as I lay in my bed trying to sleep. Sometimes I wished someone could just make the decision for me. I knew whatever I decided would be wrong.

The next day, as I ate lunch, it hit me that the first time I would see Mark and Anthony again would be in court, with them giving evidence against me from the witness box. I felt miserable, especially knowing I could spare them the ordeal by pleading guilty. I knew I had put them through enough torment already, so why was I even considering going to trial? I knew why, of course: I couldn't bear the thought of being locked up in this prison for years, so I was putting myself first. I knew it was incredibly selfish and could only further damage what little chance I had of the boys ever forgiving me. But what else could I do? If I didn't at least give myself a chance by going to trial, I would be languishing behind bars for years. I was party to the crimes, of course I was. But it wasn't my idea, none of it was. I was always dead against the whole crackpot scheme and had been dragged into everything by John. My husband was overbearing. That was the truth and I wanted to let people know of the incredible pressure I had been under and how I had been too weak to stand up to him. It may have been pathetic, but it was the truth.

I wondered if the boys would understand, or if they'd even care. I knew that as they'd been called as witnesses, they didn't have much say in the matter. But maybe they'd want to help the prosecution anyway after all John and I had put them through. Maybe if we were given stiff sentences, they'd feel that we got what we deserved. Maybe they wanted us to be punished. After all, we'd punished them enough over recent years.

It wasn't long before the story that they were to be prosecution witnesses appeared in the *Daily Mirror*, so now everyone around me knew my own sons would be a vital part of the prosecution case against me. I'd always been a private person and hated everyone knowing my business.

There'd been yet another story on the local TV news that one of the bars in our old home town was considering changing its name to 'The Seaton Canoe'. A guard, who was always friendly, stopped me and said that, seeing I was now a local celebrity, I should pose for photographs outside the bar and he'd sell the pictures and retire on the proceeds. It was only meant as a joke, and I knew there'd be lots more to come the following day from the women, there always were. A previous story that said there were plans to rename the bar in the hotel next to our old home 'Darwins' had brought much merriment. At least the guard had given me some time to think of a suitable retort. Another officer told me he'd read that tourism had increased in Seaton after all the publicity over our arrests and my return from Panama, so the local tourist board had plenty to thank me for. One fish and chip shop was even planning on introducing a 'Canoe Burger' for the coming season, he said.

Among the latest batch of evidence sent by Nicola were my credit card statements but also Mark and Anthony's bank statements. It was horrible to think that their affairs were being made so public. It must have been horrible for them to have detectives poring over the intricate details of their finances, particularly as they'd done absolutely nothing wrong. They had just been used by me and John, their own parents. They must have despised us.

The number of legal files I now had was immense. I was running out of room to even keep them in my cell. Reading through some of them, I came across my interview transcripts from when I first returned from Panama and they made me feel nauseous. No doubt the prosecution would make much of them at the trial. I wished I'd told the truth. They made me out to be such a liar, which of course I was, and they made very unpleasant reading.

You can't turn back the clock, unfortunately. I told myself that when the time for the trial came, I'd just have to tell the truth and put my faith in God.

With less than a month to go before the court case, Mam, Dad and Christine visited for the third time. Christine looked well, Dad looked to have lost weight, but Mam looked absolutely terrible, very drawn and grey. She told me she was worried about everything and praying I'd be cleared and released. Dad was more worried about the practicalities of where I'd go and how I'd pay the rent if I was convicted – exactly what rent I wasn't really sure. It was horrible seeing them so worried and confused about everything.

For their visit, I wore some trousers and one of the

shirts Mam and Dad had recently sent me, so they could see how grateful I was to have received them. I think that, at least, brought a smile to their faces. I was sad when it was time for them to go but happy we'd had time to talk and be together. I worried how badly the court case would affect them, knowing full well some of the coverage would make uncomfortable reading. They told me they were going to stay with Christine during the trial, which was reassuring. It was nice to know she'd be taking care of them and explaining things as best she could. Their visits meant everything, especially as the rest of the family weren't ready to have any contact with me at all. Because of the age difference, we hadn't really developed that sisterly bond that other siblings share. When I married and moved away, Christine was only 12. And when she left college she went to work in London so we didn't get to spend much time together. However, there was no rivalry between us. We had always cared for each other. I valued her support, now, when I was most in need. Christine had been exceptionally kind to me and I don't think I would have coped without her regular visits.

The following day I received a package from Nicola with some of the evidence. I read through emails between John and I, and felt they all looked fairly damning. They were friendly and didn't give the impression that he was in any way 'overbearing'. I think the police had been fairly selective with the ones they'd chosen to produce in court – but they weren't about to do me any favours, were they?

I was convinced I'd be portrayed in court as a lying, scheming, money-grubbing, unspeakable person. And to be honest, I wasn't at all sure how I'd be able to prove that I wasn't. Everything seemed stacked against me.

I'd been told by my legal team to think of examples that illustrated John's dominance in our relationship, especially things the boys might remember. I think Nicola was just trying to prepare my defence as best she could, as she knew the boys' evidence could be damning and she hoped I could remember something they'd witnessed that would help my defence. But it was difficult. I couldn't think of any instances where they'd been present. I woke up the next morning still wondering if I'd made the right decision. *I should have just pleaded guilty and had done with it*, I thought. *Maybe that isn't being true to me, but it would bring things to a close, even if I have to stay here for years.*

Anyway, I wasn't in a hurry to go anywhere right now. There was nothing left for me outside. I was beginning to understand how people locked away for years and years became institutionalised. Perhaps prison simply became their home and it was the only place they felt comfortable.

If I end my own life, will I suffer eternal damnation, or will God forgive me? It wasn't the first time such thoughts had flooded my mind and I doubted it would be the last. I was hardly sleeping, my mind in turmoil about what best to do. Outside the weather was warm but I lay in bed freezing cold, shivering and sick to the stomach.

I woke early after a particularly restless night and when I looked in the mirror, I didn't like what I saw. I looked terrible. I hardly recognised myself, or who I had become.

I thought about phoning home, to speak with Mam and Dad, but then I changed my mind. I had no news, was miserable and what else did I have to talk about?

Around lunchtime, I was informed I had a video link arranged for that afternoon with Nicola and Dean Armstrong, my barrister, who represented me in court until the trial, when that role was fulfilled by the QC. They reassured me I was doing the right thing in going for a trial, and it left me feeling a little better. *At least I have someone on my side*, I thought.

At breakfast the following morning, my bread bun had several spots of blue mould on it and I had to ask for another. Prison food could be pretty grim sometimes. I went to the morning church service. It was busy, although I'd learned many of the girls simply went to break the monotony of their day. Twice, I had to ask the girl sitting behind me to take her feet off my chair and to stop kicking me, but it still continued. I found it very annoying and distracting and didn't feel able to take Holy Communion.

I received birthday cards from Mam and Dad, Christine and one other old friend on 3 July, just ten days before the trial. But that was it: nothing from the boys. I phoned Mam and Dad after work, as I knew they'd have been thinking about me and it was nice to hear their voices. I had spent most of the day wondering about what the future held, and about returning to prison if I was found guilty. I knew it was a very likely outcome. I felt so incredibly anxious.

A few days later, 7 July, was Dad's birthday. I phoned to wish him a happy birthday, but there was no one in, so I guessed they were out celebrating, and left a message saying I'd try again in the morning.

The 'jury bundle', all the evidence that would be shown to the jury, arrived in a package from Nicola the following day. It was so I could make any last-minute comments. The biggest surprise was Mr Waters asking if we could call Mam as a witness – there was no way in the world I would have allowed that, even if my life depended on it. She would never stand the strain and would be a nervous wreck. *No, no, no, no, no. What on earth was he thinking? Why, oh, why, am I doing this?* I wrote to Nicola saying there was no way I was involving Mam.

Over the next couple of days, I gradually worked my way through the jury bundle. Reading the emails that would be presented and studying the other documents, I had to admit, it all looked fairly damning.

It was only a snapshot of what actually happened – but

who was ever going to believe me, the lying Anne
Darwin?

Chapter 21

Facing My Sons in Court

On Monday, 14 July, 2008, at Teesside Crown Court in Middlesbrough, using the defence of marital coercion, I denied nine charges of money laundering and nine of deception. John, for once in his life having taken the sensible option, had already pleaded guilty to seven charges of obtaining cash by deception and a separate passport offence. Nine charges of using criminal property, which he denied, were allowed to lay on file.

The day that had occupied my thoughts for so long started early, after a largely sleepless night. I was up and dressed by 5am, having showered and washed my hair the previous evening. Most of the women on my wing had come to wish me luck, but I wondered whether they'd feel the same way the following week, after reading all the evidence that would come out during my trial. I'd been escorted to reception, for the ritual strip search humiliation, and then collected by a prison bus before 7am. The first 'drop' was a girl at Hartlepool Magistrates' Court, then we continued along the coast road and through, unbelievably, Seaton Carew. I was on the sea side of the bus, and fortunately couldn't see the houses that had been our downfall, and that held so many unhappy memories for me. We reached court so early we had even beaten the press, so thankfully there were no cameras there to record my arrival.

Later, inside Court 11, was a different story altogether. With more reporters than there were seats on the press benches, they were even allowed to spill over into the public gallery. I was collected from the holding cell by a court officer, and led along what seemed like endless narrow corridors, up a flight of stairs to a light, bright waiting area. We waited about five minutes before being called into the courtroom. I stepped through a door at the back of the court which led into the defendants' box, which was directly opposite the judge's bench. There were two rows of seats and a glass partition between me and the rest of the court. I was told to sit in the front row and two dock officers sat behind me.

There was a buzz about the room and I was aware there were people in the public gallery, but I tried hard not to look in that direction for fear of seeing someone I recognised. My legal team were seated in front of me but facing the judge. Their bench and that of the prosecution was piled high with papers and files, all neatly stacked. Nicola came to ask if I was OK and told me Mark and Anthony would not appear in court until they gave evidence. I didn't know whether to feel relieved or not. I was dreading that moment both for them and myself.

Feeling nervous and anxious, I watched as one by one the jury was sworn in. I could already feel my ankles starting to swell because I had been sitting still for so long. As hard as I knew it would be, I just wanted to remain as calm and focused as possible. I never truly felt very confident in my case but I didn't want people to know that. Although I had played a huge part in making the deception possible, it was most certainly not my idea and I was not the driving force behind the crimes, which had all been John's doing. Letting that be known was important to me.

As the trial started, and the whole sorry saga of our greed, deception and lies was outlined in graphic detail, what little faith I had in my case quickly dissipated. It wasn't at all pleasant listening to the prosecution paint a very bleak picture.

Opening the trial, the prosecuting barrister, Andrew Robertson QC, told the jury that while the initial idea may well have been John's, it was a scheme in which I not only played an equal and vital role but it was a role which I played with 'superb aplomb'. He said I had shown a considerable amount of 'guile, convincing pretence, persistence and guts' to see it through. John, after supposedly disappearing, had simply to keep his head down so the falsity of his disappearance would not be rumbled by anybody. I was the one who had to take all the positive steps. But I had coolly kept my nerve, knowing the rewards were going to be considerable – sufficient not only to discharge the debts but to finance a potentially idyllic life abroad together. 'We submit this was a convincing performance and one which obviously required no prompting, let alone coercion, from her husband – a performance born of her own initiative and her determination to see the fraud through.' He said, the plot had been hatched out of financial desperation.

From the outset, it seemed obvious from his comments that the judge, Mr Justice Wilkie, had no sympathy for me or my decision to plead not guilty. I had served as a juror and knew how influential a judge's words could be in any trial – and every word uttered by the judge seemed to condemn me.

In truth, I don't think my defence ever stood a chance and I could sense it crumbling around me before we had really got underway. First, evidence proved I was not even in the same country as John when some aspects of the crime were committed, so there was no way he could have been 'physically at my side', and, secondly, a string of loving emails between us, sent throughout the time the offences were being committed, undermined any possibility that John had been totally overbearing. Those emails were mainly one-sided, but I occasionally responded with what I thought John wanted to hear. Now I regretted even doing that. There was no way of proving I wasn't totally committed to John and the fraud.

My lawyers had been the ones who came up with the defence, but, of course, it was ultimately my decision to plead not guilty and fight for my liberty. I'd always known that it had not been a good decision, but it had seemed worth pursuing if there was a possibility of being released. The marital-coercion defence was abolished from English Law in 2014 after the Law Commission said it was 'no longer appropriate' and widely regarded as a relic from a bygone age.

I arrived back at Low Newton, at 7pm, totally drained. I had some toast and just wanted to go to bed, but all the women came in to see how things had gone. They were supportive but they wanted to talk, and I really didn't, although I did want to watch the late news to see what was being reported. As it was the trial's first day, there wasn't a great deal for them to say. I was bracing myself for what would come over the following days. I hardly slept and was again up at 5am – I knew it would be my daily routine until the trial ended.

Day after day, judge and jury listened as I wriggled and squirmed, as the prosecution described how I repeatedly changed my story in the police interviews. They said I was prepared to 'lie, lie, then lie again' in a bid to evade justice, which, as painful as it is to admit, had been true. Worst of all, because I had pleaded not guilty, Mark and Anthony had been forced to attend court, to once again relive the horrendous ordeal that had already blighted their lives for many years. They even agreed to give evidence for the prosecution.

I hadn't seen the boys since I had left Seaton Carew the

previous October and, despite the circumstances, I was still eager for sight of them. After all, they were my sons and I loved them both dearly. Mark, dressed in a smart dark blue suit, was first into the witness box, but not once while giving evidence did he look in my direction.

'I couldn't believe the fact she knew he was alive all this time and I had been lied to for God knows how long,' he said, as I hung my head in shame. 'It crushed my world.'

It was only as he was leaving the box that for a fleeting second our eyes met and I was totally shocked at how dark and full of anger they were. I'm not quite sure why I should have thought differently, but I just hadn't expected it and it jolted me.

Then came Anthony, who said after the picture of John and I together in Panama came to light, he thought it was faked and must have been doctored by an internet prankster. It was only when he read my newspaper confession that he realised he had been so badly duped. With Anthony, there was no eye contact at all. I didn't know what was worse, another angry set of eyes, or no eyes whatsoever.

I wasn't at all upset with the boys for giving evidence against me. How could I be? I knew how hard coming to court must have been for them and totally understood why they had done it. After all, they were only there, being put through this public ordeal that I knew they'd both hate, because of me. I could have saved them so much grief and anguish if I had only chosen to plead guilty. It was another terrible decision that I regret to this day.

After they had finished giving evidence, Mark, who was then 32, and Anthony, 29, sat listening intently to the rest of the proceedings from the public gallery. They heard the prosecution tell the court that I had played a 'vital and equal' role in the crimes, had an equal partnership with John and enjoyed the fruits of our scheme. It had all been very much a husband-and-wife team effort – and we should each pay accordingly. By cashing in the pension and life insurance policies, my fraud amounted to £250,820.75. But, said the prosecution, by the time the fraud was uncovered in December 2007, the amount of money, land and property owned by us amounted to a hefty £500,000. Had we been forced to sell our properties and cars at the time John vanished, we would have barely had enough to pay off our debts. As it was, by staving off bankruptcy and selling our property portfolio at the height of the market, we had doubled our money and were sitting on a small fortune.

The day on which I had to take the stand was horrendous. I couldn't stop shaking. I knew that, from that point onwards, I wouldn't be allowed any more contact with my legal team until the end of the trial. I was on my own. As I started speaking, there were complaints that my voice was so soft no one could hear what I was saying and I was instructed to speak up into the microphone. I wasn't being deliberately difficult. This was my natural voice in very daunting circumstances. After giving evidence, it was time to be cross-examined, the thing I had been fearing more than anything and, of course, the prosecutor ran rings round me. It was hard to even concentrate on what I was saying and I kept losing my train of thought. Holes were picked in virtually every single word I said. I wanted to be able to expand on my replies but the questions were put in such a way that I could only respond with yes or no. By the end of the day, I felt hopeless and helpless. It was a truly awful experience and I was way out of my depth.

Court ended early, at 1.15pm, on the Friday and I spent the weekend at Low Newton, cleaning, dusting and doing my usual prison duties, despite being in the middle of a trial. I felt everyone's eyes on me the entire time and knew that everyone around me had been following every step of my trial. The weekend seemed to last an eternity. I just wanted the trial to be over.

Monday and part of Tuesday's court was taken up with the defence and prosecutions' summing up, followed by that of the judge, which was most unpleasant. It was obvious what Mr Justice Wilkie thought of me and my defence. After the conclusion of the eight-day trial, the jury was sent out shortly after 3pm and I was led down to the courtroom cells.

In my mind the entire time had been a sentence of two to three years, but suddenly my legal team were suggesting four or more. I had completely forgotten that they had advised me, at the start, that this could be the case if I was found guilty. Now, I tried to get to grips with that possibility. At 4.30pm, having been unable to reach a unanimous verdict, the jury of nine women and three men was sent home for the night but early the next morning, after less than four hours of deliberation, I was told they had reached their verdict.

On Wednesday, 23 July, 2008, I was led back into the courtroom to hear the jury foreman pronounce that I was guilty on each and every count.

I actually felt some relief that it was finally over, or so I thought. The court adjourned to allow the judge to consider sentencing. Then, once again, I was lead through the winding corridors to the waiting area before being called into court.

At my request, in the defendants' box where I had sat during the trial, a custody officer stood between me and John, who was appearing in court for the first time since pleading guilty. Then Mr Justice Wilkie passed sentence. I knew the sentences would be tough but never for a moment could I have expected how severe they would be. John would serve six years and three months, while I, who had forfeited any possible reduction by trying to shift all the blame onto John, would serve even longer: six years and six months. It wasn't the guilty verdict that was crushing – I had expected that – but I was aghast at the severity of the sentence. The judge said the maximum sentence he could have imposed was actually ten years and if John had pleaded not guilty, he would have jailed him for eight-and-a-half years.

I felt absolutely numb, and was struggling to breathe and stay composed, as I listened to the judge say the boys were the 'real victims' of our duplicity. He said: 'Although the sums involved are not as high as some reported cases, the duration of the offending, its multi-faceted nature and in particular the grief inflicted over the years to those who in truth were the real victims, your own sons, whose lives you crushed, make this a case which merits a particularly severe sentence.'

I didn't for one moment look at John, and was shaking like a leaf as I was led down to the cells by the custody officer. A few minutes later, I was taken to a private interview room, where Nicola and Dean, my barrister, and Mr Waters, were waiting. I was devastated and broke down in tears, barely able to speak. My legal team said they were outraged, and a decision to appeal had already been made. But I don't think I could even take in what they were saying. All I could think about was a prison sentence of six-and-a-half years.

Outside court, Detective Inspector Andy Greenwood told the press that the police were now concentrating their efforts on recovering the money and assets we had in Panama. He admitted that when the investigation initially started, he and other senior detectives were convinced the boys must have known about their parents' plan. But the more they investigated, the more they realised Mark and Anthony knew absolutely nothing, were treated in a disgraceful way and had in fact been through a particularly horrendous sequence of events.

I couldn't dispute those comments. We had put them through a torment that lasted for years, but it was still a bitter pill to swallow. Mark and Anthony probably thought we got what we deserved, and I couldn't blame them. I would, somehow, have to come to terms with the sentence and the consequences.

Chapter 22

A Little Joy after the Misery

John and I were driven back to our respective jails, just four miles apart, to begin our sentences. I'd been told that with parole and good behaviour, I would probably spend only half that amount of time in jail, but that was of little consolation and there was another black cloud hanging over me. If, for some reason, the Crown Prosecution Service's Proceeds of Crime team was unable to recover my assets from Panama, the courts had the power to increase my sentence, possibly by as much as another ten years and without parole. Everything was in my name, so this would only affect me, not John. The thought of even more time behind bars was a terrifying prospect.

On arriving back in prison, I was initially placed in a holding cell. Everyone at Low Newton knew about my sentence, of course, from having watched the TV news. When one of the officers came in to see if I was OK, I broke down again in floods of tears, unable to say a word. I just sat there, huddled over and shaking. The officer left and returned shortly afterwards with a mug of tea. She said she'd keep me separated from the other women for as long as she could, to give me some time to compose myself, which was incredibly kind and considerate. I was seen by a doctor, had my fingerprints taken to complete my criminal record and given something to eat. It was several hours before I was taken back to my cell on G Wing.

As I walked along the corridor a great cheer went up. Some women shouted my name, as my fellow inmates showed their support for me. I hadn't witnessed anything like that before, and the show of solidarity was touching, but I didn't want any fuss. I didn't speak to or even look at anyone as, head bowed, I quietly made my way back to my cell. One of the women I'd befriended was waiting outside to comfort me and said everyone had been shocked at the length of the sentence. I sat down on my bed and cried, still unable to speak.

A number of officers popped their head round the door to sympathise and to check I was OK. 'Take tomorrow off work and get yourself sorted out,' I was told, but I wanted to try and just carry on as normal. I hated being the centre of attention.

That night I decided I needed to ring Mam as there had been reports on the news that I was on suicide watch. I didn't think it was true, but I knew she would be worrying herself sick.

'It's OK, Mam, I'm fine and everything is going to be all right,' I told her. 'There's no need for you and Dad to worry.'

I knew my call wouldn't stop them from worrying, especially Mam. John had also heard about the suicide watch and called the prison to make sure I was OK. I didn't want to talk to him but told the officer to tell him I was fine. Next day in reception, where I worked, most of the women could see how upset I was and left me in peace. Only one of the more mouthy girls yelled out, 'Anne Darwin, you're famous. Can I have your autograph?'

'Only if you can pay for it,' I responded. 'And it will be expensive as I'm penniless now!'

I had to at least try and put on a brave face.

That Saturday, which was the day that Mass took place, there was only a small group for church. Because one of the readers was missing I was asked if I'd read the psalm. I agreed but there couldn't have been a worse, or maybe more appropriate, psalm to have picked for me that day. It was about living for the word of God and not for money. Once I'd started to read I couldn't stop but, as I reached the line, 'The law from your mouth is more precious to me than thousands of pieces of silver and gold,' I felt horribly ashamed and wanted the ground to swallow me up, knowing the words wouldn't have been lost on anyone at the service.

Probably, in God's eyes, it was the perfect psalm to have chosen for me. It's said that money is the root of all evil and I suppose that's true. If John hadn't been so incredibly materialistic, and I hadn't been so stupid in agreeing to help, we'd probably still be living in our lovely house in Witton Gilbert, comfortably off and with no worries in the world. Instead, I was Anne Darwin, the evil lying mother who had betrayed her two sons in the cruellest way possible and was now languishing in jail, where I belonged.

From the moment of John's return, Mark and Anthony had refused all offers to talk to newspapers. But now they had decided to set the record straight, giving an interview to the *Mail on Sunday*, in which neither pulled any punches. Mark, once fiercely protective of me, said he always believed he had the best parents anyone could ever ask for, but now: 'The mother I had respected and loved all my life seemed to have transformed into a hideous lying bitch who had gone to outrageous lengths to con us. She let us believe our dad was dead, she encouraged us to believe this. I thought she was a wonderful woman who loved me and would always protect me. Before then I would never have traded them, I thought they were the best parents, but then they both lied to us in the cruellest way possible. She even dragged our names into it by buying Premium Bonds in our names. She didn't need to do that. I have been had completely and I feel bitter about it. It will take a lot of time to come to terms with what they have done. At the moment I want nothing to do with them.'

Anthony said: 'It's bewildering. Nothing seems real any

more. It's as if our whole life has been a lie. They have tarnished all the good times that came before. I can't ever forgive them for putting us through the torture of mourning. They were in it together and they deserve the sentences handed down by the judge. They're as bad as each other. Dad told one nasty lie and disappeared and said he was dead but she lied for six years, she was the face of the lies, she kept on lying even when the evidence was so overwhelmingly against her. She dragged us through hell by forcing a court case. I don't think they planned to do it to us – we were a consequence; we were collateral damage. They trampled over our lives for the sake of money. That is not something you do to people you love.'

I was mortified when I read their words. Of course, they were right about everything and who could blame them for despising me? I was sure, now, they'd never speak to me again.

I also knew Mam and Dad would have been extremely saddened by the court case, the newspaper article and me being portrayed in the press as the liar I knew I was. I had tried to warn them they'd be shocked with everything that would come out at the trial but I don't think I realised how bad it would be. I was sick of everyone asking if I was all right – I was far from all right. I was an emotional mess, embarrassed, humiliated and distraught, and things were still far from over for me because I still had the confiscation order to deal with and the threat of more jail time. Everyone, even some members of the family, seemed to think I still had a secret stash of money hidden in Panama. It simply wasn't true and I had accounted for every last penny to my name and was desperate for it to be recovered. But why should anyone believe me? I was a liar.

It may sound hard to believe but I actually received many letters of support and comfort from strangers across the country, which did help. I even received a letter and a little teddy bear from a woman in Australia, although the bear was confiscated. The letters expressed outrage at the sentence and hope for the future, saying blood is thicker than water and Mark and Anthony would forgive me eventually. They offered support and prayers and said I could correspond if it would help. Often they would write that murderers got lesser sentences. And if I needed anything sending into prison, I only had to say and it would be provided. And over the next few days, everyone at Low Newton was kind and sympathetic and even officers said they were shocked at the severity of my sentence.

Somehow, I now had to try to pick up the pieces of my life and get back to 'normal' – whatever normal was anymore. But the next few days and weeks all seemed to pass in a blur. I had been assigned a job as a cleaner, but some days I couldn't even remember what I'd done and what was still left to do. I was oblivious to everyone and everything around me. It was, without doubt, one of the lowest points of my life.

John had written to me throughout our time on remand and letters continued to arrive almost daily. On some days, three or four would come together, having been delayed in the prison mail. They were all first read and vetted by officers but I'm sure they must have found them incredibly boring, as they were usually full of John's same rambling thoughts, always professing his unstinting love for me and basically saying the same thing. He always seemed to be feeling sorry for himself and hard done by. I was angry with myself for not being strong enough to stand up to John, but even angrier with him for getting me into this nightmare. I didn't reply to his letters. I just wanted to be given some space, but John was relentless. He insisted that now we had a release date we should plan where we were going to live together.

He would call once every few weeks, but eventually I stopped taking them. I knew the calls were monitored and, though he was happy to, I didn't want to discuss personal matters with him, or anything to do with the CPS efforts to recover our assets in Panama. As far as I was concerned, everything needed to be repaid, and the sooner the better. I was doing all that I could, through Nicola, to assist. I didn't want to hear him complaining about everything or telling me what to do or what I should say to my lawyer. Look where listening to him had got me in the past.

He knew all the money from our – my – bank accounts

would have to be returned, but what was most incredible, even then, was that John was convinced we'd be able to keep hold of the apartment in Panama City, and maybe the land at Colon, because they were in the name of a corporation. He didn't seem to appreciate that without the sale of the Jaguar Lodge assets, I'd be languishing in jail long after he'd been freed to continue his life. He said we could still return to Panama and pick up the pieces when we were released, as we had nothing left in England anymore, but I knew I'd never go back. I had no wish to return. That part of my life was over. But John was forever trying to work out what he could still get away with. He was incapable of putting the past behind him, atoning for his sins and making a fresh start.

Nicola was keeping me updated on the recovery efforts but it was a long, slow process and the authorities in Panama, who prided themselves on secrecy for 'wealthy' foreign investors, didn't appear to be in any rush to help. The thought of spending many more years in jail if the recovery was unsuccessful was always in the back of my mind.

On other occasions, John would suggest in a letter that we should forget about Panama and instead return to live in Blackhall, where we had started married life. But there was no way I wanted to go anywhere near the village in which we still had family and knew so many people. I would be too ashamed to show my face. There were people living there who I had lied to, and I couldn't contemplate the thought of going back.

I had no idea where I'd go but I wanted it to be somewhere I could disappear into obscurity. For some time, I had wondered whether I would be better off without John and, as time passed, those feelings grew. There had been a gradual deterioration in our relationship and, deep down, I knew my life would be better and easier without him.

On the advice of our lawyers, we both appealed against the length of our sentences. But instead of showing contrition, John, astonishingly, remained resentful that Mark and Anthony had – he believed – refused his requests to help with the appeals. In one letter, he wrote: 'They are depriving both of us from seeing our fathers alive again.' The irony that he was complaining about not getting to see his own father, when he'd caused both his father and his two sons to grieve for him for nearly six years, seemed lost on him.

In fact, John never again got to see his father, Ronnie, who died after a series of strokes in a nursing home in December 2008, aged 91. Actually, he never even tried. Before he died, John wrote one short message to Ronnie from his prison cell, the first contact between the pair since he disappeared all those years ago. The note read: 'Dear Dad. Just to let you know, please don't worry.' They were the only ten words Ronnie ever heard from his son again. Ronnie had said: 'Every time the phone rings, I grab it thinking it might be John but it never is.' Relatives said Ronnie never got over the shock of discovering his son had lied to him and even cut John out of his will.

In fact, unbeknown to us both, Mark had actually written letters on our behalves to the Court of Appeal, asking for leniency in the jail terms. I was astonished when Nicola informed me, as, after all that we had put him through, it was such an incredibly generous thing to do – and he did it without even telling us. I wrote immediately to thank him and, although I heard nothing back, it did at least give me some hope. So maybe, just maybe, everything wasn't quite lost.

And then, thank God, Mark wrote to me. The letter arrived on 14 August and I had to keep re-reading his words to make sure I wasn't imagining them. Finally, my prayers had been answered. It was only a short letter but he asked if he could visit the following month. I was excited but nervous, as I knew Mark and Anthony would naturally still be upset and angry with me. I lay awake at night wondering whether Mark would come alone or bring Flick with him, and whether or not he would show any forgiveness.

The stress of dealing with what we had put them through had taken a heavy toll on both boys. Mark had just started a new job when he learned of his father's return from the dead and subsequent arrest. He'd had to deal with his name and picture being plastered all over the newspapers. Having all his new colleagues see such stories must have been humiliating for him. It was equally hard for Anthony because he worked in insurance and defrauding insurance companies played a big part in our crimes. For months, both had to live with the constant whispers about what they really knew. They were well aware many were pointing the finger of suspicion at them, and it was all our doing.

I had asked the governor if there was any way Mark's visit could be in private, maybe in the chapel. I was desperate to shield him from any more hurtful publicity and I knew nothing that happened in the visits hall ever stayed private for long. But my request was turned down on the grounds that the prison service couldn't be seen to be giving special favours to anyone, not least to a high-profile inmate like me.

Anthony's 30th birthday came and went but he still sent no word. Every day I wished I could speak to him or he would just at least acknowledge me and tell me how he was. He had always been quieter and more introverted than his older brother and I wondered how he was dealing with the shame of what we had put him through.

As I counted down the days to Mark's visit, I could think of nothing else. I tried to distract myself wherever possible by reading or watching television. The summer Olympics, from Beijing, were on and I enjoyed watching the competition most days. Someone pointed out an article from a 'lads' mag' called *Nuts* that had a picture mocked up of John and I paddling in a canoe, in which we were billed as the next Olympic hopefuls. I actually found it quite funny and was able to laugh at it. One of the wardens who'd seen it cheekily asked me how many medals I'd won. 'Two for rowing and one for running,' I replied. 'And 20 for making teas.' It was a case of either joining in with the laughter or being ridiculed.

One day I learnt that details of the money in my prison bank account had been leaked by someone. I found out when one of the girls stood outside my cell one afternoon saying, 'Anne Darwin's rich, she is, Anne Darwin's rich.' I actually had £256 in my account – all the money I had to my name – and every penny had been earned from my prison work. The only difference between me and most of the other girls was that I didn't spend my money on cigarettes, chocolates and sweets, or buying phone cards, as I had virtually no one to call.

It was Saturday, 20 September, and I was so nervous as I sat in the visiting room, midway down the centre row of tables, awaiting Mark and Flick's arrival. As soon as I saw them walk in, I broke down in floods of tears. They both had tears in their eyes as Mark, perhaps a little frostily at first, said, 'Hello, Mam.' We all sat down and talked, though I found it hard to stop crying.

After about ten minutes, with everyone a little more relaxed, Mark said, 'We've got something to tell you,' and he broke the wonderful news that they were getting married. Although I had read an article in one of the papers in which Flick was described as Mark's fiancée, I hadn't been sure if it was true, and news of the wedding was still a total surprise. They were so well suited for each other and I could see how happy they were. I was thrilled for them.

Then Mark brought me down to earth with a bump by saying, 'Of course, you and Dad will both miss this wedding.' The date had been set for the following month.

But on the whole, the visit was wonderful. Just to have Mark talking to me once again was more than I could ever have wished for. I asked after Anthony and Louise, and Mark said they were upset but coping, and it was up to them whether they wanted to get in touch or not. I asked Mark to send them my love.

When it was time to go, we all hugged, which we hadn't done when they arrived, and Mark promised to stay in touch.

A week later, I had just finished writing a letter to Mam and Dad, enclosing a wedding card for Mark and Flick, when I received a short letter from Anthony. It took me completely by surprise and I wondered if it had been prompted by Mark's visit. It was short and didn't say a great deal, just that he and Louise were fine and he hoped I was coping. But it was the breakthrough I had been praying for and I clutched it close to my heart. That night, I thought long and hard about my reply, and the next day I wrote back, struggling through my constant tears and choosing my words incredibly carefully, for fear of saying one slight thing that might upset him. Now all I could do was pray the communication would continue.

For some reason I wasn't entirely sure of, John had been transferred to HMP Everthorpe, near Hull. But shortly after his transfer, on Friday, 26 September, there was a front-page story in the *Sun* saying he had been attacked and punched in the face and was going to be moved yet again, to an open prison, for his own safety. I was shocked to read this and asked one of the guards if there was any way they could find out how he was. The guard told me that, next to being a paedophile, being a former prison officer was the worse thing to be in jail. John would be constantly in danger from other inmates.

On the day of the wedding, 17 October – my Mam's birthday – I woke up thinking about Mark and Flick and hoping they would have a perfect day. It was hard to accept that I couldn't be there. They were going to be married at the register office near their home in

Hampshire. I phoned Mam the day after to see how it had gone. She said the wedding had passed without a hitch and everyone had thoroughly enjoyed themselves. I heard from Mark and Flick by postcard, a week or so later, saying they were on honeymoon and having a great time.

I may not have been there for the most important day in Mark's life but, with his visit and Anthony's short letter, words couldn't describe how happy I was to at least now be included, in some small way, in both my sons' lives again.

Chapter 23

Mistaken for a Murderer

The legal papers granting me leave to appeal against sentence arrived on Saturday, 25 October. I was busy ironing when one of the more senior guards called me into her office and personally handed them to me, which was thoughtful. She knew I'd been waiting on them and didn't let them just sit around for hours. I sat down, tentatively opened the envelope and saw straightaway that, while I could appeal against the length of my sentence, the application to appeal against the actual conviction had been turned down. No great surprise there, I thought to myself. Now I needed to speak to Nicola about the next steps to take.

Later that day, a card arrived from John, and on it was a poem he'd written for me. He also enclosed a newspaper cutting about Mark and Flick's wedding. I could tell he was feeling rather low and it would have been easy for me to write back, but I wasn't going to. I wanted to do it when I was good and ready and not when I felt under pressure to do so. Playing on my mind was the last conversation I'd had with Mam, in which she'd said she and Dad were worried about what would become of me when I was released. She mentioned how they both probably 'wouldn't be around for much longer' – a phrase she'd often used for years, but given my current position it was the last thing I wanted to hear. I know she hadn't meant to upset me, and probably didn't even realise she had, but it was such a horrible thing to contemplate. I was only too aware of their limited time, and the fact that I was languishing in jail, unable to see them. That made everything so much worse and more painful. I missed them both so much.

The following day, a letter from Nicola arrived saying I could challenge the decision not to allow an appeal against conviction. But I wasn't in the least bit interested in doing that. She also said John had been refused permission to even appeal his sentence, which I knew he wouldn't be at all happy with. I headed to the gym, which often helped clear my mind.

I worked out as often as I could. I usually started on the treadmill but also liked to use the rowing machines, which gave the girls another great opportunity to have a laugh at my expense. 'Where you off to today, Anne? Panama?' was the usual joke. 'Yes, not far to go now,' I'd usually reply.

That morning, one of the girls, who I liked to cut my hair, asked if anyone wanted to do a step-aerobics class. I said I'd join in, if she didn't mind a complete beginner taking part. I warmed up on an exercise bike, while she set up and worked out a routine. Then we started, first with some fairly basic steps. To my great surprise, I managed to keep up, although I was occasionally wrong-footed and almost beaten by the star jumps. I really enjoyed it and hoped we'd get to do it again the following Sunday. It was only later in the day that my legs started to ache and I wondered if I'd pushed myself too hard.

The following Wednesday, by which time my legs had just about stopped aching, I decided to go to the gym, to get myself going again – and got the shock of my life.

It was just after 8am and I was on the treadmill when I became aware of someone getting onto the machine next to me, so turned to say good morning. But as I looked round, there was the plump and rather squat figure of notorious serial killer Rose West, with the usual attendant officer close by, just a few feet from me. She didn't say anything, just stared straight ahead and carried on walking. After about 15 minutes, she stopped, took a bit of a breather, and used one of the exercise bikes. Then she had another brief rest, and got back on the treadmill before leaving. *Crikey*, I thought to myself, *now there's a sight you don't see every day.*

The woman jailed for life for collaborating with her husband Fred in the torture and murder of at least ten young women, at their home in Gloucester, had arrived at Low Newton about eight weeks earlier. She was smuggled in by a back door and taken straight to F Wing to join the other lifers. Her arrival was the only thing anyone could talk about. The inmates seemed to find the thought of having such an infamous killer in our midst incredibly exciting. I just found it creepy.

Everyone, it seemed, was desperate to get a glimpse of her. A lot of the women weren't in the least bit frightened at the prospect of having her at the prison, and there were a lot of serious hard cases who would have loved to have been able to boast of attacking her. There was a lot of hatred among the inmates for people, like Rose, who'd been a part of such barbaric killings. Some of these girls weren't to be messed with, that's for sure, and if they didn't like someone, they'd spit in their food or make snide or threatening comments. And when someone was attacked, all hell would break loose and there'd be complete pandemonium, with alarms sounding and officers descending from every corner.

Not that it would have been easy to get to Rose. Along with the other lifers, she was kept on a separate high-security wing. Whenever she left her cell, a prison officer was always detailed to her for her own protection and, at least when she first arrived, she had to wear a bright yellow jumper or top to mark her out as a high-profile/high-risk prisoner. You didn't talk to Rose, no one did, except for a few of the lifers on her wing. There she was known as 'Baker Rose', because one day a week she was allowed to bake cakes on the wing. Quite how she had managed to get such a privilege I have no idea, but she was well known for sharing her cakes with her fellow lifers.

I went to the chapel whenever there was a Catholic mass, which was always on a Saturday, and occasionally Rose would turn up with her officer in tow. It was a rather strange sight, and always turned heads, but no one ever said anything. At meal times, she would sit alone, or maybe with one or two of the other lifers. There was always plenty of space around her in the dining hall.

On a couple of occasions, I was even mistaken for her, despite the fact we looked nothing alike, other than we both wore glasses. Two new, much older women had arrived on the wing, and when they first saw me, one of them asked if I was Rose West. 'No,' she was told, 'That's Anne Darwin.' 'But she's a murderer as well, isn't she?' the woman replied. She was in her seventies and in jail for stabbing her female partner. I'd never imagined I'd be mistaken for a serial killer. At least murder was something I could never be accused of. But it made me start thinking that perhaps I should grow my hair a little longer. If I could wear it in a ponytail, perhaps there would be no more identification mistakes.

Another high-profile prisoner who came to Low Newton during my time there was Tracey Connelly, who was jailed for letting her lover and his brother torture to death her toddler son, Peter, known in the press as 'Baby P'. Many of the girls would have loved to have got to her, as anyone who had harmed or had anything to do with child cruelty was hated and a marked woman in jail.

You quickly learned which women to avoid and which women you could trust. I kept myself to myself as much as possible but made one or two friends: just ordinary women who had taken a wrong turn in life or made a bad choice. I never asked anyone what they were inside for but if they volunteered the information that was fair enough. It was interesting hearing about their lives and I quite enjoyed having someone to talk to. Many of the women were repeat offenders and seemed proud of their criminal records. Others, like me, had made one bad decision that led them down the wrong path.

I did see a whole new side of life I'd never before been witness to.

Like most women's prisons, I learned, Low Newton had its fair share of lesbians. Some were lesbians before entering jail and others got together with other girls after being locked up, as a way of finding companionship. There were quite a few who had boyfriends or husbands waiting for them on the outside and who'd come to visit every week. I used to wonder what their partners would make of it if they ever found out. Some of the girls were quite open, while others tried to hide it, but no one paid an awful lot of attention to it really. They'd stroll around holding hands, or kiss as they walked along, and I'd hear stories that so-and-so was sleeping with so-and-so in one of the cells that had more than one bed. It certainly wasn't encouraged by the officers but, to be honest, they were a bit powerless to do much about it.

In November, two officers from Askham Grange, a nearby open prison that specialised in preparing inmates for rehabilitation back into the community, visited Low Newton, touting for recruits. They'd been before but because I knew I wasn't eligible for a move, I'd never felt inclined to sit and listen to what they had to say. Askham usually took inmates with less than two years of their sentence remaining, and I had just over that. The prison helped with finding jobs and opening new bank accounts, in preparation for being freed. Nicola had said I was likely to be released in early 2011, to carry out the remainder of my sentence on probation. As I was just a few months away from the demarcation line, I decided to ask how soon I could put my name down on the waiting list. To my great surprise, my name was added immediately and I was told my case, and that of one other girl who had applied, would be discussed that afternoon, but that it may be some time before a decision was made.

I received a letter from Anthony. It was friendly but I was upset to learn he'd changed jobs because it had become too awkward speaking to clients – all totally my fault. I was sure he must feel very resentful towards me and his dad. He said he'd write again soon.

Christmas came and went and, as the weeks passed, I grew upset at not hearing any more from Mark or Anthony. They had both given me a ray of hope but now that once again seemed to have disappeared from my life. I knew they were busy trying to rebuild their lives and wondered if they'd changed their minds about being in contact with me. If only I knew that for sure, I thought, I wouldn't have to spend every day praying for letters that would never arrive. It was agony not knowing and it was eating away at me. Many days, I felt like crying all the time. When I woke up, my pillow was often damp from my tears. *Am I such a bad person? Maybe I don't pray enough? Please, God, I implore you to help me. I don't want to lose my children. Please, anything but that. I can't do this on my own anymore.* I saw nothing but a miserable and lonely existence ahead.

I decided to apply to be a 'listener', a prisoner who helped new arrivals with any problems or issues they were having. Listeners were trained by the Samaritans and performed the role of Samaritan for any prisoner, not just new ones, which I know seems a little ironic, given that I was so depressed myself for much of the time. One of the chaplains and several officers had put my name forward after hearing how I had helped new girls out on a number of occasions. It reminded me of my work at the doctor's surgery, and was something that just came naturally to me. I had always preferred to look for the good in people and help whenever or however I could.

As we sat playing cards one afternoon, a Vietnamese girl said she was fascinated by my 'soft' hands, and before I knew it, she was reading my palm. I'd have a long life, she told me, I had a loving family and two men loved me. She said I was a good person: I certainly didn't feel like one. The only important men in my life, were my boys. If there was any truth in what she was saying, it could only be my sons.

Then Shrove Tuesday arrived with some wonderful news – a letter from Mark saying he was coming to visit the following month. I could hardly believe it and read the letter three times and then went to tell one of the girls. I was so happy I had to share the news with someone. The letter was short but friendly, and Mark said he had lots of news – I only hoped it was good news. I put a VO (visiting order) in the mail that evening. I was so excited and rang Mam to tell her. She and Dad were in regular contact with the boys, but never conveyed messages or divulged information to me. Mam was pleased I'd heard from Mark, and sounded much brighter than of late. She said Dad, who had recently undergone surgery, was doing well and sent his love. All in all, it was the first good day I could remember in a long time.

But, someone obviously wanted to make sure I was never too happy, as the next morning I awoke with a painful swelling just below my hairline, and was diagnosed with shingles. I was seen by a prison nurse but all they could offer me was paracetamol and ibuprofen, and I was given nothing for the itching, which got progressively worse.

Although I was still in a lot of discomfort, I was very excited and happy on the day of Mark's visit, if a little nervous. I needn't have worried, as he arrived smiling and relaxed. He proudly showed me his wedding ring, told me all about the big day itself and the honeymoon. He said, 'The best thing we ever did was to get married.' I could see from his face how happy he was. He'd also gained a bit of weight and looked better for it, although he did need a haircut! He said it was all change on the home front too, as he and Flick were buying a new house and Anthony and Louise were also moving.

I thanked Mark for the letters he'd written to Nicola and to John's solicitor supporting our pleas for a reduction in sentence. He actually said we had both been good parents – obviously not taking the last few years into account. I told him I'd be forever grateful, even if the appeal was unsuccessful, and that I took enormous comfort from knowing he was supporting us.

Mark said he'd recently been to visit John. 'He wants to know that you're OK and coping.'

'I'm coping as best as I can' I replied, not wanting Mark to worry about me.

'Dad spent the whole time talking about you and

seemed close to tears for much of the visit.'

'Mark, I really don't know what the future holds for us. Things are difficult between us. I have a lot of thinking to do and decisions to make.'

'If you love each other, what is there to think about?'

'That's the big question. This is not an easy thing to say, especially to you, but I'm not sure that I do love him anymore.'

Despite this, I was glad that Mark had visited John. I didn't want him to be all alone in the world.

All too soon it was time for Mark to go. But his visit had done wonders in lifting my spirits. I hoped it wouldn't be long before he came to see me again. Less than a fortnight later, Flick wrote a lovely letter, giving me their new address and telling me all about the new house and various other news. She said if I wanted to correspond with Anthony and Louise, I would have to send my letters via her and Mark, at least for the time being, but I still took great comfort in being told that at least I could write. I was still quite down at not hearing from Anthony, especially as in his last letter he'd told me he'd write over Christmas and we were now well into the New Year. But I knew I had to be patient and at least he hadn't completely cut me out of his life.

For much of March, I was prescribed RIC (Rest in Cell) because of my shingles. I spent the days writing letters, reading and doing word puzzles. It was during this time that I learned my appeal date was to be 18 March, although it was later deferred to the 26th. I had already resigned myself to the fact that I probably wouldn't get a reduction in sentence, but if it did happen, and I was lucky enough to have it shortened by six months, that would mean only one more Christmas behind bars.

The result of my appeal played constantly on my mind. I'd been expecting the result on the Thursday, but when it got to 4.30pm and I'd still heard nothing, I rang Nicola, who explained that the judges had decided to extend their deliberations overnight.

The next day, before I could speak to Nicola, one of the officers told me it was being reported on the news that my appeal had been turned down. It was crushing, of course, even though I hadn't really expected any good news. I spoke to Nicola, who offered to send me the 14-page judgment but I told her not to bother. I really didn't want to read what was bound to be a load of derogatory comments. According to Nicola, The Lord Chief Justice said it was a 'unique crime that deserved a unique sentence'.

I now knew that I'd be detained until 9 March, 2011. That would mark the end of my custodial sentence and the remaining 1,186 days would be served on the outside, on licence, but under close supervision from the Probation Service. Plus, I was still living with the possibility of added time, for non-payment of the proceeds of crime. That black cloud was ever present.

I phoned Mam and Dad, who hadn't heard the news and were extremely sad and disappointed. I managed to contain my emotions until I told them about Mark's letter of support, and then I lost it and sobbed. Christine came to see me, which I was very grateful for. She had been a tower of strength for me and I'm really not sure I could have coped without her visits. John sent me a card a few days later, saying he loved me and always would. But I wasn't sure I could believe him. He didn't exactly have a very good track record, what with his affairs and smutty letters – and they were only the things I knew about. I wondered what else he might have done. A week later I received a ten-page letter from him. It was rather rambling but he claimed he'd already got some employment prospects lined up for when he was eventually freed. I knew it was way too soon to have anything official through the Probation Service, so I guessed it must have involved one of his fellow inmates, or perhaps an old friend. I supposed he was always looking ahead.

I quickly fell back into a deep depression, wondering why everything always went wrong for me. After one of my visits to see the prison doctor, the wing officer, who had always been kind to me, asked if everything was OK as I seemed very down.

I broke down and, in floods of tears, told him I didn't

think I could go on anymore. I needed help. A visit was arranged for me to see the community psychiatric nurse and I started to see her on a regular basis. It was the first time I had been able to talk about how lonely and utterly worthless I felt. She arranged a prescription for antidepressants and suggested seeing a psychologist. I was initially reluctant but then I reasoned with myself that if it was the only way to get myself out of this hopeless situation then perhaps I needed to do it. I had spent so many years bottling everything up that I found it hard to talk to anyone. My first appointment had been made for the following month. I was very nervous about the meeting and knew it wouldn't be easy for me to speak freely about my life and the mistakes I'd made – and the lies I'd told. It had been years since I'd properly opened up to anyone but, if I was to gain any benefit from the sessions, I knew that's what I'd have to do.

Chapter 24

A Future without John?

Having worked as a cleaner since arriving at Low
Newton, at the start of May 2009 I applied for and
got a job working in the prison gardens. It was, quite
literally, a breath of fresh air. I'd spend my days tending to
the flowers and concentrating on trying to live as
anonymous an existence as the surroundings allowed. It
was so lovely to be outside. Indoors, I'd spent hours
reading or writing letters, and suppose I must have cut a
rather sad and lonely figure, with few friends or visitors.
The occasional letter from the handful of people who had
stood by me at least offered some comfort.

I loved working in the gardens, whatever the weather.
Just being outside seemed to make everything less stressful.
I mowed the lawns, separated and planted baby tomato
plants, which smelled lovely, and potted begonias in the
greenhouse. It was good to be doing something different
and, it felt, rewarding. I and one of the other women
became the 'dynamic duo' of potters, although the other
girl was twice as quick as me. As summer approached, we
potted begonias, coleus and cordylines – bringing back

memories of the ones we had in the garden at Seaton Carew. It was hard to believe that they started life as such tiny, fragile seedlings. There were an awful lot of hanging baskets and wall baskets to plant up, which was really enjoyable. I knew they'd bring some lovely colour to the prison gardens over the coming months. In one two-day period, we planted over 500 wallflower seedlings.

There was a corner in one of the old greenhouses that was home to some harvest mice, which I discovered were actually an endangered species. Kirklevington Grange Prison, in North Yorkshire, also had them but had lost their male mouse and, as we had plenty, two of ours were caught and transferred – there were lots of jokes about them being 'shipped out'.

Other things happened to lift my spirits that May. I started to see Eva, the psychologist, and although it was very hard at first, we built up a rapport and I began looking forward to my sessions with her. We usually met in one of the upstairs association rooms. There would be a notice on the outside of the door, saying 'No entry', but it didn't always prevent people from entering and then making a hasty retreat. Another unsettling fact was the room was surveyed with CCTV. Although sound was not recorded, it took a while for me to feel comfortable, knowing the officers who were downstairs, could see us. But I knew I had to be completely honest, something I didn't exactly have the best track record in, or the visits would be pointless and of no benefit at all. So, probably for the first time in my life, I opened up completely and felt that I laid bare my inner self.

At first I found it incredibly stressful to talk about my feelings and anxieties in so much depth. I shed tears over my miscarriage and John's affairs in the early years of our marriage. It was very draining. But Eva would give me all sorts of mental exercises to do when I was on my own, and slowly, gradually, over a period of several months, I started to improve and the depression that had engulfed my life began to lift.

We talked about my life, my boys and my relationship with John. I'm sure having someone to listen and talk to helped me towards an awareness that I needed to live my life independently of him. It would be some time till I got there, because I had never really been independent. I had lived with my parents until I married and moved in with John, meaning I had always had someone sharing my life. I had many doubts about whether I'd be able to cope living by myself. But with Eva I began to realise that perhaps I didn't want to be with John anymore. Just thinking this was a huge step to make – but one I needed.

And yet – I began corresponding with John again. How could I be so stupid? I was still torn on whether we had a future together or not, and frequently changed my mind. After all, he was the only man I had really ever known and he was the father of my two children. I found it hard to imagine life with no John, and I suppose that's why I began writing to him again. But I wasn't at all sure that he could change. As soon as I was locked up, I knew I had to do things to change the person I'd become. I wanted to come out of prison a better person, so I could have a fresh start and try to put what had happened behind me. It was still too early to say what the future held, but we did have an awful lot of history. But I think, deep down, I knew John could never change and, if I was totally truthful with myself, I knew I had to face up to a life without him. It was just such a hard step to take.

Also in May 2009, I received a letter from Christine saying she would come and visit one weekend and, just a day later, a letter from Mark, saying he and Flick would also like to. Both letters did wonders for me.

I woke on the Saturday of Mark and Flick's visit feeling very grateful to be alive. I was expecting the visit to be relaxed, especially in light of Mark's previous visit and the news-filled letters that Flick had begun sending me.

Waiting in the visitors' hall, I spotted Mark walking through the door, smiling, but there was no sign of Flick.

We hugged and greeted each other warmly but when I asked where Flick was, Mark said she'd been too angry to come, so he'd dropped her off in Durham to look at the shops. I was a bit confused and asked what she was angry about.

'Angry at you, Mam,' Mark responded. 'Angry at everything that's happened. Some days she's OK and others she's angry. And today she's angry.'

I accepted Mark's explanation, it was entirely understandable. There had been stories in the papers about the sale of the Jaguar Property assets, and Mark had written to ask me about it. I'd been unable to answer some of the questions and I'd advised him to ask Nicola. I'm sure that couldn't have helped anything. I was sad that Flick couldn't be there, of course, but still happy to be able to spend time with Mark, and grateful that he had decided to come and see me.

It was only later, long after he'd gone, that I started to get upset again. I wondered if Flick not wanting to see me would affect our relationship in the longer term. If Flick decided she wanted nothing more to do with me, would that stop Mark coming to see me? Would I lose him from my life again – something too painful to contemplate. 'Please, God, don't let that happen,' I prayed. And what about Anthony? Would he, too, decide I was more trouble than I was worth? I hadn't heard from him in many months. Would I finally lose both my sons forever, as I was sure many people felt I deserved. I felt absolutely desperate but at least I now had Eva to talk to about everything.

In early June, I began to think about applying for a Release on Temporary Licence (ROTL), basically a day out of the prison, which could be spent with family or friends. I knew I would be eligible to apply in July and thought Christine might be able to take me to see Mam and Dad. But I wasn't sure if I'd need to be escorted by a prison officer and, if that was the case, I certainly wouldn't be visiting them with an officer in tow.

I received a letter from Nicola. She said the date for a Proceeds of Crime hearing had been set for 10 November, in Newcastle Crown Court, and that investigators were holding out for the recovery of £1.7million – well over the money we had received in pensions and insurance in the fraud itself, and also well over a million pounds more than the property and my assets were worth. She said it was ridiculous and she was doing all she could to get them to lower the amount. If whatever figure was agreed on wasn't repaid within 12 months of the hearing, there was a possibility of my sentence being increased by anything between five to ten years. I read and reread the letter three times. I couldn't stop shaking. It just wasn't fair that I could be punished twice for my crimes.

Hadn't I paid a heavy enough price already, and what else could I possibly do? Since the day of my arrest, I had cooperated at every step of the way about the recovery of our assets. *I could be 67 years old by the time I'm eventually released. I'd be completely institutionalised and ready for nothing but an old folks' home – if I survived that long.* I wanted to tear up the letter but instead I flung it across the room and dissolved into floods of tears.

One of the women came to see me. To try and cheer me up she said I should write to the Queen! But, more wisely, she said I should warn my parents about the possibility of an additional sentence, rather than let them hear it from the media.

A few days later there was a big story in one of the papers, complete with a picture of me and John, saying we were refusing to cooperate with the Crown Prosecution Service, which simply wasn't true and left me furious and upset. The paper said we had half-a-million pounds stashed away and there was no way of recovering it, which was nonsense. There was a quote from a 'police source' saying they had written to the Panamanian government for help months ago but still hadn't heard back. That bit may have been true but it was certainly not my fault. More than anything else, I was worried it would affect my chances of getting a ROTL visit and being transferred to Askham.

I wrote to Nicola asking her if there was anything she could do to put the story right. She wrote straight back, saying she'd written to the CPS pointing out that there was absolutely no truth in the story that had appeared. I didn't really think it would make any difference but I was pleased she'd written.

I tried to distract myself by focusing on my studies. My IT course had actually been going so well that the instructor, Clare, suggested I should consider an Openings Course, designed as a taster for Open University studying.

I found two suitable options: Understanding Management and Learning to Change. I didn't really like the second option, I was already doing enough of that in my psychology sessions. Clare even suggested I should consider studying at degree level. Me – a degree! I couldn't have been more surprised.

On Friday, 12 June, I was overjoyed to receive a letter from Anthony and Louise, which, according to the postmark, had taken a month to arrive. It was a good letter, telling me about their new home, and also asking lots of questions about what I was doing with my time. It was so lovely to finally hear from them and, as the tone was friendly, it gave me a great deal of hope. I wrote back, choosing my words incredibly carefully, desperate not to say anything that would upset them.

Feeling in slightly better spirits, I filled in my application for ROTL to spend a day at Christine's house with Mam and Dad. One of the officers told me my request for transfer to Askham was under discussion by the various prison and probation services, and lots of reports about my behaviour and suitability were being considered. I was so excited I could barely sleep, even though, as usual, I was expecting the worst.

The following day, while we were all in the association room, someone looking out of the window spotted a rainbow and we all went over to look. I never would have thought a simple rainbow could cause so much excitement.

At the end of June, I needed to go to hospital for breast

screening. I was driven to the Queen Elizabeth Hospital in Gateshead by car, which was the usual mode of transport for attending hospital appointments and certainly beat the usual 'sweatbox'. Before leaving the prison, I was handcuffed to a female prison officer. The cuffs were briefly removed, to allow me to undress, but then immediately put back on and attached to a long chain, a bit like a dog leash, so the officer could stand behind the screen with the technician while the X-rays were taken. Did they really think I was going to make a daring escape bid while being screened for breast cancer? Did they really think I was the type of person who would try to escape at all? I'm not really sure where they thought I'd go. I didn't exactly have a queue of people who'd be willing to harbour a runaway convict. I think the fact that I wasn't more upset just went to show how accustomed I'd become to such degrading treatment.

The hospital staff didn't enter into any conversation with me, other than to give instructions on how to position myself for the mammogram. After the X-rays, I was re-handcuffed directly to the officer and led out of the hospital. I kept my head down and avoided any eye contact as we walked back out to the car, but I could sense lots of people looking at me. I'm sure I gave them something to tell their family and friends about later, even if they hadn't recognised me.

On the eve of my birthday, 3 July, I was delighted to receive a card from Mark and Flick and another, containing a nice letter, from Mam and Dad. One of the girls who'd recently been released sent me a parcel containing a T-shirt, underwear and socks, which were always very welcome. On the day itself, I was woken early by one of the women knocking on my door to wish me happy birthday and to give me some shower gel and a lovely card. Only a handful of people knew it was my birthday because I wasn't one to broadcast such occasions. I spent the entire morning watering the greenhouses and then went back to my cell to prepare for a visit from Christine.

She arrived with a chocolate muffin – the closest I got to a birthday cake, which made for a nice surprise – and filled me in with the latest family news. I phoned Mam and Dad that evening and was pleased to hear them both sounding quite cheerful. I returned to my cell and the day was almost over when there was an announcement over the tannoy, telling everyone it was my birthday. I wasn't sure who'd let the cat out of the bag but I didn't really mind. In no time at all, a number of cards were slid under my door, two women delivered pieces of fruit and then everyone on the landing sang 'Happy Birthday'. It was nice for the day to end on such a high note. It was quite humbling to know that so many people wanted to share some happiness with me. Above everything else, that's what made the day special.

On a visit by a probation officer, I was told that my ROTL shouldn't be a problem but that Askham was a different matter altogether, because of the publicity my transfer was bound to generate. 'You seem a lot more relaxed than the last time we met. Is that because you have accepted your sentence?' he said.

I replied, 'It's more a case of understanding how probation can help me, rather than acceptance.'

I was always quite suspicious of the Probation Service, but wanted to come across as being more positive, and extremely grateful for any help they could give me.

Thursday, 23 July, 2009, day 593 in Low Newton, officially marked the halfway point of my custodial sentence. I was now on the downward slope!

I woke on the morning of 16 August to discover John was front-page news in the Sun. Rather than keeping his head down and trying to make amends with the boys, he had done the complete opposite. The story said he'd bragged to his fellow inmates about how he was going to 'make a million pounds' by selling his life story – despite the fact that profiting from his crime was impossible under the Proceeds of Crime Act (my own fee for this book is being split between two charities, the RNLI and the RSPCA). He'd spent many hours beavering away on two books – an account of his 'Panama adventure' and another on his prison diaries. He even designed what he saw as the front cover of the main book: a man in a red canoe paddling towards an idyllic tropical island, laden with palm trees. And then he'd set about trying to beat the system by smuggling his books out of jail, using a bogus law firm set up by a fellow inmate. He had trusted a prisoner, another fraudster, to act as his 'agent', which spectacularly backfired.

But, far worse than that for me, was that he also smuggled out of jail and into the arms of potential publishers my private letters, ones in which I had opened my heart, saying I still loved him. I had written about a possible future together when our time was served and we were deemed fit to be released back into society. They were personal letters and certainly never meant for publication. It seemed to me that he enjoyed making the headlines and had no regard for the devastation that was likely to follow. *How many more times do I have to forgive him? I can't continue 'sweeping things under the carpet'. How can I possibly live with him after this?*

How could I love him? I'd married him 'for better or worse', but the words cut right through me. I didn't want to continue to live my life with everyone looking at me as if I was some kind of a freak. I'd told him a thousand times I couldn't take any more bad publicity. He was driving the wedge between us ever deeper.

The story was picked up by TV and radio stations, so there was no chance of anyone not knowing about it. I was summoned by one of the governors to the office, to see what I knew. I'm sure he could see I was absolutely devastated and he asked if I had any thoughts of self-harm. I said I'd had a good cry and would be OK and asked if it would affect my chances of ROTL or transfer to Askham, as both were constantly on my mind. He promised to look into it.

A little later he passed on a message from John that I wasn't to worry if he didn't write or phone for a couple of weeks, as he wanted things to quieten down. How rich was that! Not even an apology or explanation… thanks, John. Thanks for nothing. John showed no regard for me whatsoever. I knew I simply couldn't go on this way.

Two days later, I was informed that my application to transfer to Askham had been turned down *and* my RTOL had been rejected. I felt as if the bottom had dropped out of my world. The reason given was 'ongoing police investigations' and I was told I could apply again in November. When would this nightmare ever end? I wrote to Nicola asking if the police investigation really was ongoing. I'd waited almost three months, but then, straight after John's stupid story had appeared in the papers, both my applications were almost immediately turned down. Some coincidence, I'm sure. My own prison record was exemplary. I was being penalised for John's actions.

I'd said it before, but this time I meant it. I really did. It was time to forget about John and start planning for a future by myself. After reaching this conclusion, I actually felt strangely calm. I took down from my pinboard two cards he'd sent me. I had to get him out of my life. I received a letter from John, not so much an apology, more a list of excuses, but it meant nothing. There were more stories in the Sun all week, and more revelations about our private life. I was being stripped of what little dignity I had left. I could not forgive him. Not this time.

I phoned home and was very happy to be told by Mam that Anthony had phoned and said he was thinking of me and would write soon. What must he and Mark have thought about their father's revelations? I'm sure they must have been as embarrassed and disgusted as me. Who wants to read about their parents' sex lives – even if most of John's stories were make-believe? I only wished I could have spoken to Mark and Anthony. I felt like a complete failure.

Shortly after, I was summoned to see one of the governors. She told me there was an article in the *Daily Mail* about me having been refused a transfer to an open prison. She insinuated the leak had come from my family. I told her that only Mam, Dad and Christine knew that

I'd applied and they never spoke to the press. She then asked if it could have been Mark or Anthony. 'Absolutely not, they had no idea that I'd applied.' Then came the question, 'What about your husband?' I again said that he had no idea I'd applied. Of course, the prison wouldn't accept it, but the leak could only have come from prison staff.

On top of this, it had become clear that several letters from Nicola had been opened before they reached me. They were marked with 'Rule 39 Applies', just as letters would from anyone's legal team, meaning they should not have been opened in any circumstance. I wrote in my diary at the time, 'I may as well stick all of my correspondence on the prison gate.' Nicola put me in touch with a specialist law firm, dealing in prison law, and in due course I received a verbal apology from the head governor, Paddy Fox. But it was excruciating to know that I couldn't rely on any aspect of my life being private.

Then, I received an eight-page letter from John with an ultimatum to reply by 1 October or he'd instruct a solicitor to send papers of separation. So much for him always loving me and being there for me. He seemed to have forgotten that this whole mess was his making…

A few days later, I agreed to take a phone call from him. As usual, this call was in the wing office, sitting in the presence of a prison officer. No privacy whatsoever.

'We need to get our names onto a housing list, or we won't have anywhere to live when we're released,' John insisted.

'It was only last week you threatened me with separation papers! I don't know what you want anymore,' I replied.

'I was annoyed. You never write to me. I need to know that you still love me and we can be together.'

'I don't know that we can be together, after everything that's happened. You will be released before me anyway, so it's probably best if you apply for your own housing.'

'You can't, surely, give up on our marriage now?' he said.

It seemed to me he'd given up a long time ago, and I was just beginning to realise it.

Christine came to see me and when I asked for her honest opinion of what I should do, she made me realise some painful home truths.

She said, 'Just think about how you've ended up in prison. Whose fault is it that you're here?'

She also asked…

'Can you ever trust John again?'

'Would you be in this situation if it wasn't for John?'

'Could you have come up with such a plan?'

And the biggest question of all: 'Do you really think John loves you?'

When I returned to my cell, Christine's questions helped me to crystallise my thoughts.

She helped me to understand what I'd known in my heart for a very long time. It didn't make it any easier, but

A Future without John?

I knew I couldn't go on this way. Thank God John and I would be released from different establishments, at different times, and to different areas. I couldn't take any more humiliation. I was finally done with John and the shame he continued to heap on me.

Chapter 25

Countdown to Freedom

I was overjoyed to, at last, be transferred to HMP
Askham Grange in June 2010. It is an 'open prison'
situated in Askham Richard, an historic village, with
picturesque stone cottages sitting around a village green,
complete with a duck pond, six miles from York. There
are acres of gardens, around which we were allowed to
freely wander until early evening, and a weekly treat was
the Sunday roast, with fresh vegetables grown and
nurtured in the grounds by my fellow inmates.

Life at Askham was different to Low Newton in just
about every respect. Rather than being confined to my
own cell, I found myself sharing a room with three other
women, which did have some disadvantages, especially
when watching TV. I always liked to watch documentaries
and programmes like Panorama, but at Askham the
women preferred soaps and Big Brother, although I have
to admit I did quite like Strictly Come Dancing. Never
one to rattle cages, I usually just went with the flow. One
TV programme none of the prisoners on my wing got to
watch was the BBC dramatisation of my story, Canoe

Man, starring Bernard Hill and Saskia Reeves. The authorities very kindly made sure no one got to see it. I certainly didn't want to watch it, especially with other people about, and I think it was felt it would be a little cruel to let the women watch a programme about one of their fellow inmates.

The main focus at Askham was in the reintegration of prisoners back into the community and preparing us for life after prison. Once transferred, we knew we really were finally on the home straight. As part of our resettlement, we were offered work placements, which was exciting, if a little daunting. Women prisoners are not required to wear a uniform, we mostly wore jeans and joggers with T-shirts. With work placements on the horizon, I needed to find some decent clothes to wear.

After two-and-a-half years behind Low Newton's razor wire-topped, towering, prison walls, I was finally given a taste of freedom. I was even allowed to leave the prison grounds by myself, either to do voluntary work, having found a placement with the RSPCA, or to spend the day with visitors. The only requirement was that I had to stay within a 50-mile radius of the jail, which was a small price to pay.

I could have a mobile phone, which I had to buy, and had to keep switched on whenever I was out of the prison, in case they decided to call and check up on my whereabouts. I had my grey hair dyed auburn, not out of vanity or wanting to look younger, but because I thought it would change my appearance a little. I was absolutely paranoid about people recognising me and often felt they were staring at me, even when they weren't.

We were only allowed to bring certain things back into the prison but, from time to time, girls would try to smuggle in cigarettes and other things, concealed about their body. I'm sure they got away with it sometimes. There was a pub in the village, The Rose & Crown, but we were strictly forbidden from the premises. Those who ignored the ban and staggered back to the jail drunk, quickly found themselves shipped off to more secure premises.

Just a few weeks before my transfer, Anthony had made his first visit to Low Newton. It was the first time I had seen him and Louise in over two years – since the horror and humiliation of my trial in Middlebrough.

It was a very emotional visit. They were both clearly still very angry and wanted to know why we had caused so much pain. All I could do was to say how sorry I was, I didn't have a suitable explanation. It was then I learned that they'd had a baby, my first grandchild. I will never forget the question asked by Louise: 'How could you do this to your sons? As a mother, surely, you want to do everything you can to protect your children?' I was so overcome with shame and emotion, I couldn't speak. I hadn't known anything of the pregnancy, and eventually was able to ask when their son was born: the beginning of March 2010.

Now, a couple of months after arriving at Askham, I received some wonderful news. Anthony wrote saying he'd like to visit me again and take me out for the day. I was thrilled.

It was August, and I sat waiting in the reception area, a complete bag of nerves. Askham Grange was far removed from anything you might imagine a prison to be. It is an imposing building, with many of the original features you might expect to find in a rather grand country house – high ceilings, plaster coving, elaborate fireplaces and a staircase that would grace any film set. When I saw his car pulling up the gravel drive, I got up, steadied myself and went outside to greet him. As I walked out the grand front door, I suddenly stopped in my tracks, my heart missing a beat. There, standing by the car's rear door, was Louise… and she was holding my grandson. It was such an overwhelming moment I burst into tears. Louise came over and passed the baby to me, and I cradled my first grandchild in my arms.

It was the most wonderful moment imaginable.

We went into town and found a teashop and they let me hold this beautiful, tiny child, now five months old, and even bottle-feed him. I didn't want to ever let go. It was just so amazing. It brought back fond memories of

Mark and Anthony as babies, and I felt like the luckiest person alive that Anthony and Louise had driven 200 miles from their home down south to introduce me to my first grandchild. It was an incredible gesture, given all that I had put them through. Both my sons were now slowly, and very gradually, letting me back into their lives and I couldn't have been happier or more grateful.

On another occasion, I went to stay with my sister for the weekend. When I arrived, Mam and Dad were there waiting for me. It was such a lovely surprise. The prison visits had been very stressful for them – they were both in their eighties – and they were so much more relaxed and at ease in familiar surroundings. I always called them every week but it was so nice being able to sit and talk to them, face to face.

It was having tasted this new-found freedom that I finally plucked up the courage to tell John what I should have told him years earlier. It was during a brief and difficult telephone call in November 2010 that I told my husband that our thrity-seven-year marriage was over. It was the first time we had actually spoken in nearly a year, and John was angry and belligerent, telling me not to be 'daft' and that we could still 'work things out'.

'No, John, you're not listening,' I told him firmly, as he continued his rant. 'I don't want to be with you when I get out of here. It's over, I'm not coming back.'

John furiously slammed down the receiver. I felt nothing but a tremendous sense of relief. I knew it wouldn't be long before he did something stupid again. He couldn't help himself. I'd known him since I was eleven years old but I had to make a fresh start on my own and couldn't go back to how things were. If he'd done the sensible thing, back then, and declared himself bankrupt, the shame would have been over a long time ago now. But that's not what happened and you can't turn back the clock. We all have to live with the decisions we make in life.

It was as if a great weight had been lifted from my shoulders.

Through my lawyers, I continued to cooperate with Cleveland Police's asset-recovery team and was relieved to learn that Panamanian authorities were also now cooperating. All the money from the Panama bank accounts was in the process of, or had been returned to, the UK. The flat in Panama City was in the process of being sold; and the land, really nothing more than nearly 500 acres of uninhabitable jungle, was up for sale, though there wasn't exactly a rush of foolish get-rich-quick investors queuing up to buy it. I suppose the likes of the pipe-dreaming Darwins didn't come along every day of the week. All I cared about was that with all the assets being gradually recovered, the chances of my prison sentence being extended were lessening by the day.

Nonetheless, my time at Askham was not without incident. About a week before telling John our marriage was over, photographs of me had appeared in a newspaper alongside another even more notorious Askham inmate, Tracie Andrews, who had been jailed for 14 years for killing her fiancé. She had stabbed him thirty-seven times before slashing his throat, then claimed he had been the victim of a road-rage attack. Like me, Tracie, who was also shortly due to be released, happened to be among Askham's Catholic inmates, who regularly attended Sunday service at The Church of Our Lady, in the suburb of Acomb, about five miles away. Someone had tipped off the press and photographs had been taken of us smiling and chatting as we left after the service. There followed a rash of stories, saying we were best friends and planning to move in together when we were released, which was fabricated nonsense – yet more newspaper headlines I could well have done without.

The following week, our priest, Father Pat Smith, addressed the story during morning mass, saying the Askham women had every right to belong to the church. The rest of the congregation burst out in spontaneous applause. Quite a few came up and shook our hands after the service, which was reassuring, and we were invited for coffee and a cake. But I'm sure it was no coincidence that, shortly after the story appeared, the church trips were stopped by the prison. After that, Father Smith would instead come to the prison once a week to say mass. I missed my weekly trips to church. The parishioners were warm and welcoming, and by attending mass, it gave us a sense of belonging and normal life.

It might sound hard to believe, given what she'd done, but although she certainly wasn't my new best friend, Tracie was actually all right. She was just one of the women at Askham – I even let her cut my hair once! She was a trained hairdresser and I never felt at all nervous in her presence. She kept herself to herself, but we sometimes talked about being in similar situations, as far as our notoriety was concerned.

Then I had something to look forward to. Mark had written, saying he and Flick would be visiting the following week. The day came and we drove into York. We were wandering through the streets, browsing in shop windows, when Flick stopped, turned to Mark and said: 'Are we going to do it then or not?'

Mark turned to me and smiled, then broke the news that Flick was expecting their first child. I was overcome and hugged them both. I think we all had tears in our eyes. We were all so excited. Flick told me they'd needed to tell me as she wouldn't be able to conceal the rapidly growing bump for much longer and they wanted me to be among the first to know. The thought of having a second grandchild filled me with pride.

With our Panama City flat now sold, Mark very kindly

agreed to fly to Central America to recover some personal, mainly sentimental, belongings we had left behind, including a gold chain given to me by my parents. He flew alone, booking into a nearby hotel, and visiting the apartment I had fled with two strange journalists, after the story about John first appeared in December 2007. He said he found it a strange experience, seeing all his dad's clothes spread out on the bed. Everything was covered in dust and there were lots of dead cockroaches lying around. It was very hot and humid and he spent several hours inside, sifting through our belongings. I don't think he enjoyed it at all. He called both of us in our respective jails, to check he had what we wanted, before flying home to the UK with paperwork, jewellery and family photographs.

As I counted down the days to my release, I started to feel nervous at the thought of returning to life outside the prison walls. I decided to stay at Askham that Christmas. I would have been allowed to leave for a few days, and Mark and Flick had invited me to stay with them, but I'd never been one for imposing, and I thought it probably best to stay put and ready myself for my release, now only three months away. It was quiet and peaceful but also strange – and a tremendous relief – to know I'd spent my last Christmas behind bars.

On 17 January, 2011, John was released from Moorland open prison in Doncaster, and wasted no time in moving straight back to the scene of his crimes. He quickly found refuge with perhaps his one true friend, Paul Wager, in his home in Easington, just 13 miles from Seaton Carew. And it wasn't long before newspapers ran photographs of 'The Canoe Man' walking a dog along the beach from which he staged his own death. John seemed to relish being back in the limelight.

Flick suggested that when I was released, two months later, I could stay with her and Mark, at least until I'd sorted myself out. It was an incredibly kind gesture but one I couldn't accept. I knew the newspapers would find out – they always did – and I didn't want to bring any more unwanted attention on to my family or disrupt their lives more than I had already. Mark said he couldn't bear the thought of me being released with no one being there to support me and he didn't want me to have to walk out the gates alone. But I firmly told him that I wouldn't allow him to be put back in the spotlight and, somehow, I'd sort it out myself. I was dreading being part of the media circus again but I felt that, hopefully, it wouldn't last forever. I didn't want anyone else to be a part of that.

As it turned out, I wasn't going to have to walk out the gates of Askham at all. My release, initially to a bail hostel in Leeds, was going to be handled by a prisoners' support charity called Women in Prison. With the press well aware that I was due out any day, photographers were camped out in their cars around the village green, desperate for a new picture of me. But they were no match for the women from WIP, who had planned my 'escape' like a military operation. After discussing ways of getting me out unseen – unnervingly, it was a bit like Panama all over again – they decided to use a small van, which the night before they parked in the rear grounds of the prison. I was ushered out of a rear door and packed into the back of the van, with an old piece of carpet to sit on and a blanket to keep warm. It was pitch black, so they gave me a torch, and told me to stay down. They'd arranged for a 'decoy' car to tear off in one direction and divert the journalists, which worked a treat, and a few minutes later we pulled out of the drive unseen and headed off towards Leeds. It had even been arranged for me to enter the bail hostel by a rear entrance, just in case someone had tipped off the press that that's where I was going. It all worked like a dream.

Having served three years and three months of my sentence, I was finally free. The date was Wednesday, 9 March, 2011. A month beforehand, I received a court order to surrender my passport. Although I was being released on licence and couldn't legally travel abroad for the remainder of the term of my sentence, the recovery of my assets was still not entirely complete, and I suppose no one was taking any chances. It would be another 12 months before the Crown Prosecution Service announced that the asset recovery was now complete: the apartment and land in Panama were sold, and every last penny from bank accounts in Panama and the UK had been recovered. In total, it amounted to £501,641.39.

I had to spend nine weeks and two days in the halfway house bail hostel in Leeds, which I didn't enjoy at all. I quickly returned to the days of nervously looking over my shoulder the whole time, as I'd been told journalists were frantically looking everywhere for me. I'd served my time and just wanted to be left alone. Will that ever happen?

The hostel was supposed to allow for a period of 'personal adjustment', supervised by the probation service, but I couldn't wait to get out. It was an old period, terraced house, at the top of a long hill. The facilities were basic but clean – we all had single rooms but still had to share bathroom facilities. Once again, I was not allowed to have medication in my possession. This time, it was because a lot of the women had a drug habit. Knowing that didn't really make me feel very safe. I had to sign on at the job centre for employment and, for the first time in my life, claimed benefits. We were allowed out, as long as we didn't have any supervision appointments, but there was a strict curfew. If we broke any of the terms, we would be immediately transported back to a secure establishment.

During my second week there, I told my probation officer that I'd really like to continue my voluntary work with the RSPCA, as York was where I was planning to make my home. Everything was agreed, and I was provided with return rail tickets so I could start looking for somewhere to live. As luck would have it, a part-time position at the animal home became available, so I applied and was thrilled to get a paid job, working three days a week. It involved dealing with the public on reception, which reminded me of my work in the doctor's surgery. It almost felt too good to be true.

The coming weekend was Easter and I'd been given permission to spend a few days with my family. Christine and her husband, Phil, and Mam and Dad, came to Leeds to pick me up and we all drove south to Hertfordshire, where Mark and Flick had invited everyone, including Anthony and Louise, to spend Easter together. It would be the first time I would meet my two new grandchildren – Mark's newborn son and Anthony's second, a daughter – born a week apart. We spent the weekend passing the babies round, talking and having fun, and it was lovely to see Mam and Dad so relaxed and happy and enjoying their great-grandchildren.

The boys both had some questions they wanted to ask about the recovery of our assets, life in prison and how I saw my future. I explained things as best I could. This was the first opportunity we'd all had to speak privately, as a family, and I owed them that, at the very least. I knew the pain I'd caused them could never be forgotten but the anger they had both once felt seemed to have passed. It was the most amazing family weekend I could possibly have hoped for.

The pieces of my life were slowly starting to fall back into place, although for the boys there must have been a little sadness that there was one person missing from our happy family reunion. Anthony had cut off all contact with his father and, while Mark was still in touch, I knew we would never all be together again as a family.

I was finally allowed to leave the hostel and on Friday, 13 May, I moved into a rented ground-floor bedsit in a converted house in the York suburb of Heworth. It was tiny, but adequate. It meant I had my own home, a job and had been reunited with my family. I couldn't have asked for anything more. It was a dream come true.

But I still couldn't escape John, not yet. Over the past year, letters from him had stopped arriving. I think I only received one or two during my entire time at Askham. I had made up my mind that once we were released, there would be no further contact. Being a Catholic, I didn't really agree with divorce and just assumed we'd go our separate ways in life.

Then, some time in July, I decided to ask my probation officer, Nicola, for help in arranging a meeting with John. Finally, I felt strong enough to speak to him, face to face, about ending our marriage. Nicola kindly agreed to help and started liaising with John's probation officer about finding a suitable venue.

But much to my surprise, John suddenly served divorce papers on me. On Saturday, 13 August, 2011, I received a petition for divorce. I knew it was pointless continuing with arrangements to meet John, so, instead, I made an appointment with a divorce lawyer.

In December that year, there was an incident that left me in no doubt that I had made the right decision. I have no idea how he got my address, but just before the divorce was finalised, I received a letter from John at my bedsit, the tone of which was quite threatening. He said he knew where I was and knew how to find me whenever he wanted. He even included an old photograph of me, and across the front of it he'd stuck a copyright symbol, which seemed to be suggesting that I was his property and belonged to him.

I was very worried over how he'd managed to find me and asked the boys if they'd given him the address – they assured me they hadn't. I was frightened that perhaps he had arranged for someone to follow me from work, or that he might just turn up on my doorstep and do something stupid.

I didn't think he'd harm me, but the letter and photograph left me feeling very uncertain. I was still adjusting to life on the outside and it was all very unsettling. One day soon afterwards, I was walking home when I spotted a man with a shaggy beard walking towards me. I stopped in my tracks, convinced it was John. It wasn't, but I had had enough of living in fear. I decided to show the picture and letter to my probation officer.

Nicola said there was sufficient reason to be concerned and suggested I talked to the police, who sent an officer round to interview me. He took away the letter and soon afterwards John was served with a restraining order, forbidding him from coming within a certain radius of me, my home or my work. I wrote to the boys to let them know what I had done, explaining that I needed peace of mind. I said I was not acting out of malice but, given their father's unpredictable track record, I had been sufficiently concerned and felt the need to do something.

My marriage of thirty-seven years was ended on 11 January, 2012, the day the decree absolute was declared.

I never heard from John again.

Chapter 26

It's Never Too Late

As the tourist coach edged its way along the narrow North Devon lanes, I gazed out of the window, admiring the lush, hilly countryside and, once again, thanked my lucky stars that the madness that had plagued my life for so many years was now behind me. That madness, or, to be precise, mad man, was John. He, for some reason I could never fathom out, seemed to crave the spotlight I myself so despised.

This time around, now aged 64, he was again making newspaper headlines, having married a Filipina girl half his age. I could only shake my head in disbelief. I'd been warned by my family that the story was about to appear in newspapers and knew that meant reporters would be banging on my door at any moment, as indeed had happened. At least John was now on the other side of the world, living with his new young bride, the charmingly named Mercy May Avila, in her native Philippines. The papers said Mercy had been busy posting messages about John on her Facebook page: 'I love you so much sweetheart… Our life is great and happy! Remember we are sign of Libra very lucky ha ha ha!'

Poor girl, I thought to myself. *Being married to John, she's going to need all the luck she can get.* Whether she knew about his past life, I had no idea. John was very much a part of my former life and long gone now, thank goodness. It was the summer of 2015 and I'd had virtually no direct contact with him for nearly six years. It was his problem, his life and nothing to do with me anymore. But, of course, I still got to hear about all the stories that appeared in the newspapers. There was one about him going back to Panama, but I really couldn't see it. I guess with John you never really know: practically anything seems possible.

I had been planning to go to my sister's but at the last minute, when all the stories started appearing in the papers again, I booked the trip to Devon – hundreds of miles from home. The stories about John's wedding were all pretty ghastly and brought back painful memories. I felt so physically and emotionally drained, I needed to get away. For me, the more time that passed and I didn't need to constantly look over my shoulder, the harder it was when something like this happened. It was like being hit with a brick.

It was a lovely break. It was the first time I had ever holidayed alone. Although I had been slightly nervous at the prospect, I enjoyed my first proper holiday since being freed from Her Majesty's pleasure. I stayed in the North

Devon seaside resort of Ilfracombe, and the weather was glorious as the coach, packed with my fellow tourists from the north-east, ventured out on day trips to such places as the port town of Bideford and the village Combe Martin, on the edge of the Exmoor National Park.

I felt invigorated. I loved the anonymity of being with people who knew me as simply a divorcee, taking a well-earned break from my job working for the RSPCA in York. Although accustomed to keeping myself to myself, I had befriended another single lady, from Sunderland, who in turn was friendly with a retired couple, and the four of us spent a good deal of time together, chatting and sharing the occasional meal during our outings.

'Are you sure I don't know you?' the only man in our party-of-four, who happened to be a retired police sergeant, asked me one day. 'You seem so familiar.'

'No, no, quite sure,' I reassured him. 'Maybe I just have one of those faces!'

The man smiled but continued looking at me quizzically, obviously not totally convinced. Eventually, I was fairly sure he twigged who I was, and I was grateful he was kind enough not to mention it.

On the day I travelled back to York, Friday, 3 July, 2015, I celebrated my sixty-third birthday. No party, no fuss. My fellow travellers had no idea that 'Anne Stephenson' – I had long since reverted to my maiden name – was even celebrating her birthday. But there were calls on my mobile phone wishing me a happy birthday from the two most important people in my life: Mark and Anthony.

How long John's marriage lasts to Mercy May Avila, only time will tell. I'm sure it will be no great surprise to anyone to see him returning from the Philippines with his tail between his legs. Quite where he got the money to pay for his ticket is anyone's guess. As I returned to work after my summer holiday, the Crown Prosecution Service obtained a court order ensuring John would have to forfeit his pension funds, worth £40,000, after they matured – the very last of his assets. Thirteen years after he faked his death in the North Sea, the CPS ensured they'd got their hands on every penny they could.

John doesn't appear to have learned any lessons and continues to show scant regard for anyone's feelings. He has shown little or no remorse and to this day, as far I know, he still feels he didn't really do anything that wrong. He probably continues to blame the banks and financial institutions for his downfall: nothing is ever his fault. Instead of keeping his head down and trying to make amends after being freed from jail, he has continued to bring unwanted attention on the family. It is his life and he has every right to live it as he wishes, but I am glad I'm no longer a part of it.

I don't need anyone to tell me I've made some terrible choices in my life. It has taken me to the very depths of despair on numerous occasions, but I cannot continue to look back and dwell on the past. Now is the time to look forward. Yes, I took the decision to go along with John's scheming plan and I deserved to be punished, and I will never, ever forget. I am truly sorry for the part I played. I served a lengthy prison sentence and, for a while, lost everyone I held dear to me. It has taken a long time to regain the trust and love of the family I so cruelly deceived. I will never permit myself to be put into that position again.

Abuse can take many forms and quite often the victims themselves don't realise what is happening until it is too late. I believe it's possible to know that what is happening is wrong but still feel you have no power to prevent it. In my case, I had no self-confidence and low self-esteem, and didn't have the courage to do the right thing. I put all my trust in the man I married and could not perceive a life without him. As a result, I committed a crime that will haunt me for the rest of my life, but of greater regret is the impact it had and continues to have on other members of my family.

In November 2013, Dad died after a long illness, which was a devastating time for me. John – with his impeccable timing – had made front-page news. He had flown to the Ukraine to meet a girl he'd met on an internet dating site. I'm sure the 25-year-old, tall and blonde and looking to marry a wealthy foreign husband, had no idea the man who wooed her would be a balding, penniless ex-con with a dubious history. It seems that as soon as she found out, she sent him packing. As John arrived back in the UK, he was promptly arrested and sent back to jail for 28 days for leaving the country without authorisation and thereby breaching the terms of his release licence. It does seem amazing that the authorities hadn't, at the very least, confiscated his passport. After all, he did have a well-documented history of disappearing... The press attention that naturally followed really was the last thing I needed at that particular time. But, as I was staying with Mam while arrangements were being made for Dad's funeral, at least I wasn't at home or work, and journalists quickly gave up trying to find me.

Everything that happened – from the moment John went missing, until I was released from jail – was so hard for Mam and Dad. Mam had been virtually housebound before Dad's death, and after his passing she deteriorated. It's been very, very hard for her. Today, she struggles with many aches and pains but, thankfully, she has carers in every day to help. I try to get up and see her as often as I can. Thankfully, my sister is only 40 minutes away, so gets to see her every week, as does my brother.

I'm sure many people will wonder whether I really deserve a second chance. Mark and Anthony decided I did, and to me that's the only thing that matters. Words cannot describe how happy that makes me feel, especially when I thought I had lost them forever. Looking back, I cannot believe I put them through such torment and it's entirely possible they will never fully understand how or why I did what I did. I accept that our relationship may never be quite the same again, but it means everything to me to be part of their lives once more and to be able to know and love my grandchildren. No doubt, one day they in turn will have questions of their own to ask.

Going to prison was the end of my life as I knew it, and something from which I never expected to recover. Yet it turned out to be a fresh start. Following the ordeal of the trial and realising just how long I would have to spend behind bars, I resolved to take advantage of the time, of which there was plenty, to examine my life and find out where I had gone wrong – and put it right. There was no one to rely on in prison and no one to trust. I had to become resilient and self-reliant. Being thrust into an alien environment where most of the inmates were in their twenties or thirties with convictions for drug offences or crimes of theft was a disturbing experience. I had to learn a whole new language in order to understand what was going on around me.

Education offered me the escape that I needed and gave me something positive upon which to focus. After I completed the assessments for basic maths and English, Clare, from the education department, saw potential in me and encouraged me to apply for an Open University course. This was my turning point. I began to believe in myself and was determined to give myself the best opportunity for success after release. Gaining qualifications in IT, at the same time as doing the OU course, was a stepping stone towards that goal. I could only hope and pray that I would one day be reconciled to my family but I knew I had to give myself the best chance of finding employment to earn a living.

Being in prison, I learned what it means to be lonely, even though I was surrounded by hundreds of people twenty-four hours a day. I was the butt of many jokes made by inmates and staff alike, but I soon learned to accept it and to respond positively. I did various jobs, cleaning, cooking and gardening, and found pleasure in them all. But I got the most pleasure in welcoming new prisoners, especially those jailed for the first time in their lives. My experience of being in the depths of despair had given me the insight needed to know exactly how they were feeling. I was able to offer hope and encouragement and in doing so I became aware of just how much I had changed.

Home for the last three-and-a-half years has been a small but comfortable flat in a pretty village just a few miles from York. There's a fish shop, library, post office, three pubs and a small supermarket – just about everything I could need. I have finally got around to giving the flat the lick of paint it had needed since I moved in, making it more homely. Most importantly, it is my home, and Mark and Flick and Anthony and Louise and my four grandchildren have all been to visit and stay. It's more than I could ever have dreamt possible.

I still work at the RSPCA York Animal Home, where I first started as a volunteer while at Askham. Now working five days a week, I split my time between looking after the charity's local website, working on invoicing and two or three days a week on reception, reminiscent of my many years working for the doctor's surgery in Gilesgate. I could have retired last year and claimed my state pension but I wanted to stay busy and carry on working. Besides, I really have no idea what I'd do with myself if I was sat around all day with nothing to do. I'd go potty! Whether or not I continue to work when I turn 65 I'm not sure. I'll tackle that when the time comes.

In the village, no one has ever said anything. I'm left in peace and if people know about my past, they don't say. Of course I sometimes wonder who knows and who doesn't, but it doesn't really matter. The people at work know, obviously, but they have accepted me for who I am now and not who I was. I have become a more confident, independent person, in charge of my own life and destiny.

I am not proud of what I did and would like to apologise for the pain and anguish caused to everyone, including the rescue services for wasting time and putting their lives at risk. I am, truly, very sorry. But I am proud of what I have achieved in recent years. With the help and support of friends and colleagues, I am trying to put the past behind me and to live in the present.

The decision to write this book was not an easy one to make. It will, of course, put me in the media spotlight again, but it has become clear that this will happen to me whether I choose it or not — John will doubtless make headlines for years to come. Now that I have found a way to build a new life, it felt like the right time to tell my own story in my own words. Mark and Anthony and Flick and Louise have supported me in my choice.

Over the last ten years, what I have learnt, above all, is that while I do need my family, I don't need a husband. It is possible for me to be self-reliant, and even happy, on my own. I know how obvious this will sound to some, but it took me thirty-seven years of marriage and a six-and-a-half-year jail sentence to discover this.

After years spent out of my depth, not knowing who to confide in besides my increasingly delusional and unpredictable husband, or where to turn, it was only when I hit rock bottom that I turned my life around. If there's one thing I'd like readers to take away from this book, it is that it is never too late to start again. If I can do it, anyone can.

Acknowledgements

My grateful thanks are given to Nicola, my probation officer, who was tireless in her support; and to the staff of the RSPCA York Animal Home who offered me a position as a volunteer while still serving my prison sentence and later as an employee.

I would especially like to thank David Leigh. If he had not knocked on the door of my apartment in Panama, in December 2007, this book may never have been written. That night, I denied him entry as long as possible, but he persisted to paint a vivid but accurate picture of how the next hours and days were likely to unfold. So, I took a gamble and accepted his offer of help. The events that followed are well documented in this book. From the day we first met, David treated me with dignity and respect, even in the face of my lies, but more recently, we have become firm friends. I am grateful for the support he has given to me throughout the process of writing this book, especially when reliving painful memories. I hope our friendship will endure well into the future. Lastly, I would like to apologise to David's family for taking up so much of his time and I wish you all well.

Most of all, words cannot express my gratitude towards my family, especially my two sons, who have allowed me to be part of their lives once again. Nothing else matters without their love and support.

The boys have steadfastly refused to speak publicly about family matters. The past is the past, as far as both are concerned. Canoe and Panama are words they would rather forget, and both have made clear that their life today is nobody's business but their own. They have had to shoulder the greatest burden of all, and deserve to be left in peace.

Anne

Also by Mirror Books

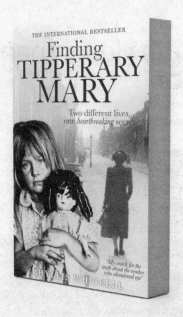

THE SUNDAY TIMES BESTSELLER
FINDING TIPPERARY MARY

The astonishing real story of a daughter's search for her own past
and the desperate mother who gave her up for adoption.

Phyllis Whitsell began looking for her birth mother as a young
woman and although it was many years before she finally met her,
their lives had crossed on the journey without their knowledge.
When they both eventually sat together in the same room,
the circumstances were extraordinary, moving and
ultimately life-changing.

This is a daughter's personal account of the remarkable
relationship that grew from abandonment into love,
understanding and selfless care.

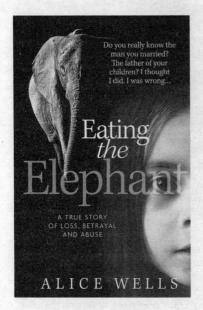